GOD'S LAUGHTER

Gerhard Staguhn

GOD'S LAUGHTER

Man and His Cosmos

TRANSLATED FROM THE GERMAN BY
Steve Lake and Caroline Mähl

KODANSHA INTERNATIONAL
New York • Tokyo • London

Kodansha America, Inc.
114 Fifth Avenue, New York, New York 10011, U.S.A.

Kodansha International Ltd.
17-14 Otowa 1-chome, Bunkyo-ku, Tokyo 112, Japan

Published in 1994 by Kodansha America, Inc.
by arrangement with HarperCollins Publishers.

This work was originally published in Germany in 1990 under the title
Das Lachen Gottes by Carl Hanser Verlag. The first English translation
was published in 1992 by HarperCollins Publishers, New York.

This is a Kodansha Globe book.

Library of Congress Cataloging-in-Publication Data

Staguhn, Gerhard, 1952–
  [Lachen Gottes. English]
  God's laughter: man and his cosmos / Gerhard Staguhn:
  translated from the German by Steve Lake and Caroline Mähl.
      p.   cm.
  Originally published: New York : HarperCollins Publishers,
  © 1992.
  Includes index.
  ISBN 1-56836-045-2
  1. Cosmology. 2. Religion and science. I. Title.
  [BD513.S7913   1994]
  113—dc20   94-39916

Book design by Barbara DuPree Knowles

The cover was printed by Phoenix Color Corporation,
Hagerstown, Maryland

Printed and bound by Quebecor Printing Fairfield,
Fairfield, Pennsylvania

Printed in the United States of America

94 95 96 97 98   10 9 8 7 6 5 4 3 2 1

CONTENTS

ILLUSTRATIONS

GOD'S LAUGHTER

Is the riddle of God, Man, and World, then, so arcane?
No! But no one wants to hear this; thus a secret it remains.

—Johann Wolfgang Goethe

Wanderer at the World's Edge
Rejoicing, our spirits strove upwards, breaking bonds, and as they
looked about, alas!, there was but infinite emptiness.
[FRIEDRICH HÖLDERLIN]

INTRODUCTION

My first "cosmic" experience took place in 1957. I was five years old. The memory is astonishingly clear and accompanied by a strong emotion. It is night. I am standing in the garden with my parents and a few neighbors. Together we gaze up at the stars, looking for something. I am looking, too, without knowing what I am supposed to look for. The excited babble of the grownups tells me it has to be something hitherto unexperienced. Even though I don't understand what they are talking about or what purpose this scanning of the night sky might serve, my childish mind strongly registers their excitement and the subliminal fear in their voices. Time and again they use a word unknown to me, alien and mysterious-sounding: *sputnik*. As I don't know what to make of this word, I promptly convert it into "spit-nik." This, however, doesn't make the affair more comprehensible. So the grown-ups were looking for "spit" in the tangle of twinkling stars. How strange. "Spittle" in the sky, that didn't sound too good, particularly as the creator of this celestial phlegm, this sputnik-sputum, was identified as "the Russian."

"The Russian"—at the time, the ultimate metaphor for fear and menace; in my imagination I saw him as a monster, waiting only for an opportunity to attack and destroy. So the monster had spat, and "spittle" now circled the earth—a threat materialized.

My first "cosmic" experience, then, may be dated with some exactitude. It must have taken place in the days after the sputnik shock of October 4, 1957.

The year of my first "microcosmic" experience, on the other hand, cannot now be determined; I might have been ten, maybe even twelve years old. But I know the day for certain: Christmas Eve. Santa Claus had brought me a microscope. Surprising perhaps, since it is not in Santa's best interests to awaken a child's scientific curiosity. My insights into the universe of small things, however, were extremely modest and did not shake my faith too much. At a magnification of 150, the simple device reached its limits. But what did that matter! What the eye could see was enough to fill me with enthusiasm. Suddenly even the most banal things surrounding me were imbued with a completely new sensual quality. What had seemed without mystery revealed an entire cosmos of strange shapes.

I remember that all Christmas, my spirit of research kindled, I was totally absorbed in the microsphere that was our *Gabentisch*, the table where presents were displayed. Wax flaked from a Christmas candle, a crumb of Christmas cake, a piece of fluff rescued from the ashtray—under the microscope, these turned into optical miracles.

I was lost in wonder. But, in time, this too came to an end. Gradually, my interest in the microscope faded; it was dismissed to a corner of the room, finally to a crate in the attic. My awakening scientific curiosity had been stymied by the limitations of the means at my disposal.

Probably everybody can tell little "cosmic" and "microcosmic" tales like these. Presumably, everybody will have noticed too that only the "cosmic" stories have really developed intellectually, gaining in depth with the passing of years, whereas the understanding of small things has refused to unfold properly, unless obliged to do so in the course of a professional career as a biologist, chemist, or physicist. Everybody reflects on the cosmos in one way or another, but only few on the microcosmos. One reason for this is, of course, that the sky above us, particularly the clear night sky, symbolizes the inconceivable so impressively. He who gazes at the stars unavoidably starts thinking.

He compares himself to the infinity above. He asks for the meaning of his speck-of-dust existence but won't find an answer. Where reason reaches its limits, belief in God or any kind of faith is likely to arise. This is fortunate, because faith helps. Suddenly, a narrow earthly existence has a focal point outside itself. This is why man, speaking of or to God, instinctively lifts his eyes skyward, and keeps on doing so even if he has long since said good-bye to the bearded God-behind-the-clouds of his picture books—as if God, if He exists, could only be hidden somewhere in this infinity above us.

There is another kind of infinitude with which God could be identified just as satisfactorily: the infinitely small. But in most people's minds, this infinity does not exist. It does not force itself upon us sensually. In the finite and limited—in a stone, a plant, or in myself—I do not expect to find infinity. My logical thinking tells me that something limited can never harbor infinity. Through a microscope, however, one might begin suspecting that this logic becomes the more precarious the farther one enters the cosmos of small things. For one never comes to an end. Where optical devices reach their limits, electron microscopes take over the exploration of the smallness of things. And though even they eventually come to a limit, we know that the smallness continues beyond that. We know of the existence of atoms and that they consist of even smaller particles. And those parts are still divisible, and the parts of those parts as well, and so on. Infinite space there, too.

Modern man has therefore no choice but to determine his intellectual and spiritual standpoint on the basis of two infinities, at the intersection of which he himself exists. This is even more true for the determining of a religious standpoint. Whenever a human being seriously looks for God, seriously meaning independent of ideology and dogma, he has to integrate both infinities into his search. This alone makes the claim that science has banished God from the world a foolish one. Science has only banished certain views of God, or rather, it has declared any concept of God untenable, but has given Him back His essential quality, which is to exist beyond all conceivability. From that point of view, modern science has done great service to the concept of theism: It has made it nonobjective. If God exists, He can only be where human knowledge cannot reach Him.

But it is not easy to believe in something that reason cannot grasp. Strictly speaking, even Christianity represents a refined form of idolatry; it is not God one believes in but a picture of God, and if it is not made of wood or stone, it is at least made of words. Man's inclination to idolatry already tested the God of the Old Testament. What answer could He give when Moses, on behalf of his people, asked Him for His name? If a picture was out of the question, the people demanded at least the name of their God. In a way, a name, too, is something that can be grasped both physically and rationally, that can be adored. God solved this difficult problem in a truly divine manner. He gave His name without giving it away: "I am that I am" (Hebrew: *ehje asher ehje*).

This touches upon a dilemma basic to every religion. Each tries to convey the inexpressible, but this is only possible indirectly, by way of symbols, allegories, and tautological phrases, which may be understood or interpreted quite individually. There cannot be a universal picture of God. One is inclined to speak of the irony of fate when one reflects that modern science, which allegedly destroyed faith, is itself occupied with topics and questions beyond the scope of human imagination. Like religion, science looks for the sources of everything, the ultimate things, for a total explanation of the universe. So physics is also, ultimately, a kind of metaphysics.

Science, as well, depends on symbols and allegories when trying to make its findings accessible to the general public. Physics' authentic symbolic language is mathematics; when the more complicated facts of scientific research are discussed, however, this language is understood only by specialists. If science wants to communicate itself on a broad scale and affect the public's picture of the universe, it cannot avoid transforming its mathematical language of equations into a language of allegories. This unavoidably leads to simplifications that in turn contain the danger of falsification. Complex matters cannot be arbitrarily simplified.

Thus, to the layman, the terminology of modern science sometimes appears to be a crutch supporting our thinking as it inches along the borders of the inconceivable. For that reason, the layman interested in modern science must also be willing to believe; he must believe that the universe is as scientists describe it. Like any belief, this also represents an act of faith.

Blaise Pascal, the great French mathematician and philosopher, once said that to believe in God means to doubt God. Science provides important intellectual equipment for this doubt. On the other hand, the scientific view of the universe can also be questioned—at least insofar as one does not consider the physical world all the world there is. Something like spirit or soul does not exist in this world picture. At best, it appears as some sort of after-product of material things or, to be more precise, a result of electromagnetic currents in the brain. The reduction of the spiritual to energy processes in material things, however, is not truly satisfactory. This picture's disturbing aspect is its one-sidedness, its undialectical aspect. If the spiritual is based on material things, why should not material things be based on the spiritual? And why should it not be possible to resolve the contrast between spirit and matter in a primary unity that would necessarily be of a metaphysical nature?

Whoever thinks this way must tolerate being accused of mysticism. Quite rightly, in my opinion. A view of life that refuses to restrict itself to the physical world unavoidably assumes metaphysical traits. These enrich, rather than diminish, our understanding. It is important to free the term *mysticism* from the tangle of superstition and esoteric mystery-mongering surrounding it so that mysticism basically means nothing but the acknowledgment of a scientifically unexplainable mystery-cause underlying the world.

Erwin Schrödinger (1887–1961), one of the initiators of quantum physics, said that a purely rational worldview totally devoid of mysticism is absurd. He insisted that this opinion complied to a large degree with the findings of modern physics. In his book *Mind and Matter*, Schrödinger also points out the strange fact that on the one hand all the elements of our world picture are creations of the conscious mind, including science itself, but that conscious

mind or "personality" is not contained in that same world picture.
Schrödinger's subsequent thoughts on the matter are so convincing that they should be quoted here:

> We have entirely taken to thinking of the personality of a human
> being, or for that matter also of an animal, as located in the interior
> of its body. To learn that it cannot really be found there is so amaz-
> ing that it meets with doubt and hesitation, we are very loath to
> admit it. We have got used to localizing the conscious personality
> inside a person's head—I should say an inch or two behind the mid-
> point of the eyes. From there it gives us, as the case may be, under-
> standing or loving or tender—or suspicious or angry looks. I won-
> der has it ever been noted that the eye is the only sense organ whose
> purely receptive character we fail to recognize in naive thought.
> Reversing the actual state of affairs, we are much more inclined to
> think of "rays of vision," issuing from the eyes, than of the "rays of
> light" that hit the eyes from outside. You quite frequently find such
> a "ray of vision" represented in a drawing in a comic paper, or even
> in some older schematic sketch intended to illustrate an optic instru-
> ment or law, a dotted line emerging from the eye and pointing to
> the object, the direction being indicated by an arrowhead at the far
> end. Dear reader or, better still, dear lady reader, recall the bright,
> joyful eyes with which your child beams upon you when you bring
> him a new toy, and then let the physicist tell you that in reality noth-
> ing emerges from these eyes: in reality their only objectively
> detectable function is, continually, to be hit by and to receive light
> quanta. In reality! A strange reality! Something seems to be missing
> in it. It is very difficult for us to take stock of the fact that the local-
> ization of the personality, of the conscious mind, inside the body, is
> only symbolic, just an aid for practical use. Let us, with all the
> knowledge we have about it, follow such a "tender look" inside the
> body. We do hit there on a supremely interesting bustle or, if you
> like, machinery. We find millions of cells of very specialized build in
> an arrangement that is unsurveyably intricate but quite obviously
> serves a very far-reaching and highly consummate mutual communi-
> cation and collaboration; a ceaseless hammering of regular electro-
> chemical pulses which, however, change rapidly in their configura-
> tion, being conducted from nerve cell to nerve cell, tens of thou-
> sands of contacts being opened and blocked every split second,

chemical transformations being induced and maybe other changes as yet undiscovered. All this we meet and, as the science of physiology advances, we may trust that we shall come to know more and more about it. But now let us assume that in a particular case you eventually observe several efferent bundles of pulsating currents, which issue through the brain and through long cellular protrusions (motor nerve fibers), are conducted to certain muscles of the arm, which, as a consequence, tends a hesitating, trembling hand to bid you farewell—for a long, heart-rending separation; at the same time you may find some other pulsating bundles produce a certain glandular secretion so as to veil the poor sad eye with a crape of tears. But nowhere along this way from the eye through the central organ to the arm muscles and the tear glands—nowhere, you may be sure, however far physiology advances, will you ever meet the personality, will you ever meet the pain, the bewildered worry within this soul, though their reality is to you so certain as though you suffered them yourself—as in actual fact you do!

As the acre that is to be ploughed in this book has now been roughly demarcated, I would first like to ask the self-critical question whether I, as a layman, am in any way qualified to handle the intellectual iron plough of science. Must it not appear as an incredible presumption if a layman writes a book about modern cosmology and its relation to religion? Is that not a topic exclusively reserved for the specialist? I don't believe so, for who, after all, is specialized in physics *and* religion? There is no professorship for astrophysical theology yet. But that is not the point anyway. The point is as simple as this: If scientists make their knowledge accessible to laymen by means of popular books, this can be construed as an invitation to join the discussion.

Science should not remain the exclusive concern of scientists. In the long run, it must touch public thought on as broad a scale as possible. The understanding of nature cannot be the scientist's privilege. Of course, the reach of the layman's intellect is limited; his knowledge is always a simplified one. This, however, does not make conclusions drawn from his simplified knowledge less valuable. On the contrary, even his failure to understand may be interesting; it can bring forth questions pointing far beyond the merely scientific. For even the best-founded knowledge of the researcher is never absolute knowledge; it is always the consolidated knowledge of a particular era. Strictly speaking, we are all laymen anyway.

The close relationship between modern science and religion has been one of the natural consequences of scientific research. Time and again, the great physicists of our century have stressed this relationship strongly and with great seriousness, and have developed their thoughts on the matter. On the subject of religion they were just laymen like all of us. Furthermore, particularly in modern nuclear physics and astrophysics, the individual scientist has been condemned to a kind of layman's specialization.

Each scientist has enough to do in keeping track of his limited field and trying not to fall behind. This, however, entails losing the broad perspective. Scientists often remind us of laymen staring through the keyhole at the secrets of the universe without noticing that behind them the room is already on fire. Or, to quote Hölderlin: "Rejoicing, our spirits strove upwards, breaking bounds, and as they looked about, alas!, there was but infinite emptiness."

Research is primarily based on the principles of remuneration. In today's research laboratories it is not the noble, pure truth that matters anymore but ignoble prestige and pure profit. Pure science, that is, "science for science's sake," has long since ceased to exist. The goal is to be quicker than one's competitors. Science is all frantic activity. Results are marketed as sensations before they have been thoroughly checked, this being the best way to secure marketing rights. Research is undertaken in competition rather than cooperation. It becomes more and more difficult, particularly for the layman, to maintain a faith in science. It is losing its credibility. One has the impression that scientists, in their feverish and unrelenting research, have already dug the ground from under their own feet. This spiritual chaos in modern research seems to be accompanied by a decline in researchers' ethics. Research is undertaken blindly.

The much-mooted crisis in science seems to be, above all, the scientists' moral crisis. The result is a loss of confidence on the side of the public and an accompanying slackening of general interest in scientific research. A disquieting development. Albert Einstein once said that the restriction of scientific findings to a small circle of specialists weakens a people's philosophical spirit and leads to its intellectual impoverishment. Today, one might ask oneself if there still is a philosophical spirit to weaken.

The frantic activity and confusion in scientific research is yet another aspect of the spiritual crisis apparent on all levels, not merely the religious. There is a general lack of orientation, a general collapsing of values. Crisis, however, is not at root a negative phenomenon. The original meaning of *krisis* indicates that a decision is demanded; a decisive turn of events is imminent. If the modern spiritual crisis confronts matters as crucial as the survival of the species, this is a call for all to contribute their critical reason to combat it. Yet in the meantime, many have lost their confidence in human reason and are seeking salvation in irrationalism. This, too, illustrates the comprehensive character of the crisis. Man has nothing universal left to believe in and orientate himself by, neither in the field of human reason nor in the field of traditional religion. Above all, there are no utopias anymore, neither wordly nor otherwordly, toward which human hopes might be directed. Our final utopian dream is of somewhat negative character: the belief that this planet may yet be saved.

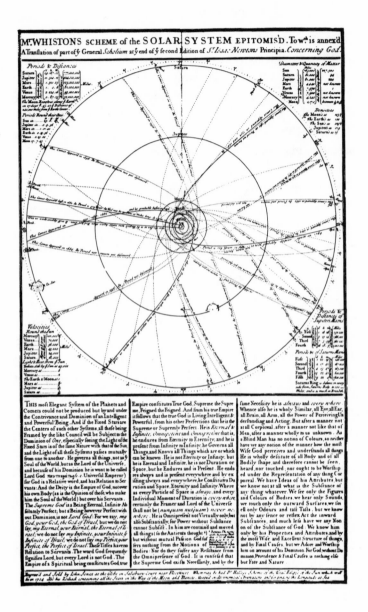

Newton's Solar System with Comet Orbits
The most beautiful system of the Sun, planets, and comets, could only
proceed from the counsel and dominion of an intelligent and powerful Being.

[ISAAC NEWTON]

{ 1 }

THE RENUNCIATION OF
APPEARANCES

A Short History of Cosmology from Preantiquity to the Nineteenth Century

The oldest preserved maps of the world originate from Babylonian times, that is, from the third millennium before Christ. On these maps, the Earth is depicted as a flat disk floating on the ocean. Babylon is at the center of the disk. To make a center of power the center of the world, just because it is one's own, is essentially a religious act. It expresses something extremely important, something that remained valid until the founding of our modern cosmology.

Man, observing the cosmos, always places himself at its center. Moreover, in viewing the world, he ultimately always views himself. This seems to be the only way for man to free himself of the oppressive sensation of being small and isolated. In the center he effortlessly acquires a regal position. Man represents not only the final stage in the development of life on Earth but the crown of a cosmogenesis. Thus, the old Babylonian maps also show us what has driven mankind toward religious beliefs: a desire for security and comfort, for a permanent position in the center of things. To find one's own center, whatever that means, is still a primary motive for many a religious quest. For at the border, chaos, dissolution, and destruction loom.

PROTECTION AGAINST CHAOS,
ALIENATION, AND MYSTERY

Religion seems to be basically a man-made phenomenon. In many archaic cultures, the village, the temple, or the house was regarded as "the center of the world." It is unhelpful to dismiss this archaic belief as nonsensical from our enlightened standpoint by pointing out, for example, that there is no such center, let alone that several villages or temples could be at the center simultaneously. What is important is the metaphysical center of which the geographical center is but a symbol.

It is evident that in earlier times man was part of a world that seemed to him profoundly alien and frightening. By placing his familiar and comforting home in the middle, he was able to ward off the world's strangeness and to establish a whole and holy order. At the root of religion—to this day!—lies fear. More precisely, the fear of death, which is but a synonym for chaos. Religion is nothing but a heroic negation of chaos and death, man's attempt to oppose world-chaos by establishing a permanent center, and to define thereby a reference point for everything—in short, a meaning.

Cosmology, for the very fact that it was a vessel for basic religious needs, was closely linked to theism from the outset. The constellations in the sky, particularly those that caught the eye because of their movement and remarkable appearance, were elevated to deities whose favor man tried to curry by means of sacrifices. Religion was cultish, and pompous ritual and extravagant procession were the means by which its priests mesmerized the people. Clairvoyants, augurs, fortune-tellers, spiritists, and sorcerers were others who benefited from this naive religiousness. That many people today practice these primitive forms of belief with a dogged seriousness shows the depth of our contemporary crisis. It is as if there had never been an age of enlightenment.

Yet even in preantiquity, some outstanding thinkers tried to go beyond a solely mythical understanding of the cosmos. In doing so, however, they had to deprive the celestial bodies of their godly nature and turn them into objects of rational observation. A bold step. Astronomical research within a religion-based cosmology was practiced not only in Babylonia but also in ancient Egypt, China, and in South America's advanced civilizations. Amazingly, all four cultures independently arrived at an almost identical level of astronomical knowledge and were able to incorporate their findings effortlessly into their respective religious theories of life. Astronomy served both scientific and ritual purposes; the boundaries were fluid.

By discovering and measuring periodically repetitive movements in the sky, astronomy enabled mankind to put its wordly social order into close relationship with a stricter heavenly order. Earthly conditions could be structured and strengthened via the heaven of the gods. This relationship becomes most evident in the calendar based, in most cases, on the lunar cycle. In ancient China, for example, the calendar presented the highest law. Nature had to obey it, and so did mankind.

THE PHILOSOPHICALLY INCLINED HEAVEN

With antiquity, astronomy acquired its essential scientific quality, which means that it became a critical science. It stopped accepting observations as given facts, and attempted to evaluate and to ask: Why are things the way they are? Since one can question and search in different directions, astronomy in ancient Greece did not develop as an integral whole but split into several, partly opposing schools. The so-called Ionian School, named after the coastal area in Western Asia Minor, succeeded to an astonishing degree in liberating astronomy from the chains of ancient theism, simply by assuming that celestial bodies are made of the same materials as the Earth and are therefore subject to the same processes of change and decay. Furthermore, this school was the first to argue that the Sun rather than the Earth might be the center of the universe.

In contrast, the Athenian School and its most famous representative, Aristotle (384–322 B.C.), followed an entirely different trail.

It based the whole realm of cosmology on a single and even meta-physical platonic thesis: The planets move in regular and circular patterns and must therefore be governed by a divine soul. Aristotle simply reversed this metaphysical argumentation, maintaining that the planets are divine beings and therefore imperishable and unchangeable. These qualities demand that they move in circles and be of spherical shape because only circle and sphere are perfect—that is, divine—shapes, and they too have no beginning and no end.

Thus, for Aristotle, the cosmos as a whole was a sphere as well, consisting of planet spheres and the outer fixed star sphere. Inside the global sphere, these spheres are layered like onion skins; they, too, perform circular movements, and, from the outer layer inward, each sphere transfers its movement to the next. The outermost fixed star sphere, however, is moved by God who himself remains unmoved. Unlike the cosmos of the Ionian School, the Aristotelian cosmos was not deduced from exact observation but from philosophical speculation. Basically, only two hypotheses in Aristotelian cosmology were correct: that the Earth and the other planets are spheres, and that the moon circles the earth. Everything else was wrong.

Although this cosmology was comprehensively inaccurate, it dominated man's view of the universe for almost two thousand years. It did so because it had a major advantage over other cosmologies: It corresponded with what was visible. In addition, it was internally logical. Before it was finally accepted, however, and became determinative and in every respect disastrous for the Middle Ages, it temporarily fell into disfavor after the death of Aristotle and the resulting decline of the Athenian School.

Other schools and other cosmological theories appeared: above all, the Alexandrian School and its most important teachers, Euclid (ca. 300 B.C.) and Aristarchus of Samos (ca. 310 to ca. 230 B.C.). Aristarchus placed the Sun at the center of the cosmos, circled by the planets, including Earth. This heliocentric theory, even though correct, was nevertheless unsuccessful, probably because it could not be reconciled with contemporary religious views and even less with so-called common sense. Every child could see that the Earth was static and the Sun was moving! How could one trust a view of the universe that did not admit what the eye could see! And yet, all this would have been insufficient to prevent the victory of the heliocentric thesis. Even at the time, too many scientific observations spoke for it.

TRIUMPH OF THE WRONG

The revival and ascendancy of the incorrect Aristotelian world-picture was engineered by antiquity's most important astronomer, Hipparchus of Nicaea (ca. 190 to ca. 125 B.C.), who invested all his energy to strengthen the Aristotelian system and rid it of its inconsistencies. Hipparchus is a classic example of the scientific genius who unfortunately backs the wrong horse but, in this case, does it with such fervor that only two thousand years later is his error apparent.

One could, of course, suggest that Hipparchus might not have been such a genius if he was unable to distinguish between the "right" and the "wrong" cosmological horse. That, however, would do him injustice. First of all, he examined the heliocentric theory thoroughly because he believed it to be the scientifically more credible one. The central problems in ancient astronomy, whether it placed the Sun or the Earth at the center of the cosmos, were the observed irregularities of the planetary movements. How could these be explained if one believed that the planets moved in harmonious orbits?

For the observer on Earth, the planets do not move regularly across the firmament. Their movement toward the East is interrupted by periods of retrograde motion toward the West. Even if one assumes that this phenomenon can only be an illusion caused by the interplay of two circular movements, this does not explain their nature. The heliocentric picture automatically includes these circular movements: The Earth orbits the Sun, and the observed planet orbits the Sun as well, although on a different orbit. For the observer on Earth, who, naturally, does not perceive his own circular motion, the planet's orbit is distorted into a kind of pendulum swing; this distortion is caused by his own movement.

It is to Hipparchus's credit that he first tried to prove the correctness of the heliocentric theory. It is even more to his credit that he was finally obliged to abandon this fundamentally correct thesis, for his calculations showed that the heliocentric theory could not explain the irregularities of the planetary movements in a mathematically exact manner. A single yet decisive basic assumption was still incorrect: The planets' paths are, in fact, elliptical, although those elliptical orbits are very similar to circular orbits. The circular orbit that is not strictly circular proves fatal for the heliocentric theory. Hipparchus's calculations were so precise that the difference between assumed circular orbit and actual elliptical orbit took effect. His only mistake was that he abandoned this theory completely where he should have abandoned only the theory of the circular orbits. The fixation with the circle, ultimately a religious fixation, prevented the breakthrough of the heliocentric theory, even in antiquity.

So Hipparchus settled decisively on the Aristotelian system with an immobile Earth at its center. If, however, the Earth was immobile and the planets moved around it on circular orbits, what was the reason for their apparent pendulum movements? In order to solve this contradiction, Hipparchus used a theory that already existed but had yet to be mathematically proven: the so-called epicycle theory. According to this theory, the planets do not move one circular orbit but on two orbits simultaneously. The planet itself does not move on the main orbit around the Earth but on a smaller epicircle, the center of which moves on the main orbit. The planet, therefore, moves around an imaginary point in space, which in turn moves around the Earth! A rather laughable theory! The extraordinary thing is, though, that by choosing appropriate velocities on the smaller epicircle and the big carrier circle, the planets' apparently elliptical movements can actually be explained. Here, Hipparchus pulled off a brilliant arithmetical feat.

In the second century, Ptolemy (ca. 87 to ca. 170) gave the epicycle theory its final shape. Per se, this was the greatest intellectual achievement in early astronomy, although the results were completely wrong. Nevertheless the Ptolemaic world-picture survived all through the Middle Ages. Throughout this long period nothing happened in the astronomical field, although the church periodically attacked the Ptolemaic theory, according to the whims of the pope in power. Above all, it was the concept of the Earth as a disk that the church was reluctant to abandon because it fitted more neatly the religious concepts of Heaven and Earth, angels and devils. The Hellish Below and the Heavenly Above could not be reconciled to a spherical Earth and cosmos because a sphere has no above and below, and offers no fixed location for God's throne.

It was Thomas Aquinas who, erecting a huge, inherently logical edifice of thought, reconciled the Christian religious system with the Aristotelian-Ptolemaic theory. As a result, cosmology became a part of theology. Since the cosmological system was entirely inaccurate, however, there had to be something wrong with the theological system as well. Of course, one can speak of "wrong" only from a modern point of view. For the Middle Ages, this "wrong" was absolutely right, and served to explain everything that demanded explanation. From the start, this fixed, dogmatic system did not admit any questions that led beyond its frame of reference.

SO LONG, THEOLOGICAL COSMOLOGY

It is therefore even more remarkable that a single man, Nicolaus Copernicus (1473–1543), was able to wrench this enormous, seemingly unassailable system from its very foundations. The Copernican shock waves impacted decisively with the much more powerful shock waves of the Lutheran Reformation. The rigid Catholic system was shaken from two points simultaneously. This made the shaking particularly effective, not least because both shocks took place absolutely independently and with completely different objectives.

Copernicus's goal was an accurate astronomical system, while Luther aimed at a correct, or rather sincere, theology. Both were concerned with exactitude, a fact bound to have fatal repercussions for a religious and philosphical system rooted in so much wrongness. Initially, the effect of Copernicus's findings remained limited to a close circle of scientists. Around the year 1512, he had sent his *Commentariolus,* a paper on the structure of the planetary system, to several acquaintances. That was all. In this paper, his thesis that the Earth revolves around its axis and that the Earth and the planets orbit the Sun was formulated for the first time. Shortly thereafter, in 1517, Luther issued his *Ninety-five Theses.*

Copernicus apparently was not interested in destroying the world-picture of his era. He simply considered a few of its inherent assumptions too artificial. In addition, considerable discrepancies between observed and precalculated planetary orbits had become apparent in the previous centuries. The deviations were not large but big enough to prompt Copernicus to look for other solutions. A strict science does not allow for contradictions between observation and calculation, even if they are very small.

Copernicus took up the old heliocentric theories and combined them with the concept of an Earth revolving around itself. This concept was also not new but was incorporated already in the rationalizations of several of the ancient philosophers. Basically, this was Copernicus's only justification for the daring theory of a revolving Earth. It was so completely contradictory to sensory perception. Why did human beings fail to perceive this rotation?

Copernicus could not offer a convincing physical explanation for the spinning of the Earth. Both of his basic assumptions were correct but insufficient to explain the old problem of the irregularities in the observed planetary movements. The extremely complex mathematical system that Copernicus developed was logical and aptly described the nature of the planetary movements, but was no more able to predict the exact position of a planet at a given time than the old Ptolemaic system had been. In this respect, his system offered no improvements on the geocentric system. As Copernicus's first priority was to preserve at all costs the holy principle of circular movement, his theory also failed to correspond completely with reality.

Another fifty years had to pass before Johannes Kepler (1571–1630) discovered that the planetary orbits were elliptical and, at the same time, found a simple law with which one could calculate the planets' speed on these orbits. At last the Copernican theory had been given a mathematical foundation, although this meant relinquishing antiquity's belief in the divinity of the circle to which Copernicus himself had clung so passionately. That it was Kepler who destroyed this belief is remarkable, for he was filled with an almost mystical faith in the divine harmony of the heavens. Such are the qualities of a great scientist: He refuses to sacrifice scientific findings to divine concepts merely because these concepts cannot be reconciled with his findings. In such cases, it is the religious concepts that have to be modified.

My earlier claim that the prevalent religious system had almost simultaneously been shaken by Luther's and Copernicus's theses is not entirely correct. Initially, the Catholic church completely overlooked Copernicus's theories. The Copernican tremor was drowned by the much stronger quake caused by the Wittenberg monk. At first it was the Protestants who tried to suppress the Copernican worldview. The Reformers were themselves so little reformed that they believed it to be irreconcilable with the Bible. Seventy years passed before the Catholic church also began to suspect how much intellectual explosive was concealed in Copernicus's theses. When it finally became aware of the extent of the threat, its hostility had to be directed full force against the man who was, at the time, the most fervent advocate of the new astronomy: Galileo.

THE VIEW THROUGH THE TELESCOPE

In the year 1616, Galileo Galilei (1564–1642) had to justify himself before the Court of Inquisition for the first time because he was able to present more, and increasingly indisputable, evidence for the accuracy of the Copernican theses. This evidence threatened to give the coup de grace to the already enervated Aristotelian physics and, as a consequence, to destroy the entire Catholic theology that the Reformation had already pushed against the wall.

What made Galileo particularly dangerous for the Catholic church was the fact that he was already a highly respected celebrity. At the University of Padua he sometimes gave lectures to more than two thousand students. Knowledge about his theories and findings did not remain limited to a small circle of scientists. His fame reached new proportions when, in 1609, he built a telescope and made sensational observations with it. He provided obvious proof for the correctness of the Copernican theories for a large public. The view through the telescope has an incredible authority.

All at once astronomy had become everybody's business. The church, however, paralyzed by thousand-year-old dogma, could react to new findings only with suppression, making unavoidable the rupture between a religion and a science that had hitherto formed a perfect unity. For theology, this signaled the beginning of a slow decline, while science began an increasingly fast ascent. The view through a primitive telescope had been enough to blow away two millennia of inaccurate science.

Basically, the old picture of the universe was overturned by five observations: the sunspots and the fact that they moved across the Sun, the moon craters, a variety of new stars in the galaxy, the Jupiter moons, and the phases of Venus. Particularly the last two observations supported the heliocentric theory in a convincing manner. From the fact that Jupiter's four big moons changed their positions every night one could conclude that they moved in orbits around the planet, which meant that smaller likenesses of the solar system existed in space, heavenly bodies that did not orbit the Earth. With that, the geocentric system was toppled. But the discovery of the Venus phases provided even stronger evidence. To the naked eye, Venus had always presented itself as a bright, unchanging dot, but now, looking through the telescope, one could see that the planet, depending on its position to the Sun, passed through various phases of differing brightness, from narrow crescent to full disk. According to the Aristotelian system, an observer on Earth should have seen Venus only as a crescent.

These observations, however, were not the only cause for the church to wage such fierce war against Galileo, a man who had been received by Pope Paul V in full honor in 1611. For the church was not in a position to doubt everything that anybody who looked through a telescope could see. Perhaps the church could somehow have managed to integrate these new findings into their dogmatic system with a little intellectual sophistry. There were quite a few influential men in the clergy who took an open-minded view of the new theories.

Galileo, however, had overturned not only parts of the Aristotelian theory but the entire system, and not so much on the basis of his telescope observations as through his theoretical work on the dynamics of moving bodies. His laws of gravitation and of pendulum oscillation represented an intense provocation for the old physics of appearances. Galileo's findings constitute the real beginnings of classical physics. According to the old Aristotelian physics, heavy bodies fall faster than light ones; everybody could prove the correctness of this thesis experimentally. As a matter of fact, a stone does fall to the ground faster than an equally sized body made of paper.

Galileo's brilliant mind mistrusted the apparently convincing visual evidence. By a succession of logical arguments he arrived at the conclusion that every body, no matter how heavy, falls to the ground with the same acceleration and that the observable differences can be attributed simply to air resistance. In a vacuum,

Galileo argued, even the most different bodies, whether a lead ball or a feather, would fall to the ground with the same acceleration. Unfortunately, it proved impossible for him to generate a vacuum in order to demonstrate the correctness of his theoretical considerations. This was achieved after Galileo's death by his student Torricelli. The mere assumption of a vacuum was absolutely irreconcilable with the Aristotelian school. How could one prove God's perfection in the emptiness of the vacuum?

THE GREAT LAW OF THE HEAVENS

On the first anniversary of Galileo's death, Isaac Newton (1643–1727) was born. His epochal achievement was to combine Galileo's dynamic laws of moving bodies and his telescope observations with Kepler's laws of the planetary movements, and to develop, as a synthesis, the law of universal gravitation, that is, to explain without contradictions how bodies as big as the planets can be put into motion at all and kept on an orbit around the Sun.

The old universal system had been shattered, but the new one confronted science with a frightening host of theoretical problems that demanded a solution. Newton actually found the solution to all these questions on the basis of merely two universal laws: the law of gravity and the law of motion. Simply put, the first law states that a planet is constrained on its solar orbit by the same force that also acts upon an object falling to the ground. This force acts between all masses in space. Its force is directly proportional to the product of the two masses attracting each other and inversely proportional to the square of the distance between them.

The second law, the law of motion, also concerns all the masses in space, whether they be falling stones or orbiting planets: The force acting upon a moving body is equal to the product of its mass and its acceleration. In school we were told, "Force equals mass times acceleration." By combining these laws one can explain why the planets move on fixed solar orbits, neither colliding with the Sun nor vanishing into space. The gravitational force with which they are attracted by the Sun is exactly equal to the centrifugal force that tears them away from it. This does not explain, however, who put the planets in motion in the first place.

With these simple laws a universal synthesis had been discovered that unambiguously explained and summarized all mechanical movements on Earth, the movement of the Earth itself, and the movements of the celestial bodies. In 1687, Newton's epochal findings were published under the title *Principia Mathematica*. This book is still regarded as one of the greatest scientific works ever written.

Newton's laws were so perfect that there was little work of real importance left for the following generations of physicists. For them, it was difficult enough to understand and master the details of Newton's complex work. Essentially, the entire eighteenth century is marked by the endeavors of physicists, French physicists primarily, to apply and perhaps extend Newton's principles. Of particular importance was Pierre Laplace (1749–1827) who, in a thirteen-volume work, tried to prove that the universe is nothing but a gigantic clockwork with Newton's laws as the formulae that regulate it. This clockwork runs perfectly smoothly and will do so eternally. Development and change did not fit into this system. The universe was pure mechanics, no more.

SPACE AS LABORATORY

For the time being, a definite physical description of the cosmos had been obtained, at least as regarded the movements of the bodies contained within it. The way in which the clockwork functioned was clear enough but, with the telescope rapidly developing, questions concerning its size worked their way into the center of astronomical research. To simply state that it was infinitely big, contained an infinite number of objects, and was centered around the Sun left at least one question open: What was the nature of these objects?

In the second half of the eighteenth century, Wilhelm Herschel

(1738–1822) became the dominant figure in this area of research. Born in Hanover, he left Germany as a young man to earn a living as a professional musician in England. He was already thirty-five years old when he discovered an interest in optics and, finally, in astronomy. He borrowed a reflector telescope and was moved to design his own, based on the system that Newton had developed. Using an alloy of tin and copper, he finally succeeded in building a very good reflector with a focal length of 214 centimeters. With this telescope, he discovered a new planet, Uranus, in 1781—a discovery that made him famous.

He then concentrated on the so-called nebulae and star clusters; scanning the sky, he found twenty-five hundred figurations of this kind. The strength of his telescope enabled him to resolve many of these nebulae into numerous single stars. Others, however, like the Orion nebula, resisted resolution. Herschel arrived at the conclusion that these nebulae had to be very distant systems that his telescope was not strong enough to break up into single stars. Today we know that this assumption was only partially correct. There are unresolvable nebulae, purely gaseous nebulae, even in our galaxy, for example, the above-mentioned Orion nebula or gaseous nebulae that are remainders of exploded stars.

But Herschel's importance as the founding father of modern astronomy is not limited to the discovery and classification of stars and nebulae. He also discovered, for example, double star systems, that is, two stars orbiting each other. His research has provided an important theoretical basis for modern astronomers throughout the twentieth century. The entire nineteenth century, however, yielded few new findings, mainly because no significant developments took place in telescope technology. Meanwhile, theoretical physics, too, was paralyzed by Newton's huge legacy. Not until the second half of the nineteenth century did new and trailblazing ideas emerge in theoretical physics, ideas that, further developed, would eventually supplant mechanistic thinking at the beginning of our century.

This makes Herschel's achievements as a theoretician all the more impressive. He was the first to introduce the concept of development and change into cosmology, thus contradicting Newton's strict mechanics. The observations of differing types of nebulae induced him to think that forces other than Newton's gravity might be at work in the universe. Herschel wondered, for example, whether collisions between stars might generate celestial bodies of a new quality. Here, he had at least a notion of what was to form the modern theory of stars being generated from gaseous nebulae.

And something else is concealed in Herschel's considerations that is of central importance for our modern understanding of the universe: the element of time. For Herschel, our galaxy, scanned so meticulously with his telescope, was no longer a mere mechanism, running as it has always done, but also an index of cosmic time. The universe is the clock with which we can measure the duration of its past and future existence. What we can see out there through the telescope has not always been what it is now and will not remain the same forever. In his dynamic thinking, Herschel was more than a hundred years ahead of his time. He raised questions in the eighteenth century that remained unanswered until the twentieth.

A NEW HOMELESSNESS

What to do now with this rough summary of five thousand years of cosmological history, as far as the subject of this book is concerned? When I presented the first preserved map of the world as the beginning of cosmological thinking, this was a little arbitrary because one can assume that human beings already related themselves to the world around them and the sky above them much earlier. Unfortunately, we know nothing of their conclusions nor do we know much about the beginnings of religion. If one takes a look at the development of religion, however, it becomes apparent that man continued to distance himself from the objects of his worship, whether spirits, demons, or gods.

In its beginnings, religion was, above all, a means of explaining nature, an archaic form of "natural science." Natural phenomena were the raw material of religion, so to speak. Or, more precisely, phenomena that defied rational explanation were "explained" with the help of supranatural and supernatural beings. Thus, man brought into nature, perceived as impenetrable and chaotic, a magical, holy order. This provided security. It was a means of triumphing over fears and anxieties. The spirits, demons, and gods were very close; they dwelt next door; they lived in almost every object man came into touch with, not to mention the animals. The more mysterious the habits of an animal, the more holy it was. But as human reason developed, making it possible to explain more and more of the unexplainable, the demons' and gods' scope of influence and duties shrank proportionally.

The phenomena in the sky, however, remained unexplainable. The sky became a kind of reservation for the gods driven from the immediate vicinity of human life. Man nominated the heavens the place of residence for the gods. The artists of antiquity beautifully symbolized this by turning the gods into constellations in the sky, and there they remained until renaissance artists brought them back to Earth.

In Aristotle's philosophy, the gods have already been melted into a single god, the immovable moving force whose throne is located somewhere far behind the fixed star sphere. Now an entire, though still conceivable, cosmos separates man from God. The gods-next-door have metamorphosed into a faraway, absent god. In order to preserve some kind of godly presence, the cosmos itself is elevated to a mirror of godliness, and serves as evidence for God's existence. With God now so distant, His existence needs to be proven. And so theology is born. What is at first its strong point, namely its indivisible fusion with a cosmological science, finally turns out to be its ruin. With Copernicus, cosmology and theology become separated.

It is surprising that the creators of this new cosmology, the men who liberated it from theology—Copernicus, Kepler, Galileo, and, finally, Newton—did not believe that their theories contradicted theology's ultimate goal, which is to prove God's existence. For all these great scientists, a world with the Sun at its center was no less godly than one that is centered around the Earth. Copernicus, for example, tried almost passionately to save the circular planetary orbits as a symbol of divine harmony.

Even Kepler, who discovered the less divine elliptical orbits, regarded the wonderful simplicity with which the mathematical laws presented themselves as a visible expression of divine will. In his enthusiastic conviction that he has been chosen to discover the beauty of these works of God, he almost resembles a mystical zealot. (Kepler was also a committed astrologer.) Galileo's new knowledge, too, ultimately provides him only with a new understanding of divine order.

And even Newton, who turns the universe into a smoothly functioning machine, is still convinced that it was God who put this machine in motion. "We know him only by his most wise and excellent contrivances of things, and final causes," he writes. The evidence of the eye has merely been replaced by mathematics. In mathematics, translated into physical laws, the divine *logos* expresses itself. In Newton's opinion, a limited amount of knowledge leads one away from God, but with increasing knowledge one finds the way back to Him.

The church, on the other hand, still believed in the power of visual evidence, although God, its central "object," is beyond perception. From a clerical point of view, this is understandable. Perhaps it would not have been impossible to update theology, adapting it to the latest scientific findings, but that would have contradicted its fundamental claim to offer man something that is durable, fixed, and imperturbable, something that provides spiritual support. The church could not assume the new science's dynamic, questioning, searching nature without dislodging a formal spirituality that was established and consolidated.

Additionally, it must have feared that the partial truths discovered by the sciences might obscure the view of the whole. Every religion claims to advocate the universal that is beyond all science. Moreover, the old Aristotelian worldview was, from a certain standpoint—a religious one, that is—not really so wrong. For man, the Earth *is* the center of the universe because it represents the world he lives in. For our lives, it is not so important whether the Earth orbits the Sun or vice versa. What is important is that the Sun is there, that it shines, rises, and sets.

Today we know that, strictly speaking, the Copernican doctrine was also incorrect. The Sun is *not* the center of the cosmos, nor is it motionless. The cosmos does not have a physical center; its center is, at best, a metaphysical one that every human being might define individually. Copernicus's intellectual achievement was, in a sense, the final incarnation of an ancient sun-mythology consciousness that has never completely been lost to humanity, regardless of the church's persistent support of the geocentric concept.

Copernican teaching represented the transformation of myth into science. The real mistake the church made was to underestimate the effect that the new scientific findings had on the minds of the people. The rapidly developing sciences caused radical social changes and influenced the intellectual climate; they helped man to place himself at the center of his universe, to make him self-confident and (literally speaking) self-conscious. Additionally, the religion-based medieval culture had long been in a state of disarray. The church, too absorbed in power politics, did not notice that it belied its own theology, undermining it from within. In discovering the strength of his intellect, man could not help but regard a theology that relied on dependency as an obstacle, in particular for the central human goal of mastering the spiritual problems of existence.

The triumph of reason that inaugurated the age of enlightenment abolished a central fear: the fear of punishment and damnation, the fear of an angry, punishing God. It was this fear that had tormented man in the Middle Ages, making him seek shelter in the bosom of the church, a church that did its utmost to kindle this fear and to profit from it.

Of course, other elementary fears survived even in the age of enlightenment: fear of fate and death, fear of a meaningless and empty existence. But the old, decaying theology could not provide shelter from these fears; its obsolete concepts failed to offer convincing answers. It lost its social effectiveness. It was no longer able to withstand the weight of the facts unearthed by the enlightened intellect.

In the age of reason, God is, as a matter of fact, no longer relevant. The belief in God has been replaced by the belief in human reason. A radical intellectual reorientation has taken place. Whether God has created the world or not is of minor importance for the enlightened human being. What counts is that the world exists and that the human intellect can discern, understand, and improve it. Social utopias replace the religious utopia of paradise. The optimism of the eighteenth and nineteenth centuries was a secularized messianism that was supposed to liberate mankind once and for all from the curse of original sin, proclaiming redemption not in the hereafter but through progress in this world. From this perspective, the history of mankind supplants the history of salvation in the nineteenth century and becomes "the last religion of the educated," as Benedetto Croce said.

This "de-godding" of nature by the scientific intellect results in a despiritualization of nature. Both phenomena probably find their strongest manifestation in Darwinism. One could exaggerate and say that here God is replaced by the ape. But that would do Darwin an injustice since he never actually claimed that man descended from the ape. He stated merely that man and ape have common ancestors. Moreover, one should not forget that Darwin was a deeply religious man.

The entire nineteenth century, then, is marked by an optimistic-materialistic worldview even though opposition movements emerge, directing attention back to the spiritual. Optimism and materialism were a perfect match; they amalgamated into faith in a significant and limitless evolution in all areas of human existence. Even in spiritism and theosophy, typical pseudoreligious movements of the late nineteenth century, a basically materialistic attitude expressed itself. The soul, above all the soul after death, everything spiritual and supernatural, is treated like matter that can be demonstrated by means of "positive evidence." Anthroposophy, too, which developed from theosophy, wants to prove the spiritual with scientific methods.

Whether the spiritual needs to be proven at all is a question never asked. The occult movements of the late nineteenth century owed their popularity—which is renewed today!—to strong discontent with a Christianity that had been completely debilitated by science and the philosophy of the enlightenment. When optimism and the belief in progress were slightly dampened for the first time, this religious vacuum attracted a host of materialistically based parareligions. In this context, even Marxism can be regarded as a materialistic parareligion: The history of mankind ultimately ends in paradise. Marxism might be compared to a "history of salvation, translated into political economy," as Karl Löwith said.

In an enormous philosophical synopsis, Friedrich Nietzsche had held a passionate funeral oration for Christianity, proclaiming the death of God. Man would now have to take God's place. For Nietzsche, God was only an emblem, the highest symbol for human alienation. Man had created God in order to be punished, rewarded, ordered, patronized, humiliated, suppressed, and, finally, redeemed by his own creation. Now that God was dead, Nietzsche reclaimed everything that Christianity had sold to heaven in terms of human strength and greatness. Nietzsche's atheism is therefore not at all nihilistic. Nietzsche wanted to regain this world after God and the next world had been lost. He wanted to sanctify this world; man should at last begin to look for salvation in his life and not in hypotheses for the soul in the hereafter.

Unfortunately, things did not work out the way Nietzsche had planned them. For in the last alert phase of his life, having turned into a philosphical ruffian, he betrayed his own life-affirming philosophy, thus providing a direct path to the nihilism of our century, which found its most terrible manifestation thus far in Nazi ideology. The spiritual crisis of our century is therefore rooted in a dual loss. We have lost God and the next world without being able to gain an understanding of ourselves and this world.

Albrecht Dürer, Melancholia I
"God" is infinitely big and infinitely small. He must be infinitely big
because he encompasses everything, and he must be infinitely small
because he is contained in everything.

THE UNKNOWN HERETIC

The Negative Theology of Nicholas of Cusa

B efore we enter our own century in the next chapter, and em-
bark upon the mad attempt to understand the radical changes
in physics with a layman's limited understanding, let us make a
brief trip to the beginnings of modern times. I would like to draw
attention to a man whose thinking may be very helpful in our
objective to establish a relationship between modern science and
religion. I am referring to Nicholas of Cusa (1401–1464). Probably very few readers will know what to make of this name, and I
acknowledge immediately that I, too, was not familiar with it until
I started preparing this book. This not only indicates pitiful gaps in
my education but says something, too, about the Catholic religious
instruction I enjoyed, or rather endured, in high school.

Nicholas of Cusa's name was never mentioned, the reason
being, I imagine, that this distinguished cardinal's views would
have confused entirely the logic of the Catholic curriculum. For
although Nicholas was a Catholic appointed to the highest of
offices, his philosophy was sometimes astoundingly, even hereti-
cally, un-Catholic. It was his good fortune that the supreme clerical
authorities of his time apparently either did not see this or did not
care to. One hundred years later, Giordano Bruno would take up
Nicholas's theories and be burned at the stake for it.

Who was Nicholas of Cusa? He was born in Kues on the Moselle
River, the son of a wealthy winegrower. At the age of twelve, he left

home, an early indication of exceptional willpower and decisive-
ness, and of a personality striving for self-fulfillment. At fifteen, he
was a student at the University of Heidelberg and a year later
moved to Padua, beginning six years of informal studies at the
town's famous university where Galileo would teach two hundred
years later. In Padua, he was at the center of the intellectual world
of his era.

Nicholas studied everything that could be studied there at the
time—except theology. He attended lectures on mathematics,
physics, astronomy, medicine, Greek and Roman philosophy, and
law, in which he also took his doctorate. He was then twenty-two.
Shortly afterward he took up theology, not in Padua but at the
University of Cologne. In his case, the sciences made up the foundations of the theological edifice. He then embarked upon a
remarkable clerical career. At twenty-six, he was appointed dean of
Koblenz; three years later he became secretary to the Archbishop
of Trier.

In 1432 a mission as a solicitor brought Nicholas to the Council
of Basel, finally opening a path into the center of ecclesiastical
power. Nicholas became an ardent advocate of the pope in Germany who, in acknowledgment, appointed him cardinal of S.
Pietro in Vincoli in 1448. In 1450 Pope Nicholas V made him
bishop of Brixen. In this function, he became entangled in
extremely taxing and ultimately unsuccessful political struggles
against the secular powers, personified by Count Sigismund of Aus-
tria. Equally unsuccessful was his diplomatic mission of 1451–1452
that aimed at reforming the monasteries and promoting the so-
called Jubilee indulgence of 1450.

He spent the last six years of his life in Rome as vicar-general,
the highest church office next to that of the pope. In this function
he was the closest counselor to Pope Pius II. Nicholas died on
August 11, 1464. Pius II died three days later.

The richness and commitment of this life alone is sufficient to create confidence in the philosophical work that he bequeathed to us. His thinking was not shaped in monkish seclusion as was the case with almost all of the great Christian thinkers but in severe, practical confrontation with the world. He was not only a highly educated but also a widely traveled man. If he was appointed to the highest offices, he never lost his humility. He renounced the pomp belonging to the office of prelate, but also dispensed with the ascetic strictness that makes the works of so many other Christian thinkers unpalatable. The funds his high offices yielded went almost exclusively into a foundation for old people which, after half a millennium, still exists, unchanged.

GOD—ABOVE EVERYTHING
AND WITHIN EVERYTHING

A fundamental point of Nicholas's philosophy will preoccupy us throughout this book: the question of whether God is or is not conceivable. This question arises whenever the word "God" is written or uttered. The word "God" implies that we wrestle with something that can be named, something that lies within the range of human imagination, an object in the broadest sense. This, however, is not the case, at least if the word "God" is used to designate something other than an idol. If we refer to God and not to an idol, we are confronted with the insoluble problem of wanting to understand something rationally that must, if it has divine quality, lie beyond human reason. In other words, between our thoughts and God yawns an insuperable abyss. The logical consequence would be: If nothing can be said about God we can only be silent about God.

To be silent about God was an attitude that did not satisfy the great Christian thinkers. God is, after all, the central "object" of all theologies. And if God is what matters, one has no choice but to talk and write about God. Theology can solve this tricky problem as long as it speaks of God as a personal unity—God as superior being, as superior ruler on a heavenly throne, as superior Father with a superior Son. But if God is supposed to be conceived as infinity, we are at our wit's end because infinity is essentially inconceivable.

The theological problem of God's infinity is in fact very similar to the problem represented by infinity in mathematics and physics. Although mathematics cannot reckon with infinity, there are nevertheless mathematical operations that make infinity intellectually accessible, by graphically depicting the movement of a curve against infinity, for example. Mathematical infinity appears at least foggily even though real infinity remains outside all mathematic calculations. Mathematics points a finger at infinity; one has a notion of what it means but is never able to master it intellectually.

Small wonder, then, that Nicholas, as a scientifically educated man, dealt with the problem of mathematical infinity at some length. It was in fact the only aspect of mathematics in which he was really passionately interested, as he had hoped to find access to divine infinity via mathematical infinity. He concerned himself, for example, with the quantitative relation between circular area and square area and the relation between the arc and chord of a circle. As these relations cannot be compared mathematically, they lead into the irrational.

If we enlarge the circle, arc and chord will become increasingly approximated. The "infinite" circle would be identical with a straight line. This infinite "shape," in which the opposites of circle and line would be abolished, becomes for Nicholas a symbol of the infinity of God. This infinity is beyond human imagination but remains accessible for our intellects because we approach it in a strictly "reasonable" way, in this case via arc and chord. Thus, we can understand the negation of opposites—here, again, of circular arc and chord—in infinity without being able to depict it.

Nicholas's concept coincides with the thoughts on infinity that Augustine had expressed long before: that in God's infinity all insoluble, finite opposites are dissolved. Or, in Augustine's own words: "We conceive God, if we can, as good without the quality of goodness, great without the quantity, a Creator without need for a Creation, enthroned above everything without location, being wholly everywhere without a position, eternal without time, a Creator of changeable things without being Himself subject to change." And Augustine concludes: "If you understand God, it is not God you understand."

This inability to understand, however, is in itself a way of perceiving God, in fact the only possible way. If God is beyond expression, it follows that one can ultimately only say what He is not. This is called negative theology. As early as the first century, Dionysius the Areopagite claimed that God could be conceived only by negation, silently, and in the dark. And Meister Eckhart (ca. 1260 to ca. 1328) said, referring to Dionysius: "But if you desire to see God in reality, you have to accept that He is unknown to us."

God is not a body, not matter, not a person, but nor is He spirit. God does not exist as an individual, but He is not something universal either. He is either all in one or the one in all, the "unique-universal." Negative theology therefore speaks of God in a constant alternation of positive and negative propositions; it defines God through indefiniteness. There is an undefined relation between God and what God *is*. This is why Thomas Aquinas says: "What God Himself is will remain concealed forever. And this is the highest understanding we can have of Him in this life—that we realize that God is beyond everything we might think of Him."

Nicholas hews to the tradition of this negative theology, founded by Augustine and further developed by Thomas Aquinas. His central God-idea is that God can be inconceivably conceived by the reconciliation of an infinite number of given opposites in finite existence. God is infinitely big and infinitely small. He must be infinitely big because he encompasses everything, and he must be infinitely small because he is contained in everything. God's infinity cannot be contrasted with the finite as "the other" because in the contrasting it would itself become finite.

Failure is already contained in the very attempt to imagine God. For Nicholas, however, it is in this constant failure that one encounters the divine. Man's thinking, incessantly aiming at God, does not triumph by revealing God as something struck, a target, say, but in continuously ricocheting to the thinker. To imagine God resembles running at a padded wall or trying to grasp one's own shadow. The thought-arrow touches the absolute, but in touching recoils and throws the archer back upon his finitude. The target is touched but never hit.

For Nicholas, the question of whether God exists or not is therefore not relevant because God does not fit into human categories of existence and nonexistence. "The best answer to the question whether God exists," Nicholas says, "is that he neither is nor is not and that he nonexists and does not exist." This wordplay expresses all the absurdity of the attempt to conceive God. And, what is more, by asking about God we already imply that God exists because we can only ask about, doubt, or confirm something that already exists within the categorization of our thinking. Nicholas concludes: "What is always taken for granted by the questioner, in all the doubtful questions about God, must indubitably be the most certain."

Whatever one thinks of these speculations about God, one has to acknowledge that they leave God in the dark; they do not drag Him down to the finite level of human comprehension as speculative mysticism does, bringing in an enormous variety of image-mongering. Nicholas's speculations always try to maintain the distance between man and God, not to build artificial bridges for the mind, simulating the possibility of a direct encounter of man and God. His thoughts are therefore of a sober—and sobering—nature. On the other hand, this sobriety and strictness give them a distinctly modern touch. His theology sets out precisely where modern science has arrived in the interim: at the borders of the conceivable and the precisely determinable.

THE COSMOS—
INFINITY IN MOTION

Nicholas developed his ideas about God into his own cosmology that had to abandon the medieval concept of a limited universe with a motionless Earth at the center. For how could an infinite and inconceivable God express Himself in such a primitive creation? That would surely have been beneath Him. For Nicholas, the cosmos itself had to be infinite and inconceivable to be commensurate with divine omnipotence. His concepts could, at bottom, almost be called relativistic, for example, the idea that everybody in the universe has to be in its center and outside its center at the same time.

In contrast to Aristotelian cosmology, Nicholas rejected the arbitration between man and God of a cosmos structured into layers and spheres. As a consequence, the entire hierarchy of angels living on the peg ladder of the heavenly spheres as mediators between man and God became irrelevant for him. Nicholas turned his back on this medieval picture of the cosmos that has found its most beautiful poetic representation in Dante's *Divine Comedy*.

For Nicholas, the cosmos has no center; it is absolutely homogeneous in that there is no hierarchy of nobility and purity. Everything is of God, and God is in everything. The cosmos is not static but dynamic. Nothing in the world can be motionless, including the Earth. The entire universe is subject to a motive force that Nicholas calls "nature." No object in the cosmos moves exactly like the others, but every object acts as a motive force on the others and is in turn moved by them. Thus, the entire universe can exist as a unity and does not disintegrate into an infinite multitude.

For Nicholas, every human attempt to fathom the mysteries of the universe is bound to fail. For if we managed to understand the cosmos in all its aspects, we would also understand God, which is impossible because God is beyond understanding. Thus, whenever man tries to probe into the universe's dimension of time, he will finally be confronted with eternity. Where he tries to understand the dimension of space, he will be finally confronted with infinity. And where he tries to understand matter by separating it into ever smaller particles, he will always discover something that is even smaller, and be confronted with the fact that there is no final smallest particle.

If Nicholas, referring to *creation*, speaks of the beginning and end of time, he uses the terms allegorically. It does not mean that time has a beginning and an end as if it were something that supplements creation. For Cusa as well as for modern physics, time is not an absolute in which creation takes place but a dimension, a part of this creation. In general, the idea of relativity is of central importance in Nicholas's cosmology: There is no absolute measure; all measures are relative. And because there is no absolute measure, all measurements lack absolute precision. Even the movements of the objects in space are relative; no movement can absolutely be the largest.

Everything in the cosmos, including the Sun, has to be in motion, but the movement is always different. There is no fixed resting point to which all movements may be related. And because everything in the cosmos is in motion, this has to apply to the Earth, too. From this it follows that orientation itself is only relative. To make any point the absolute center is purely arbitrary. Just as startling is Nicholas's theory that nothing in the world is absolute and exact, and that, therefore, "The Earth is not spherical although it tends to be of spherical shape." As we know today, the Earth is, because of its rotation, oblated at the poles. It is not a globe but a rotary ellipsoid.

Nicholas develops the concept of relativity even further: The Earth receives light, heat, and other forces from the Sun and other heavenly bodies, but these forces are not a proof of its absolute imperfection because, being a heavenly body, the Earth acts upon the Sun and all the other bodies as well. There are reciprocal influences everywhere. No object in the universe can exist without the others. Thus, Nicholas's theses include a basic relativistic theory of gravitation. He finally concludes that, as Earth is populated by human beings, animals, and plants, so could other heavenly bodies be a dwelling for other beings. "We assume that all stars are populated," he says. Although this is wrong, as we know now, one has to keep in mind how outrageous these thoughts were to the fifteenth century, the more so as they came from a Catholic dignitary.

SCIENCE AS KNOWLEDGE OF LOVE

Nicholas's writings are fascinating for his courage to think the unthinkable and simply sweep aside the mind-limiting dogmas of the Aristotelian world system. Nicholas is absolutely un-Catholic when his cosmology logically concludes that creation does not have to be exclusively limited to man as the crown of creation. Nicholas believes that God has not created the world merely for the purpose of creating man. That would be too enormous an expenditure for a creature that, at a closer look, appears to be rather wretched. It is presumptuous for man to believe that the whole universe receives meaning only through him, while he himself is constantly occupied in the search for a meaning.

If Nicholas gives us a glimpse of the relativity theory in his thoughts on the biggest things, the quantum theory shines through his thoughts on the smallest. For example: "We will never reach the simplest elementary units existing entirely in reality, for in the realm of the subtly differentiated there is no absolutely largest or smallest even though our reason believes in their existence."

One might think that Nicholas of Cusa aimed at pointing out the basic problem of modern particle physics: that the most elementary particles, the so-called quarks, can no longer be regarded in isolation. Moreover, they can no longer be designated as particles in the sense of material units. Quarks are located in a physical

"somewhere" between matter and spirit. But that will be the subject of a later chapter.

Nicholas succeeded in designing, through mere philosophical
speculation, a cosmology that has been confirmed as basically correct by empirical science on its long and stony path via Copernicus,
Kepler, Galileo, Newton, and Einstein. Of particular importance is
Nicholas's view that man loses nothing by knowing that he is no
longer at the center of the world, and that human existence is by
no means reduced or rendered meaningless by this knowledge. For
faithful thinking and thoughtful faith, all that really matters is a
metaphysical center, that is, the assurance of being forever rooted
in the whole of existence. In this case, faith is no more static than
science. Nicholas integrates the idea of progress into faith; to be
inspired by infinity means to move forward constantly, to cross
frontiers, not to settle back and make oneself comfortable in a rigid
religious system or even revert to the heathen creeds of occultism
and magic. What we believe in must be in harmony with what we
know; otherwise faith is debased into superstition and idolatry.

Nicholas's theses result in the necessity of a faith supported by
knowledge, from which derives the necessity of a knowledge
underlined by faith. This, however, touches upon a question that
becomes more and more pressing in our century, the question of
the purpose of science, of science and ethics. Nicholas dismisses
man's anxiety to learn in principle: "As long as the mind indulges
in vain knowledge unrestrainedly, it will no more reach the object
of a natural desire than someone who woos every maid. He must
not wed a fickle but an eternal knowledge."

Nicholas makes clear that he is not against science per se, but
demands that it be married with faith or, in other words, that it
become moral. Without this union of faith and morality, knowledge fades into many individual truths that lack meaning because
they lack unity. The numerous isolated partial truths spawned by
the human intellect only become *the* truth if a universal absolute is
added which, for Nicholas, can only be God. And this means that

science, if it strives after this all-embracing unity, is one of the means by which the human intellect can arrive at a perception of God. If science fails to do so it remains inherently incomplete because it is, as a whole, directionless.

Chaotic, riddled with conflicts, directionless—this is how science appears today. In almost all of its splintered specialist disciplines, it constantly encounters new borders and new borderline questions; all of these are solved at one time or another, but the solution only leads to new borders. A bottomless pit. Modern science incidentally designs, from its own inner conflicts, the picture of an unstable world leading into meaninglessness and endlessness. By looking for a purpose within itself or a partial meaning within a partial area of itself, modern science deprives the world as a whole of a universal meaning.

Contemporary research obeys only its own intrascientific law of problem-creation through problem-solution. The manner in which science—at an increasingly breathless pace—solves its partial problems turns it into a problem itself; and science's problem is lack of purpose. Nicholas seems to have anticipated this basic dilemma of modern science, seems to have suspected the great danger emerging when science, without a universal morality, merely obeys its own laws or simply the law of necessity. "To lead a good life in the manner of the world, all men make use of their reason as of a slave who helps them gain possessions, praise, and honor," Nicholas says. In this way, science will never establish a purpose for itself. As a whole, it has a universal quality because it can turn everything into a scientific object, but it is far from being a universal science that seeks to provide knowledge of the unity of things.

For Nicholas, it is beyond doubt that only God can be in possession of such perfect knowledge. He believes that the purpose of science is to serve this essential knowledge that is God's own. True perception is, ultimately, perception of God. Scientific observation should contain the experience of universal harmony, and this experience will then automatically influence its methods of research. For

Nicholas, this kind of perception coincides with his understanding of love. He speaks of the "knowledge of love." A knowledge that does not possess this quality is not knowledge but ignorance.

In his book on Nicholas of Cusa, to which I refer here, Karl Jaspers has summarized the problems of modern science and technology as follows:

> Almost until the beginning of our century, most creative researchers (of nature, history, spiritual reality, politics) were faithful Christians. They rarely openly admitted that, in the objects of their perception, they interpreted the world's language as the language of the deity. In their intention to keep science pure, they did not want to let this fact enter their arguments and verifiable observations. They looked for God not in mere feeling but in perceiving the nature of things. Perception was supported by feeling which, in turn, became more clearly defined. If the intellectual component within this basic state of belief is lost, science itself changes. It is in danger of losing itself, in the organized activity of the technological age, to a multitude of observations no longer spiritually inspired and to the methods of specialists who see nothing but their limited object. Even though modern science advances solely by means of specialized methods, these in turn are part of something greater, recognizable in the researcher and his achievements but, being no object, not explicitly there. If this is lost, then the specialists will, for all their sophistication, waste away beyond their particular scientific field, and spiritually in their lives. Thus a science continues to operate that not only in its methods and convictions but also in its meaning becomes self-sufficient, that aspires to be an end in itself. The impossibility of this becomes apparent in the scientific superstition that continues to grow despite the vast progress made, filling the vacuum with less-than-transcendent positivistic, naturalistic, spiritual theories of existence which lack scientific quality.

By "scientific superstition" Jaspers means the strong tendency of many scientists to make principal truths of their observations, to turn theories into "existential knowledge." Add to this the characteristic feature of science to make an end of itself, its lack of moral leadership accompanied by a preference for messages of salvation in the manner of "we will lead humanity to true happiness." No, at best science will one day tell us what this universality of the world is, but it will never be able to answer the question of the meaning of this universality. Yet it is this meaning that man yearns for in the depths of his being.

Solar Corona
What we perceive as the world is the three-dimensional shadow
that four-dimensional space-time casts upon our consciousness.

{ 2 }

THE RENUNCIATION OF ABSOLUTE SPACE AND ABSOLUTE TIME

Einstein's Theory of Relativity

To make it clear at the outset: It is impossible to present the theory of relativity in a popular way. The layman may read as many popular-science books about Einstein's theory as he likes—and there are quite a lot around—but he will never really understand it, even though the authors continue to promise just that. One simply has to put up with it; it is part of the cruel fate of being a layman. Or one studies mathematics and physics diligently and ceases to be a layman. For our purposes, however—to oppose modern science and religion—it is sufficient to have a notion of what is contained in the theory of relativity. After all, we find our way around with mere notions in the field of religion, too. And the sound of *notion* makes it a pretty pleasant word, soft and flexible. Its meaning is equally attractive: to be certain in uncertainty. In any case, this word will be our faithful companion in the labyrinth of ideas.

Language generally becomes a problem if one wants to describe something vividly that can be represented precisely only in the abstract language of mathematics. This chapter, for example, deals frequently with the terms *space* and *time*, which we use quite naturally in daily life. In the theory of relativity, however, they lose this natural quality, to the same extent as the theory itself has precious little to do with everyday experience. The theory of relativity has overthrown the traditional, classical understanding of space and time, but in order to present their new meaning nonmathematically, only the old terms *space* and *time* are available.

This problem, however, has been known in physics—in a milder form—for a long time. Where physics abandons mathematical representation, it traditionally borrows words from everyday life, not least from the abstract sphere of human existence. Energy, power, work, action, impulse, inertia—these are all terms which, strictly speaking, humanize the world of the purely physical. There is nothing detrimental in this, however, because it would not occur to anybody to attribute human inertia or human energy to an object. Nevertheless, the use of such terms reveals a certain lack of scientific accuracy. If the layman tries to give these terms a meaning he does so in analogies to human existence, and even the physicist, thinking in mathematical formulas and equations or reading values off measuring devices, will always have these analogous terms in mind. And his search for new findings would probably be absolutely fruitless if he did not do so.

WHICH SPACE WHERE?
WHICH TIME WHEN?

But now for Einstein's new world-picture. We have seen that the development of the physical world-picture can be roughly divided into two phases. The first phase was that of direct visual experience. The Earth was at rest at the center of the universe because man regarded it as the center of his world. Everything had its place or was moving toward its place. The second phase started with the changes effected by Copernicus. The Earth lost its motionless, privileged position. The Sun remained the center of the planetary system, but was no longer the center of the universe.

Parallel to the astronomical unlocking of the world, which is directly linked to the development of more and more sophisticated telescopes, material reality was redefined in mathematical terms as regards its substantial variety and its temporal and spatial relationships. These efforts were brought to completion by Newton's principles: an absolutely motionless space, a uniformly flowing time, an eternal and indestructible material substance called mass, and, finally, definite laws of cause and effect. These are—in rough outline—the basic definitions for a physcial description of nature. Even though Newton's mechanics had to be extended later due to the discovery of electromagnetism, which added the properties of charge and energy and the law of conservation to the property of mass, the foundations of Newton's system nevertheless remained unshaken until the beginning of our century.

The logical perfection of Newton's system notwithstanding, there remained a certain degree of discontent, mainly as regards the idea of absolute space, that was shared by Newton himself. For the physical laws themselves, strictly speaking, required that there was no absolute space, that is, an absolute, fixed position to which all movements could be related. Newton clung to the idea of absolute space simply for religious reasons. To abandon absolute space would have meant giving up the idea of an absolute God as well.

The religious need for an absolute metaphysical point of reference precipitated the emergence of a scientific need for an absolute physical point of reference. Absolute motionless space was, so to speak, a physical derivative of God as the "motionless mover." In this respect, the most rational of all thinkers proved totally irrational. Here, we are again confronted with the phenomenon of obsolete religious concepts blocking or misleading scientific observation.

Even in Newton's lifetime, other thinkers who were better able to separate physics and God had doubted the existence of absolute space. One of them was the Irish philosopher and theologian George Berkeley (1685–1753) who wrote: "Every place is relative, every motion relative. If all bodies are destroyed we shall be left with mere nothing, for all the attributes assigned to empty space

are immediately seen to be primitive or negative except its extension. But this when space is literally empty, cannot be described or
measured and so it too is effectively nothing." In other words:
There is no absolute motionless space.

THERE IS NO ABSOLUTE,
MOTIONLESS SPACE

The supposition that absolute space exists was, of course, not
based only on religious reasoning. Light had always played a special
role in Newton's mechanics. In the framework of these theories,
light could be understood only if one described its propagation in
space analogously to the propagation of sound. This required a
material medium in which light can travel in a wavelike pattern.
Light, however, also travels where there is no such medium; in fact,
it travels fastest in the vacuum. Sound, on the other hand, cannot
travel in the vacuum. It was therefore concluded that even the vacuum cannot be absolutely empty, that it must contain a substance
in which light waves can travel and sound waves cannot. This substance was called *ether*.

The idea that electromagnetic waves might have their own reality, that they might travel independent of a medium, did not occur
to the physicists at the time. Ether, on the other hand, could be
nicely reconciled with the idea of absolute space; it represented, as
it were, the absolute substance of absolute space. Thus, classic
mechanical physics had killed two birds with one stone: There was
now an absolute motionless reference for light traveling in the universe as well as a medium, although a mysterious one, in which it
traveled. There was even something more: an absolute point of reference to which all movements in the universe, not only those of
light, could be related. Ether represented absolute, motionless
space.

Physicists could have been content with this beautiful solution,
but unfortunately other questions arose. One question that sprang
to mind immediately was: What does ether consist of? It had to be
a very light substance, neither visible nor tangible, filling both

empty space and space filled with air, water, or transparent solid bodies. Here, a certain contradiction already manifests itself. Why does ether fill a solid body made of glass—because light can spread out in glass—but not a body made of stone or metal?

In general, ether had to possess characteristics that lay somewhere between the material and the purely spiritual. If it was of material nature, it had to put up a certain amount of resistance, however small, to every body that passed through it, even if one imagined ether as an incredibly thin gas consisting of unknown elements. Employing an unknown quantity to support a thesis rarely leads to satisfactory scientific results; it only renders the propounding of theories more and more arbitrary and uncontrollable. Finally, physicists agreed to attribute to ether the role of an immaterial but consistent medium, characterized by an absence of characteristics. A truly divine but unfortunately rather unscientific substance!

As ether could not be described physically, physicists invested all their energy in proving its existence at least indirectly, via its function of transferring light waves, in appropriate experiments. But all these experiments, however brilliantly devised, could not furnish proof of the existence of ether. Of course, the impossibility of detecting this substance could have been easily explained with the fact that it does not exist, but the apparent necessity of its existence had entrenched itself so firmly in the physicists' heads that this assumption, as simple as it was subversive, was definitely out of the question.

It was Albert Einstein (1879–1955) who finally relieved physics from this theoretical dilemma. His genius consisted, first of all, simply in the courage to think the impossible, which was, at the same time, the most obvious: that there is no such substance as ether. In 1905 the hitherto unknown Einstein, in his famous thesis in the *Annalen der Physik*, claimed that ether was unnecessary. Instead, one should start by simply stating that even without ether, space has the physical characteristic of transferring electromagnetic waves (namely, radio waves of different wave lengths; infrared heat radiation; the small range of waves visible to us, which we call *light;* ultraviolet radiation; soft, medium, and hard X-rays; gamma rays; and finally ultrahard X-rays).

In physics, as in all other sciences, it is of course not sufficient to simply erase a term from the scientific vocabulary. Such an erasure demands a fundamentally new approach to the problems of perception that produced the dubious term in the first place. Einstein approached the new solution through the concept of *time.* His radical thesis stated that there is no absolute time. From this, Einstein developed what is called the "special theory of relativity." This theory is based on two postulates. First: The speed of light in the vacuum is the same for all systems moving at constant velocity with respect to one another. Second: Natural laws are, without exception, true for all systems moving at constant velocity with respect to one another.

THERE IS NO ABSOLUTE TIME

The first postulate, as it is formulated here, does not reveal itself to us laymen immediately. I will therefore—at least for my own benefit—take a closer look at it. First, what is meant by "system"? As early as Greek antiquity, physicists were familiar with the idea that the motion of any given object can only be described in relation to another object. Thus, the motion of a vehicle is normally measured relative to the ground, and the motion of a planet relative to the Sun. In theoretical physics, a body that is used for referencing a movement in space is called a coordinate system. Without such a system of coordinates, the mechanical laws of Galileo and Newton, for example, could never have been formulated.

In Newton's mechanics of the universe, this coordinate system, which is used as a reference point for the motions of heavenly bodies, is anchored, so to speak, in absolute motionless space and therefore is absolute and motionless itself. Here, physics ultimately related the motions of cosmic objects to a divine absolute; God was elevated, or rather degraded, to an absolute coordinate system. In science, this is not permanently tenable. By abandoning absolute space as well as its substance, *ether*, Einstein also abandons an absolute coordinate system to which all movements in the universe can be related. Thus, now every object in the universe can be regarded as a coordinate system.

If the laws of mechanics are to remain valid, however, these objects have to fulfill two conditions in order to be suitable as coordinate systems: They must be "free of rotation" and "free of acceleration." In other words, they have to move linearly, without self-rotation, and at constant velocity. Such a coordinate system is called an inertial system. If an object in the universe complies with the requirements of an inertial system, all bodies moving linearly and at constant velocity relative to this object are also inertial systems. Reduced to a simple formula, all movements are relative. In a strictly physical sense, it is therefore not possible to state that an object that moves linearly and uniformly (= inertial system) moves at a specific speed; one can only say that it moves at this speed relative to another object, which must also be an inertial system.

In the first postulate of the special theory of relativity, a second thought is imposed onto the first one: In the vacuum, light always travels at the same speed—independently from the motion of its source—relative to every other uniformly moving system. In other words, all observers moving linearly and at constant speeds must measure the same velocity of light, no matter whether the observer and the source of light are approaching each other or separating. The velocity of light relative to such an observer is always 300,000 kilometers per second. (The exact value in the vacuum is 299,792.458 km/sec.)

THE ILLUSION OF
SIMULTANEITY IN THE COSMOS

Einstein's postulates have far-reaching effects on our concepts of cosmic space and cosmic time. In daily life on planet Earth, terms like *past, future, present moment,* or *simultaneity* do not cause particular problems. Everybody knows what they mean. Time is what the clock shows, and events are simultaneous if they take place at precisely the same time (provided all clocks keep exactly the same time). To define simultaneity in everyday life is unproblematic because the distances separating simultaneous events are comparatively small, and the velocity of light by which an event is transmitted can therefore be regarded as infinitely big.

If, for example, a traffic light 100 meters away from me switches from red to green, I can say that this event takes place in the moment of my observation because the amount of time it takes for light to travel from the traffic light to the retinae of my eyes is almost infinitely small and therefore negligible. And if a second observer is located at a distance of 300 meters from the traffic light, he and I will perceive the event at the same time. Both observers, although at different distances from the event, are temporally connected by what is called the present. The terms *present* and *simultaneity* can be safely used anywhere on Earth because relative to the velocity of light even the greatest distances on our planet are absolutely irrelevant.

This changes radically as soon as one mentally leaves the Earth and tries to apply the term *simultaneity* to the unfathomable dimensions of the universe. Relative to cosmic dimensions, light suddenly seems rather slow. To travel from the Andromeda nebula—our galactic neighbor—to Earth, light requires more than two million years, yet this galaxy is effectively on our doorstep and can be perceived with the naked eye as a small nebulous cloud in the Andromeda constellation. Compared to cosmic dimensions, everyday sensations of simultaneity become meaningless.

If one takes a cosmic event, the explosion of a star, say, then two observers, separated by a great distance both from the event and from each other, and traveling linearly and at uniform velocity relative to each other, would attribute different times and positions to the event. For the two observers, the same event does not take place at the same time and at the same place, meaning that time, which we like to regard as universal, becomes a quantity dependent on the observer's motion and position in space.

Future and past, which we experience in daily life as separated by an infinitely short time span—the present—are, compared to cosmic dimensions, separated by a finite period of time that increases with the observer's distance from the event. What happens "in this instance" anywhere in the cosmos is beyond the scope of our experience. At any given point, we observe a state of the universe that lies extremely far back in the past. Our earthly present takes place, as it were, in front of a backdrop made up of multiple cosmic pasts. This is true even for the Sun, despite its relative closeness.

If the Sun exploded *now* we would not be aware of it. Life on Earth would go on as usual—for eight minutes! Then we would notice that the Sun has exploded, and fortunately there would be no time left for terror. The "moment" between past (the Sun is still intact) and future (the Sun has exploded), which we would normally perceive as infinitely short, would have lasted slightly more than eight minutes relative to the Earth. Past, present, and future are therefore just relative entities. As our consciousness is shaped entirely by the conditions of earthly existence, it is only natural that giving up the idea of absolute time, which for us is the absolute, unchangeable measure per se, is not easy.

On the other hand, we do not experience time so absolutely anyway. On our "inner clock," time sometimes passes incredibly fast and sometimes agonizingly slowly, which very often makes us believe that our clocks are wrongly set. Of course, the psychological relativity of time must not be confused with the physical relativity of time in the universe. But it may help in relinquishing time as an absolute quantity.

The postulates of the special theory of relativity spawn other interesting consequences, but these can be derived logically only on a mathematical level. As laymen we have to accept the fact that we cannot really understand them. We have seen that the basic definitions of special relativity imply the necessity to reconsider and finally modify the Newtonian concepts of absolute space and time. As *time* and *space* have become entirely relative terms, this naturally affects also the instruments—clock and ruler—with which distances and time intervals are measured, in a manner that must strike our poor nonspecialist brains as sheer madness.

In systems moving at different speeds relative to each other, rulers have different lengths and clocks run at different speeds. And the laws governing these phenomena are the same for all systems. This sounds truly mysterious, but only for a thinking that is itself based on something entirely mysterious: absolute time and absolute space. In classical physics, it has always been understood that clocks run at the same speed in motion and at rest, and that a ruler has the same length in motion and at rest, overlooking the fact that there is no such thing as rest. A pencil lying on my desk is only at rest relative to the Earth. Relative to the Sun it performs a rather complex dance composed of two circular movements. The Sun, on the other hand, is not at rest either; it orbits around the center of our galaxy, and the galaxy in turn moves relative to every other galaxy. Viewed from a different perspective, the planets' elliptical orbits might appear as wave lines or spirals. They are only elliptical if the planetary motion is viewed relative to the central body.

What makes the special theory of relativity so hard to understand for the layman is the fact that what it says has no practical meaning for human existence because we are only confronted with bodies moving at speeds that are irrelevant compared to the speed of light. If the speed of a clock in motion and the length of a ruler in motion depend on the relative velocity of the respective object, differences in length or speed would become noticeable only if their relative velocity was very close to the speed of light. Even then the persistence of our vision would render them invisible for us.

If the relative speed of a ruler gradually approached the speed of light it would contract—in the direction of its movement—and a clock would slow down. Relative to another uniformly moving system, a ruler traveling at the speed of light would theoretically vanish and a clock would stand still. In everyday language this sounds rather absurd, but mathematically it can be presented in rock-solid equations. Higher mathematics, however, cannot easily be incorporated in so-called common sense, which works on an imaginative level. Common sense tells us that an airplane will not contract while traveling through the air, and that the pilot's watch will not slow down—provided it is a good watch. It is absurd to apply the theory of relativity to such everyday phenomena; here it is sufficient to adhere to the old Newtonian physics, and this would still be the case if our planes traveled ten thousand times faster than they do now.

Equally nonsensical are attempts to make relativity plausible by means of examples taken from an illusory everyday world. Neither rulers nor clocks can travel at speeds close to the speed of light because where would the necessary energy come from?

The theory of relativity does not make classical physics invalid but enables us to determine where it is sufficient and when it stops being exact. In a nutshell: Newtonian physics becomes inexact when we deal with speeds close to the speed of light. To apply the theory of relativity to the motion of airplanes or rockets would be as absurd as using a computer for arithmetic tasks where the multiplication table is sufficient.

THE EQUIVALENCE OF
MASS AND ENERGY

I have not yet mentioned perhaps the most important result of the special theory of relativity. The mathematical conditions derived from the two basic postulates do not only result in new, relativistic laws of motion but also in a new, relativistic law of inertia. The relativistic laws of motion imply that the closer an object's speed gets to the speed of light, the harder it is to further increase it.

In modern accelerators, elementary particles—electrons, for example—almost reach the speed of light. Almost, but not quite. If an electron is charged with an energy of 1 GeV (giga electron volt), it reaches 99.99997 percent of the speed of light. (eV is the energy unit used by elementary physicists; 1 eV is the kinetic energy of an electron moved through a potential difference of 1 V; 1 GeV equals one billion eV.) If an electron is charged with 100 GeV, it reaches 99.999999997 percent of the speed of light. Close to the speed of light, huge amounts of energy are necessary to produce a scarcely measurable acceleration. In order to accelerate a particle to exactly 100 percent of the speed of light, one would need an infinite amount of energy. The velocity of light is an absolute limit.

Among other things, Newtonian mechanics states that every body at rest has a specific mass, the so-called rest mass. This rest mass causes an object to *resist* being brought out of its state of rest, to resist in general every change of speed. This resistance increases with the mass of the body. The special theory of relativity provides an important addition to this law: The greater the speed of a body, the more it resists a change of speed.

Einstein generalized the results outlined above even further. The kinetic energy of a body resists a change of speed in the same way as mass does. What is valid for kinetic energy must also be valid for every other kind of energy because every form of energy can be converted into every other form. It follows that every form of energy resists changes of speed, and that energy and mass behave identically. In relativity, *energy* and *mass* have become interchangeable. Instead of saying that the Sun shines, one could say it emits mass. If I impart to a piece of metal so much energy that it starts glowing, I can say that this glowing piece of metal has more mass, meaning it is heavier than when it was cold.

Classical physics strictly separated mass and energy; mass was considered weighable whereas energy was regarded as weightless, even spiritual. Relativistic physics, on the other hand, has proven that there is no fundamental difference between mass and energy, that mass is only a visible, tangible form of energy, and energy an invisible form of mass. Mass and energy do not exist as separate quantities but as a coherent mass-energy or energy-mass. That this apparently simple law had remained undiscovered for such a long time is due to the fact that it could not be proved experimentally since no scales were available that provided the necessary degree of precision. Here, again, the results of the special theory of relativity lie way beyond our scope of experience. Einstein stated as an example that the heat energy necessary to convert 30,000 tons of water into vapor would only weigh about 1 gram.

Nuclear fission and nuclear fusion (as well as all the horrors they entailed) are visible proofs of the equivalence of mass and energy, which Einstein mathematically presented in his famous equation $E = mc^2$ (where E is energy, m is mass, and c is the speed of light). The knowledge that enormous amounts of energy are hidden in atomic nuclei, however, predated Einstein's revolutionary achievements, having been established in the experiments on radioactive decay conducted by Becquerel (1852–1908), Curie (1867–1934), and Rutherford (1871–1937).

COSMIC SPACE-TIME

Although, as nonspecialists, we have not fully understood the special theory of relativity, the facts so laboriously formulated here may at least have had one effect on our thinking. We no longer imagine the universe as some kind of infinitely big shoe box, that is, as a three-dimensional structure in which every movement performed by an object can be determined by means of three coordinates. In the universe, where everything moves relative to everything else and where no absolute reference point exists, a three-dimensional coordinate system would be totally arbitrary. This is also true for time.

In order to describe any given event in the universe in a mathematically exact way one cannot avoid fusing space (which is determined by the three coordinates) and time into a unity. This is what Einstein did in his ensuing theoretical work. The theory of relativity does not distinguish between space and time coordinates but combines them into a space-time continuum, also called space-time. That's easily said, but what is meant by *fusing* three-dimensional space and one-dimensional time into a four-dimensional space-time continuum? It sounds very much like hocus-pocus.

Einstein himself was aware that the fusion of space and time would pose problems for the nonspecialist mind. It is consoling to recall that at first even hard-boiled physicists had no end of trouble with Einstein's theory. "The nonmathematician," Einstein says, "is seized by a mysterious fear when he hears of four-dimensional things—similar to that awakened by images of the occult. And yet it is just a plain statement if we say that the world in which we live is a four-dimensional spatiotemporal 'continuum'." As experts in plain things, we surely should be able to find our way through this. Take courage!

First of all, one has to know what is meant by "continuum." In principle, for every number of dimensions there are corresponding continua, that is, continuous patches of space. A continuum is characterized by its uninterrupted continuity in itself. A ruler, for example, would be a one-dimensional space continuum. It can be divided into an infinite number of continuous units of measure. Most rulers give decimeter, centimeter, and millimeter as units, but theoretically millimeters do not have to be the limit. Each interval between two marks on the ruler can be subdivided into an infinite number of even smaller units. And this is the exact definition of a continuum.

A position in the one-dimensional continuum is determined by exactly one coordinate point. Correspondingly, a position in the two-dimensional continuum is defined by a degree of longitude and a degree of latitude. Seamen are therefore practitioners of the two-dimensional continuum. Airplane pilots are practitioners of the three-dimensional continuum; for them it is not sufficient to determine their position simply by longitude and latitude; they also have to take into account the vertical distance to the ground.

So far, we are still dealing with positions outside time. All natural phenomena connected to motion, however, take place inside time. If we want to represent motion in a one-dimensional continuum, for example, the movement of a train traveling on a straight route, we have to merge time and the one-dimensional continuum into a two-dimensional space-time continuum. Graphically, the one-dimensional movement of the train is representend as a continuous line in a two-dimensional diagram. Similarly, if we want to represent the cruising of a ship on the two-dimensional surface of the ocean, we have to merge this continuum and time into a three-dimensional space-time continuum. Finally, if we want to view an object's flight as a spatiotemporal unity, we have to represent it as a continuous line in a four-dimensional space-time continuum. Unfortunately, this can no longer be done graphically because in graphic depiction only three dimensions are available, and in this case time as well has to be represented as a space coordinate. The only difficulty posed by the four-dimensional space-time continuum is that we cannot visualize it; it lies beyond our imagination because our sensory perception is forever trapped in the three-dimensional.

For the mathematician, representing a continuum with any number of dimensions is easy; he represents the dimensions as numbers, and time is just one of several coordinates. In the first dimension, a line between A and B simply corresponds to the axis x: $AB = x$. On the two-dimensional plane, a line-segment AB is derived from the two coordinates x and y (length and width) by using the Pythagorean theorem: $AB = \sqrt{x^2 + y^2}$. In three-dimensional space, a line-segment AB is derived from the three coordinates x, y, z (length, width, height) by extending the Pythagorean theorem: $AB = \sqrt{x^2 + y^2 + z^2}$. This branch of mathematics is called spherical trigonometry.

To simplify matters, we have left the time factor out so far because it is not really necessary as long as we only deal with line-segments and not with continuous motion. For a representation of the cosmic dimension, however, time is essential; it is needed even if we just want to represent a line-segment AB because, as every object in the cosmos moves relative to every other object, space and time cannot be viewed separately. Thus, a "line" between A and B in the four-dimensional space-time continuum is represented mathematically as: $AB = \sqrt{x^2 + y^2 + z^2 - (ct)^2}$, where t is time and c is the speed of light. Here, time is linked to the speed of light and reflected in the fourth coordinate.

To speak of a line-segment AB in connection with space-time is not correct; hence the inverted commas. One must not think of the points A and B as position points; they are "points" in space-time that are determined by position *and* time. Points in the four-dimensional space are events in space-time. This implies that there is no absolute point of rest in the universe. As every point is an event, it is inextricably linked to the speed of light in that it communicates itself at this velocity, emitting light or other electromagnetic waves.

On a mathematical level this appears convincing, but it does not clear the fog in our heads. Our minds cannot help but separate the dimensions of space and time. If we try to combine them, we arrive at the image of a movement in space. This separation, however, is purely subjective, a consequence of our limited perception that we are inclined to regard as absolute. The special theory of relativity, however, proves that space and time, viewed separately, are only relative quantities and therefore different for every single observer. Universally valid statements on the cosmos cannot be based on human perception just because this perception has proved sound in our narrow existence on Earth, where it is is sufficient to regard space and time as separate dimensions.

Space appears to us as something external and time as something internal. On Earth, we always know what is up and what is down, what is before and what is after. In the cosmos, there is no up and down, no before and after. With regard to the entire universe, "space and time, as separate entities, have turned into meaningless, empty phantoms; they maintain their reality content only in combination," as the mathematician Hermann Minkowski (1864–1909) once said; he contributed decisively to providing a mathematical basis for the special theory of relativity, establishing exact formulae for the space-time continuum.

COSMIC SPACE-TIME IS NO CONSTRUCTION...

It would be utterly wrong to regard the space-time continuum as just a mathematical construct. On the contrary, it is our conception of a three-dimensional world that is entirely constructed. For example, all measurements of time are also measurements of space, and vice versa. Seconds, minutes, hours, days, weeks, months, years, and seasons are time measures that are inseparable from the Earth's position in the universe, relative to the Sun, the moon, the planets, and the stars.

two diff perspective.

Our experience of time is inseparably connected to movements in space, or, more precisely, the Earth's motion around its axis and around the Sun. An astronomer peering through a telescope looks out not only into space but also back into the past. He never sees the universe as it is "now." Now does not exist in the cosmos. What makes the theory of relativity so fascinating is that here, for the first time, human reason has an exact mathematical representation of a cosmic reality that lies outside its scope of sensual experience. Hence the inclination of many great scientists to regard mathematics as a key to the unimaginable.

To exaggerate: God cannot be imagined but it might be possible one day to describe Him in a mathematically exact way. Of course, mathematics is of as little help to the religious layman as it is to the nonphysicist. Even if God could be described mathematically, the layman would still have to believe in Him as he has to believe in the existence of space-time even though, scientifically, there is no doubt about its reality. To speak of a mathematically describable God, however, does not make sense, mainly because God, if He exists, would be beyond mathematics, which is merely a human

Maybe analytical aspect of God.

Color is not reducible to wavelength: we merely find correspondence.

language, albeit the most powerful and precise. To perceive God is possible, if at all, only on a metalingual level, not through mathematics but through *mathesis,* the gnostic term for the acquisition of a higher knowledge or enlightenment.

But let us abandon metaphysics for the time being and return to the nice, layman-friendly formula with which a line-segment AB (it would be better to speak of an interval between two events) in the space-time continuum can be represented: $AB = \sqrt{x^2 + y^2 + z^2 - (ct)^2}$. What is particularly striking is the minus sign before the fourth or time coordinate. The dimension of time is not just added to the three spatial dimensions, which indicates that the space-time continuum is not merely space extended by one dimension. The fusion of space and time is of a special nature, expressed by the minus sign in the formula. This also results in a special kind of geometry for the space-time continuum. The Euclidian geometry that we successfully employ in everyday life for calculating line-segments, surfaces, and bodies is of no use in the space-time continuum.

Taking a closer look at the fourth coordinate in the formula, one will notice that it is not really a time coordinate. Time *(t)* is multiplied with the speed of light *(c)* and thus converted into a distance, seconds becoming kilometers. In four-dimensional space-time, time measurement and space measurement, as I have mentioned above, are interchangeable. Special relativity makes it possible to indicate time in kilometers. *c* becomes a universally valid factor for converting space measure into time measure, and vice versa. This is permissible because *c* is the same for all observers in the universe, no matter what their position, speed, or direction.

only if there is no action at a distance

Distances between cosmic events can therefore be expressed by means of a time-dependent unit called a light-year. One light-year indicates both an interval (1 year) and a distance (9.46 trillion kilometers). Here, the fusion of time and space has entered language, or, as it is expressed in *Parsifal:* "I scarcely tread, yet seem already to have come far/You see my son, time here becomes space."

We have seen that the Pythagorean theorem can be represented by $AB = \sqrt{x^2 + y^2}$ and that its extension to three dimensions results in spherical trigonometry and the equation $AB = \sqrt{x^2 + y^2 + z^2}$. One might expect that adding a fourth dimension would result in the formula $AB = \sqrt{x^2 + y^2 + z^2 + (ct)^2}$, yet this is not the case. The mathematical linking of the three space dimensions with the time dimension makes a minus sign necessary. A plus sign would make time just a fourth dimension of space. Calculating the "distance" of cosmic events by means of four space dimensions, however, would be most confusing, because in this case, the distance as well as the velocity of light would once more be dependent on the observer's speed. This can be avoided only by placing a minus sign before the time coordinate; it guarantees that every observer, independent of his own velocity, measures the same speed of light.

Even though time appears in the equation as a spatial distance, it is not simply a fourth dimension of space. The minus sign allows for an obvious distinction between time and space, although time appears as a measure of space. As nonspecialists, we lack the mathematical knowledge to make these physical derivations plausible to ourselves. There is no other way to achieve comprehension, however. We can understand the effects of the minus sign, but not their mathematical explanation. This is our fundamental and insoluble dilemma. We have to believe what others know.

The minus sign has even more significant consequences: It determines that signals emitted by events cannot travel backward in four-dimensional space-time. The minus sign strictly separates past and future; it ensures that an event can impart itself only in the future. In other words, one can only observe cosmic events that lie in the past. What to us seems absolutely natural requires strict definitions in the structure of space-time.

As we consider it natural that the geometry of three-dimensional space allows every point to be reached from every other point, one might expect that in four-dimensional space-time every cosmic event can be reached by every other event. Time as the fourth coordinate of the space-time continuum, however, prevents this because, being one-dimensional, it can only move in one direction, namely forward, into the future, not backward or sideward as in three-dimensional space. Were this not the case, no cosmic structure whatsoever could be maintained. In such a cosmos, effects might precede their causes. It would be a cosmos upsetting itself within split seconds. The structure of space-time—that is, three dimensions of space and one dimension of time—guarantees the existence of the universe as the scene of events whose causes lie always in the past and whose effects lie always in the future.

THE CURVED COSMOS

If special relativity demands a great deal of credulity, the general theory of relativity does so with a vengeance. Here, everything becomes even more challenging and daunting for our common sense. But what is common sense anyway! "Common sense," Einstein said, "is a collection of prejudices which one has acquired by one's eighteenth birthday." Beyond this, it is questionable whether human reason can ascribe sanity to itself.

Immanuel Kant preferred to speak of an "ordinary reason" incapable of going beyond examples derived from personal experience. Common sense moves, as Einstein said, "emotionally and exclusively in analogies." Where analogies are not forthcoming, as in the case of relativity, common sense regards as paradoxical everything that mathematical abstraction holds as substantiated and absolutely necessary.

For Einstein, the general theory of relativity was the logical result of the restrictions established in the two basic postulates of special relativity, which proceeded from coordinate systems moving linearly and uniformly relative to each other. Einstein realized that the fact that this restriction was necessary in classical mechanics did not mean that it had to be valid for nature in its cosmic entirety. What has nature, Einstein asked himself, to do with the coordinate systems introduced by us? If, for the sake of physically describing nature, one cannot avoid introducing such systems, the choice should at least not be dependent on the way they move.

As a consequence, Einstein abandoned linearly and uniformly moving coordinate systems and replaced them with rotating systems that move relative to each other at variable speeds. After all, one could not take it for granted that all objects in the universe move linearly and at uniform velocities. The difficulties posed by this step in the development of a theory free of contradiction were enormous, resembling an attempt to force chaos itself into a strict theoretical framework. Einstein worked for ten years on the problem before presenting his findings in 1916.

The development of the general theory of relativity, however, did not derive exclusively from the restrictions in the special theory of relativity but was also suggested by the physical fact of gravitation, the mutual attraction of masses. In the special theory of relativity, the influence of gravitation had remained unconsidered. The decisive step Einstein took was simply to equate the force of gravitation, which relates to the weight of a body, and the centrifugal force, which relates to the inertia of a body. Although it had long been established that a body's weight and inertia are governed by the same constant, and that there existed an equivalence of inertial and gravitational mass, physicists had as yet paid this no heed. Einstein was the first to give attention to this equivalence that was to become the central postulate of the general theory of relativity.

Physicists have always been occupied with the mutual attraction between bodies since its effects have an entirely mysterious quality. Unlike the electromagnetic force, which may be attributed to electrically charged particles, gravity could not be related to a medium. Why is the apple leaving the branch pulled toward the Earth? How does the Sun keep the planets continually revolving around it? According to Newton, this force between two bodies acts in a divine manner: It simply is; one cannot say anything about it beyond the fact that it is proportional to the mass of each body and inversely proportional to the square of the distance between them.

This, however, has a very problematic consequence. If the distance between the two bodies changes, the force acting between them has to change simultaneously. If, for example, the position of the Sun relative to the Earth suddenly changed—let's assume God, in a fit of playfulness, strikes it—then, according to Newton, the Earth and all the other planets would have to make the same movement at the same time, which means that the force would have to act infinitely quickly. According to the theory of special relativity, however, it would take eight minutes before the Sun's movement affects the Earth because nothing—not even a transmission of force—can travel faster than light. Gravitation was therefore blatantly inconsistent with special relativity.

Einstein, in a logical and courageous step, abandoned the concept of linearly and uniformly moving coordinate systems, which had so far been necessary to describe the movements of material objects. As a consequence, all coordinate systems, even if they were rotating and moving at different speeds, were suitable for describing natural phenomena, including gravitation. Newtonian mechanics described the centrifugal forces acting in rotating coordinate systems as reactions to inertia. But as the centrifugal force and the force of gravitation are both, as we have seen, proportional to the mass of the bodies, it is mathematically correct to simply regard a rotating coordinate system as motionless and the centrifugal forces as gravitational forces. This is not possible in classical mechanics, which strictly distinguishes between centrifugal and gravitational force, although both are proportional to the mass of a body, that is, numerically equal. It could not, however, provide an interpretation for the numerical equality of inertial and gravitational mass.

If special relativity puts an end to the distinction between mass and energy, fusing both quantities mathematically, then general relativity mathematically merges the centrifugal and gravitational forces, regarding the former as the latter. Even in a universe exclusively filled with rotating systems, one could never say, this system rotates in this direction, and that system in another, because to do so one would have to make one of them the absolute point of reference, which would be completely arbitrary. Einstein escapes this seemingly insoluble dilemma by simply eliminating the centrifugal force. Of course, one could argue that he might as well have eliminated gravitation in order to describe it forthwith as the centrifugal force. This, however, would not have been possible because the general theory also has to be valid for all cases dealt with by special relativity, that is, nonrotating systems moving at uniform speeds. In these cases, no centrifugal force occurs.

To simply dismiss the centrifugal force from modern physics might seem a very drastic act, but it was the obvious thing to do at a time when classical mechanics was no longer useful for describing a universal cosmic reality. In terms of logic, this "drastic act" was quite correct. As mass is just a specific form of energy, so the centrifugal force is but a specific form of gravitation. In modern physics it is sufficient to use just one of the respective terms. To the layman it might appear as if this makes matters more complicated, but on the mathematical level a great simplification is achieved. And the purpose of every new scientific theory is to simplify the current world-picture while remaining valid for all natural phenomena.

Mathematically, the distinction between the centrifugal and gravitational forces becomes pointless whenever we mentally abandon the everyday world, which is only a limited, special case of reality anyway. When we examine the cosmos as a whole, with its four-dimensional structure, every force that is exerted as a reaction to inertia can be regarded as gravitation.

For the nonspecialist this is hard to accept. We cling to the centrifugal force just as we cling to the concept of mass because both can be sensually experienced. The theory of relativity does not deny that both exist; it simply claims that for a mathematical description of nature it is sufficient to speak only of energy and gravitation.

Nevertheless, the stubborn layman will argue that, for example, an astronaut traveling in a spaceship that is continually accelerating will surely feel the effects of the centrifugal force.

Einstein may have answered—certainly with a friendly smile—that the image of the astronaut unfortunately originates in three-dimensional space. Four-dimensional space-time, however, has characteristics that permit us to say that the force pressing the astronaut into his seat is a mass-attracting force. The masses acting in this case are, relative to the astronaut, at a distance very far behind him. They are therefore not visible, and the spaceship can be regarded, relative to these masses, as being stationary. "But it *does* fly!" the layman will object; the astronaut's instruments and the energy-consumption meter will certainly show that the spaceship is accelerating. To this, Einstein may have nodded assent and replied that this contradiction makes it necessary to completely redefine gravitation, not as a force similar to other forces but as a mere consequence of a characteristic of four-dimensional space-time.

"And what kind of characteristic could that be?" the obstinate layman will ask, slightly subdued already because he anticipates that embarrassing point at which his nonspecialist brain will run up a white flag, and the screen of his inner monitor will glaze over. Einstein, who would certainly have sympathized with the intellectual predicament of the layman, may have said, preceding his words with a consoling gesture: "Well, my thoughts have led me to the assumption that the space-time continuum as a whole is curved by the entirety of the mass-energy distributed within it, and that it is most curved in the vicinity of great amounts of mass-energy. What we call gravitation is only an effect of this curvature." Now the layman would love to heave a relieved "Aha!" but—alas!—he can't. How is he supposed to imagine the curvature of something that itself defies imagination?

Let us harass Einstein's genius no longer; let us stop trying to force him back into the swamps of our nonspecialist intellect. We cannot help but accept the curvature of the space-time continuum as a physical fact. What classical physics has described as the inertia of a body, general relativity attributes to a reciprocal action between the body and every other body—or mass-energy—in the cosmos. The general theory of relativity is therefore basically a theory of gravitation. It says that the universe has a dynamic structure: The curvature of space-time affects the way objects move and forces act in the universe and is, in turn, affected by every force and every movement of a body. Effect is cause, and cause is effect.

To develop the basic assumptions of the general theory of relativity—which have only been roughly outlined here—Einstein was forced to abandon the common (Euclidian) geometry. The curvature of space-time deprives the basic definitions of this geometry—straight line or plane, for example—of their exact meaning. In a curved universe, the shortest connection between two points is not a straight but a curved or *geodesic* line. On the basis of this "general" geometry, which had been developed by the mathematician Bernhard Riemann (1826–1866), Einstein could finally suggest a mathematic formulation for the correlation between the mass-energy distribution and the laws governing "general" geometry.

According to this theory, objects in four-dimensional space-time always follow straight lines but, from our three-dimensional perspective, they appear to move along curved paths. The curvature increases proportionally to the strength of the gravitational field in which an object moves. If we could sensually experience four-dimensional space-time—that is, if we did not experience space and time separately—we would see that the Sun and the planets follow straight lines. In this case, however, "to see" would be the wrong term since it belongs to three-dimensional existence.

Our three-dimensional perception of the world could be compared to watching a shadow play. What we see as the world is the three-dimensional shadow that four-dimensional space-time casts on our consciousness. In the vicinity of the Sun and its gravitational field, for example, space-time is curved to such a degree that, for us, the planets—although following straight lines in four-dimensional space-time—move on circular paths, or rather, seem to move on circular paths.

MEASURING THE UNIMAGINABLE

The layman tends to dismiss all this as a rather futile theoretical exercise, futile because the universe described here is one we can never experience. What is the use of a knowledge, one may ask, that has nothing to do with our perceptible world? Of course, it is fascinating to know that the universe reveals a different structure if we travel its unfathomable dimensions in our minds instead of staying within the boundaries of our small earthly world. Even the layman wants to know what is happening out there and finds it exciting to learn about the variety of cosmic objects, of their size, age, distance from each other, their formation and disappearance.

This information may already surpass the imaginable, but it leaves a decisive factor untouched: that we perceive the universe as space, that we look into it as we look into a gigantic room. This level of perception, which we regard as absolute, is destroyed by the theory of relativity, at least initially. A painful, disturbing loss that does not make spiritual orientation in the world any easier. In my opinion, this is also the reason why many of us do not want to be confronted with "all this cosmic stuff"; it shakes the foundations of our private worldview that we have shaped and in which we have made ourselves more or less comfortable. Modern cosmology is frightening rather than reassuring.

As the general theory of relativity describes a cosmic structure we cannot perceive, the obvious question arises whether this mathematical description must not remain pure speculation. Einstein was, of course, aware of this problem. Every scientific theory developed mathematically can only claim ultimate validity if predictions made in the theory have been undeniably confirmed by experiment or observation.

So far, three predictions resulting from the equations of the general theory have been verified by exact observations and measurements. The theory predicts, for example, that light should be bent by gravitational fields. If light emitted by a distant star passes near the Sun, its path should therefore be curved by the gravitational field of the Sun. The observational problem lies in the fact that the light from the Sun makes it impossible to observe the light emitted from other stars, unless the Sun is completely covered as is the case during a total eclipse.

The most favorable total eclipse after publication of the general theory of relativity took place on May 29, 1919. It was particularly favorable because, during the eclipse, the Sun was located in an area of stars that were bright enough to be photographed. Two British expeditions were sent out: one to Sobral in northern Brazil, the other to a West African island in the Gulf of Guinea. Both groups photographed a collection of stars in the immediate vicinity of the solar disk obscured by the moon. These pictures were afterward compared to photographs taken from the same spot after the Sun had set.

It transpired that the position of the respective stars relative to their neighbors had in fact changed; their light had therefore been deflected by the mass of the Sun, or rather, by the space-time curvature in the vicinity of the Sun. Einstein had calculated a deflection of 1.74 seconds of arc. The values observed were 1.98 and 1.6 seconds of arc, respectively. Later, more precise measurements definitely verified Einstein's predictions.

Another prediction of general relativity referred to the orbit of the planet Mercury. As the planet nearest to the Sun, it feels the strongest gravitational effects. According to Newton's theory, Mercury's orbit should have been identical to that of the other planets. Einstein, on the other hand, predicted that the long axis of its elliptical orbit should rotate about the Sun as well, approximately once every three million years. Small though this effect is, astronomers had noticed it long before Einstein. Lacking an explanation, they had attributed it to disturbances caused by other planets, but this was mathematically unconvincing.

In the case of the other planets, this deviation becomes smaller with increasing distance from the Sun and had therefore escaped the attention of the astronomers. Nevertheless, the rotation of their orbits has in the meantime been confirmed with the help of extremely precise radar installations. These measurements have been found to conform closely with the predictions of the general theory of relativity.

The third of Einstein's predictions that could be verified by measurements refers to time. Einstein's theory stated that time should run more slowly in the immediate vicinity of a massive body like the Earth. We have already acquainted ourselves with the physical fact that time is not an absolute but a relative quantity. Time is simply what one measures with clocks. The smaller the homogeneous intervals into which time can be divided, the more accurate the clock. (Correspondingly, the precision of a ruler depends on the breadth of the spaces between the marks on its scale.)

Today, the most accurate clocks are the so-called atomic clocks. One could also refer to them as light clocks since light is the visible expression of the atoms' rhythmical vibration. The atom represents the clock, so to speak, and the wave length of the light it emits determines the clock's precision. The time measure here is the interval between the crest of one wave and the next. This interval—the frequency of light—is not an absolute quantity but dependent on the energy of light. The greater the energy, the higher the frequency and, consequently, the shorter the interval between two wave crests.

According to general relativity, light loses energy when it travels in the gravitational field of a massive body, and its frequency decreases, which means that the interval between one wave crest and the next becomes longer. Time therefore runs slower if the gravitational field is stronger. As a consequence, the same atomic clock would run faster on Earth than on the Sun. Einstein calculated that one second of time on the Sun should correspond to 1.000002 Earth seconds. Although the difference is slight, physics cannot simply discard it if it wants to be an exact science. This example clearly shows the greatness of Einstein's theory: Not only does it mathematically predict this hardly measurable difference but it also provides an explanation for it.

With the accuracy of atomic clocks, it was even possible to prove that of two identical clocks the one directly on the ground ran slower than the one mounted on top of a tower. This part of the general theory is of considerable practical importance for space travel. If one ignored the difference in the "speed" of time at different heights above the Earth, the positions calculated for a docking maneuver, for example, would be wrong by several miles.

Yet all this evidence for the correctness of the general theory is not absolute. There are still minute numerical differences between calculated and measured values. A future generation of researchers will have to determine whether these differences can be attributed to systematic errors in measurement or to hitherto unknown physical factors obscuring the values required by general relativity.

THE UNIVERSE EXPANDS
TO AVOID COLLAPSING

By demanding a new geometry—it would be better to speak of a "cosmometry"—that could be used to describe the four-dimensional unity of space and time, the general theory of relativity presented old questions concerning size and structure of the universe in a new light. According to the new theoretical groundwork, the cosmos had to be imagined as a three-dimensional "space" that is curved or bent in on itself. This curvature, which is not imaginable, would represent the fusion of three-dimensionality and time.

The cosmos is therefore a three-dimensional and finite space without any boundaries. This apparent contradiction may become more plausible if one considers that there are also two-dimensional, finite but unlimited spaces. The surface of a sphere is finite in that it has a limited area, but it is also infinite because it does not have a beginning, end, or center. Following a straight path on such a finite, unlimited plane, we would never reach a boundary but would eventually end up where we started.

The surface of a sphere is a two-dimensional space that is inextricably linked to the three-dimensionality of the sphere. It could therefore be regarded as a three-dimensional surface-space continuum. A path between two points on this surface would be a geodesic, that is, not a straight but a curved line. The surface of the sphere could be envisaged as the three-dimensional "shadow" of four-dimensional space-time.

Newton had concluded from his own law of gravity that the universe possessed a certain kind of "double nature." According to his theory, there should be a finite and limited area that contained all the stars and constellations in the universe and that was located, like an island, somewhere within an infinitely big and empty space. Even in Newton's lifetime this picture of the cosmos met with objections. Particularly unsatisfactory was the idea that light radiated by the stars would disappear in the infinity of empty space. Cosmic energy would literally fizzle out into nothing, and the universe would gradually freeze to death. This concept was also contradictory to the law of energy conservation stating that energy does not die. Another inherent contradiction was that light would spread out into empty space, making it no longer empty.

Einstein proved that the Newtonian model of the universe was, for purely mathematical reasons, improbable if not altogether impossible. In such a universe, the average density of matter would disappear, that is, inexorably approach zero. If, on the other hand, there is an average density of weighable cosmic matter that is greater than zero, then the universe must be spatially finite. Science has not yet succeeded in determining the average density of cosmic matter, but at least it seems certain that it is greater than zero, which means that, mathematically, the cosmos must be finite.

Einstein's original equations, however, indicated that the universe was not static but expanding. Nevertheless, Einstein himself was convinced that the universe had to be static, and in order to support this deeply rooted belief, he introduced a so-called cosmological constant into his equations. For him, a created world had to be entirely static—that is, finished and perfect—and an expanding universe seemed to represent creative imperfection.

Einstein's cosmological constant stood for an "antigravity force" that counterbalanced the expansion suggested by the initial equations. Thus, the idea of a static universe was saved for the time being—at least on paper—but the original elegance of Einstein's equations had been destroyed. It is said that Einstein later acknowledged the cosmological constant as the biggest mistake of his life. This is another instance of how, even in the twentieth century, religious beliefs obstruct scientific findings.

In this single respect, Einstein did not take his theory seriously, although he was forced to do so later when the expansion of the universe was proven by exact observation. In fact, even Newton should have realized that the universe had a tendency to expand, for without this tendency the force of gravity—however small—between the star systems would cause the universe to collapse.

Rembrandt, Faust
Science without religion is lame, religion without science is blind.
[ALBERT EINSTEIN]

{ 3 }

"COSMIC RELIGIOUSNESS"

Albert Einstein on the Relationship
of Science and Religion

A t the end of *The Evolution of Physics*, a book intended for the layman and co-authored with Leopold Infeld, one of his closest associates, Albert Einstein says:

> We work our way through the labyrinth of observed regularities with the help of physical theories, trying to systemize and understand our sensory perceptions. Our objective is always to present the observed regularities as logical conclusions from our physical world model. Without the faith that it is possible to render reality understandable by means of our theoretical constructs, without the faith in an inner harmony of the world, there could be no science. This faith is and will always be the basic motivation behind every creative scientific idea. All our endeavors, all the dramatic conflicts between old and new ideas are supported by the eternal desire for knowledge, the unshakeable faith in cosmic harmony which becomes stronger the more difficulties loom before us.

In this short paragraph, the word *faith* appears again and again. Now this is not a term that science regards fondly. Where faith begins, science usually stops, although this need not be the case. Faith is a religious term, certainly one of the most important concepts in theology. Even when applied to mere earthly matters, indicating longing or hope, a religious connotation still reverberates. As long as man nourishes a longing or hope, designing a future for his existence, he is, in a certain sense, a religious being. His longings represent a need for something commonly referred to as *meaning*. If I hope or long for something, I wish for my existence to acquire a meaning or more meaning than it already has. Whether or not the object of my longing actually can provide meaning is another question. It seems to be one of the basic conditions of human existence that absolute meaning can neither be reached nor defined.

FAITH IN COSMIC HARMONY

For Einstein and Infeld, faith is a prerequisite for any kind of creative scientific work. One could even say that only faith gives this work, which represents an exploration into the unknown, a meaning, in two respects. First of all, as a scientist, I have to believe that all aspects of reality not yet understood or apparently unfathomable will one day reveal themselves to be comprehensible. Furthermore, I have to believe that reality is governed by a principal all-embracing harmony that can be represented by natural laws and, ultimately, by a single universal natural law.

In fact, the development of cosmology has been decisively influenced by the belief in a fundamental inner order and universal harmony. This belief caused Plato and Aristotle to design a cosmology based on the absolute harmony of sphere and circular motion. Copernicus, however, discovered in this philosophical construction extremely disturbing discords unacceptable in a true cosmology. He searched, accordingly, for a more universal harmony that did not require theoretical crutches. And he established a new harmony, maintaining the circular paths of the celestial bodies but relating them to the Sun. This new cosmology probably prevailed mainly on the strength of its aesthetic beauty because, in terms of underlying astronomical calculations, the old cosmology had been at least as precise as the new one.

Kepler, on the other hand, regarded the new Copernican harmony as still insufficiently harmonious. Of all the great astron-omers, he was perhaps the one endowed with the most ardent belief in the world as a harmonious unity that he naturally interpreted as a divine unity. Kepler freed cosmology from the fixation on sphere and circle as the only criteria for divine harmony. Ever since, harmony and perfection have been represented by abstract numerical proportions.

It was Newton who combined Kepler's laws with the idea of a universal gravitational force, transferring the harmony of the planetary movements to the whole universe. Newton believed that the cosmic harmony expressed in his laws was the work of a divine creative force. In his famous work *Principia Mathematica*, he wrote:

> The most beautiful system of the Sun, planets, and comets could only proceed from the counsel and dominion of an intelligent and powerful Being. And if the fixed stars are centres of other like systems, these, being form'd by the like wise counsel, must be all subject to the dominion of One; especially since the light of the fixed stars is of the same nature with the light of the Sun, and from every system light passes into all other systems: and lest the system of the fixed stars should, by their gravity, fall on each other, He hath placed those systems at immense distances from one another.

At the beginning of our century, it was Einstein who in turn questioned Newton's universal harmony. If Newton's system was still based on the harmonious interaction of objects attracting and orbiting each other, Einstein attributed these cosmic forces to a single "primary force," which is a property of the geometrical structure of the universe itself. It was impossible to represent this harmony in any language other than mathematics.

Although this language remains incomprehensible for the layman, he will get an idea of Einstein's world harmony by taking a look at his famous formula $E = mc^2$, which, in its simplicity, clarity, and almost aesthetic beauty, could justly be called *the* formula for cosmic harmony: equivalence of mass and energy, conveyed via a universal constant, the speed of light. Light had always been *the* symbol for the divine.

One only has to think of Dante's overwhelming heavenly vision in the *Divine Comedy*—a regular metaphysics of light, almost a mystical anticipation of the quantum and radiation theories. The "central sun" as a symbol for the "primary deity," which appears already in the mysticism of Dionysius the Areopagite, is represented by Dante as the dazzlingly white, unbearably bright spot in the midst of nine spark-shooting, spinning halos that receive direction and light from the white-hot center that is God. The primary deity is symbolically represented as a cosmic "primary particle" of infinite energy.

Einstein, like all the great physicists before and, probably, after him, was convinced that the world is supported by an inner harmony that can be described mathematically by increasingly precise natural laws. To simply observe and describe this harmony, however, was not enough for Einstein. He regarded it as something that pointed beyond the purely physical, something that became the manifestation of a higher reason. To realize this and to be amazed by it was for him no less than true religiousness.

"Every serious scientist," Einstein writes, "must be inspired by a kind of religious feeling; because he simply cannot imagine that the extremely subtle relationships he finds have been uncovered by him for the very first time. Towards the as yet uncomprehended, the scientist feels like a child trying to understand the superior actions of grown-ups." For Einstein, science and religion are not opposed but can be combined to form a single universal way of thinking. Einstein himself speaks of the religiousness of science.

Of course, Einstein does not suggest that all research is of a religious nature. He limits his assertion to those scientists who are inspired by a "deep, explorative scientific spirit." This formulation, however, is not very precise. The phrase "true serious scientist" that Einstein often uses does not make matters much clearer either. It is best to let Einstein himself explain his position in more detail. In a collection of essays and speeches, entitled *The World As I See It,* first published in 1934 in Amsterdam, he says:

> But the scientist is possessed by the sense of universal causation. The future, to him, is every whit as necessary and determined as the past. There is nothing divine about mortality, it is a purely human affair. His religious feeling takes the form of a rapturous amazement at the harmony of natural law, which reveals an intelligence of such superiority that, compared with it, all the systematic thinking and acting of human beings is an utterly insignificant reflection. This feeling is the guiding principle of his life and work, in so far as he succeeds in keeping himself from the shackles of selfish desire. It is beyond question closely akin to that which has possessed the religious geniuses of all ages.

The "true" or "serious" scientist—as Einstein sees him—is distinguished by three basic characteristics. First, he has a moral and ethical sensitivity that has absolutely nothing to do with a God but springs spontaneously from human relationships. Second, the acquisition of scientific knowledge means, ultimately, that the scientist must acknowledge the existence of a superior reason that makes his own ratiocination seem puny and insignificant. His research makes him humble rather than overbearing and arrogant. And third, he does not undertake research to satisfy selfish goals, whether they be of material or spiritual nature. One immediately asks oneself who, of the contemporary scientists, could meet these criteria. The times of heroic, selfless, and, above all, moral scientific research seem to be over once and for all.

NATURAL SCIENCE AS RELIGIOUSNESS

Einstein speaks of religiousness and avoids speaking of God. For him, the term *God* is too closely linked to the idea of a personal God with human features and human mentality. Such a concept of

God is, for Einstein, incompatible with modern scientific knowledge. This personal God may be a spiritual comfort for simple souls because one can approach Him, the omnipotent, protective, rewarding, punishing, superior Father, with all one's worries, wishes, and need for consolation. But nobody who has gained some insight into the general structure of nature can consider seriously a humanized Heavenly Father to whom man addresses only his egotistical yearnings—of which the desire for eternal salvation is, in fact, the most selfish.

Of course, even Einstein knows that science cannot disprove the existence of a personal God and world-ruler. But this God will eventually render himself superfluous as he loses his persuasiveness for more and more people. The personal God is a relic from medieval times surviving only in minds where either medieval darkness or the happy simplicity of the naif hold sway. Einstein believes that religion will have to stand its ground in the light of modern scientific knowledge if it is to have a future. For him, the age-old conflict between science and religion is mainly based on the religious concept of a personal God. But if we finally say farewell to the old man behind the clouds, we eliminate at the same time any reason for hostility between religion and science. For, as Einstein argued:

> Science can only determine what is, but not what shall be, and beyond its realm, value judgments remain indispensable. Religion, on the other hand, is concerned only with evaluating human thoughts and actions; it is not qualified to speak of real facts and the relationships between them.

Einstein is not of the opinion that science could replace religion, that, as is often claimed, faith becomes unnecessary where knowledge enters. Einstein would sooner state that faith and knowledge, while accounting for different areas of thought, have to be united. Any kind of faith that cannot survive in the face of knowledge or even claims to be knowledge itself is pure superstition. In Einstein's words: "Science without religion is lame, religion without science is blind."

Clearly, religion is blind if it seeks to avoid an encounter with scientific knowledge. It is blind to the real world in which we live and the rapid developments taking place inside it—which is not to insist that our reality is all the reality there is. A religion blinded by dogma inevitably loses its appeal for people whose existence and, consequently, thinking is geared to workaday details by science or its technological by-products.

But what, one may ask, does Einstein mean by "lame" science? One has the contrary impression that science maintains a tremendous, almost terrifying momentum, particularly where it operates far from religious or moral-ethical discussions, running a gigantic research "business" that obeys only economic and political laws. Science as it is pursued today, in huge laboratories, may be frightening or paralyzing, but it is certainly not crippled. Would it not be more appropriate if science without religion, too, was considered blind? Blind not only to the dangers resulting from research motivated by economics and power politics but also blind to the great problems confronting mankind as a whole.

Of course, one would have liked to ask Einstein which religion, in his opinion, was suitable to be united with scientific knowledge. Einstein, however, was much too wise to commit the mistake of offering any kind of formula or even preferring one of the institutionalized religions. One feels that the term *religion* did not appeal to him very much anyway. Religions have something rigid, obsessive, limiting, and overbearing about them; they are always preoccupied with doctrines laid down at some time or other by somebody or other. On the one hand, Einstein recognizes the high ethical objectives in Jewish-Christian religious tradition, which would be quite appropriate as standards of value for our actions and aspirations but, on the other hand, he also sees how religion puts the spirit in a variety of chains, mainly by imposing strict dogmatic systems with all their inherent restrictions and narrow perspectives.

For Einstein, a religion makes sense only if it is based on free and responsible self-development of the individual, not on laws and prohibitions. So he abandons the term *religion* wherever he tries to outline his concept of "true" religion, speaking instead of *religiousness*. There can be religiousness without religion. In purely relativistic terms, this, for Einstein, means that there could be as many religions or religious attitudes as there are human beings. If one assumes that human beings are religious only in asking for an ultimate goal and a higher meaning, there can be no absolute meaning applicable for everybody.

To speak of *the* meaning of life does not make sense; this would inevitably result in another rigid religious system of formulas with a strictly defined deity and a theology dictating to the individual how his faith should look to be accepted as the "right" faith. Unfortunately, many people do not seem to be able to believe without the help of theological instructions, and in this case the seed for hostility between the religions is already planted.

Immaturity and lack of independence are the main factors responsible for religious intolerance. Religion also becomes blind when it fails to realize that every religious person, simply by being religious, automatically has the "right" faith, because if this world was really created by *one* God—and not several—then every human being can only believe in *this* God, irrespective of how he imagines Him to be. Our concepts of God, expressed through a variety of theologies, are merely products of the human brain, convincing or less than convincing ancillary constructions. Each of them is, finally, as right or wrong as the next.

But I digress, and these thoughts are less Einstein's than my own. For Einstein, faith is not absolute but entirely individual. He writes: "To inquire after the meaning or object of one's own existence or of creation generally has always seemed to me absurd from an objective point of view." But not from a subjective point of view! The individual is drawn toward religiousness by thinking about his life. (Of course, his thoughts can also lead him away from religiousness.) Religiousness is an intellectual phenomenon which, like all other activities of the human mind, can be attributed to individual sentiments and longings.

"Everything that the human race has done and thought is concerned with the satisfaction of felt needs and the assuagement of pain," Einstein says. Thus, the term *religiousness* receives a pleasantly dispassionate, earthly quality; there is no room for lofty talk about the hereafter as it is practiced, in a particularly disgusting manner, by all kinds of religious or pseudoreligious sects. Where religiousness is expressed as ritual, and adheres to preprogrammed declarations, it stops being true religiousness for Einstein.

COSMIC RELIGIOUSNESS

We still do not know, however, the form that Einstein's religiousness takes. The fact that he did not talk about it much in public is to his credit. In a few instances he speaks vaguely of "cosmic religiousness" as if, by using this phrase, he wanted to express loyalty for his scientific ethos as well as the intermingling of his profound knowledge and deep faith. This cosmic religiousness, he writes, "is very difficult to explain to anyone who is entirely without it, especially as there is no anthropomorphic conception of God corresponding to it."

In any case, it demands that man perceives some kind of cosmic order or at least senses that such an order exists. At the same time, he has to realize the "insignificance of human desires and objectives": "Each of us is here for a brief sojourn; for what purpose he knows not, though he sometimes thinks he feels it." The question is whether this feeling is sufficient to give meaning to existence. For Einstein it is so. No Father God, no egoistical yearning for a hereafter, no theological constructions or esoteric sophistry but simply the notion, the vague feeling that "in nature as well as in the world of thought" a mysterious and superior reason reveals itself.

Einstein speaks of the "experience of the mysterious." The mysterious, eternally unreachable, manifests itself only as a notion. For

Einstein, it is only this vague feeling that represents true religiousness:

> A knowledge of the existence of something we cannot penetrate, of the manifestations of the profoundest reason and the most radiant beauty, which are only accessible to our reason in their most elementary forms—it is this knowledge and this emotion that constitute the truly religious attitude; in this sense, and in this alone, I am a deeply religious man. I cannot conceive of a God who rewards and punishes his creatures, or has a will of the type of which we are conscious in ourselves.

Einstein's religiousness is modest, in every respect. It contents itself with the realization that everything is, at any time, inextricably linked to everything else. More is not required. Religiousness finds its meaning on a completely different plane from pure intellectualism. True religiousness is expressed in real behavior, in practical life. The depressing aspect of all institutionalized religious systems is that wherever they could have—and should have!—proven their greatness, strength, and honesty, they almost invariably failed and continue to fail, generating, along the way, hypocrisy, dissension, hatred, and cynicism.

In Einstein's simple, even slightly naive understanding of religiousness, which offers no leeway for selfish hopes and desires, one has to lead a simple and modest life. Thus, the slightly pompous phrase "cosmic religiousness" is brought into direct relationship with everyday life. If everything is part of a cosmic unity, this includes the life of every single human being. Einstein's statement about the practical consequences of his cosmic religiousness is credible and appealing:

> A hundred times every day I remind myself that my inner and outer life depends on the labours of other men, living and dead, and that I must exert myself in order to give in the same measure as I have received and am still receiving. I am strongly drawn to the simple life and am often oppressed by the feeling that I am engrossing an unnecessary amount of the labour of my fellow-

men. I regard class differences as contrary to justice and, in the last resort, based on force. I also consider that plain living is good for everybody, physically and mentally. ... The ideals which have lighted me on my way and time after time given me new courage to face life cheerfully, have been Truth, Goodness, and Beauty. Without the sense of fellowship with men of like mind, of preoccupation with the objective, the eternally unattainable in the field of art and scientific research, life would have seemed to me empty. The ordinary objects of human endeavour—property, outward success, luxury—have always seeemed to me contemptible.

From this rather personal philosophy of life, Einstein draws his basic political views: "My political ideal is that of democracy." But Einstein puts it more precisely: "The really valuable thing in the pageant of human life seems to me not the State but the creative, sentient individual, the personality; it alone creates the noble and the sublime, while the herd as such remains dull in thought and dull in feeling."

The Primary Principles Yin and Yang
To merge and to separate, this is the way
of Nature's eternal change.

YOU ARE THE UNIVERSE

Teachings of the Tao

It is not easy to reconcile Einstein's "cosmic religiousness" with a Western view of religion shaped by Christianity. Yet in Jesus' talks, if we can trust the accuracy of the scriptures, the concept of life's unity is of central importance and is alluded to quite frequently. This could, indeed, be interpreted as a pleading for a relativistic universalism. Perhaps it is due to the influence of the apostle Paul that this philosophy never really took effect in Christianity, despite the teachings of such religious individualists as Francis of Assisi, Nicholas of Cusa, Meister Eckhart, or Giordano Bruno, variously venerated as saints or persecuted as heretics by the church.

Paul the Greek mixed the teachings of Jesus with neo-Platonic philosophy, thus initiating the corruption of a cosmological concept of unity that can still be felt in Jesus' words. The eternal unity of all things is replaced by the eternal conflict of spirit and matter. This conflict is considered insoluble. The individual can only escape it by committing himself entirely to the spirit and the spiritual, renouncing all that is natural, worldly, and mortal.

Christianity is, in fact, the first religion where a sense for nature is apparent in its separation from nature. It puts itself in opposition to nature, turns nature into an object. Friedrich Schiller expressed this relationship as follows: "The elders felt naturally, we feel the natural." Here nature, there spirit. Nature is the source of all evil; it is

Lucifer's empire. Pure spirit, on the other hand, is identical with God. The world is declared a vast robbers' den—there is something in that proposition!—ruled over by evil demons, whereas the good, that is, the spiritual, is not of this world. Lucifer's world is governed by reason and the senses. He is realist and sensualist, the defender of sensual pleasures. And that is what makes him so insidious.

What seems real is in fact only illusion, deceit, a mere dream. The true world, as opposed to this illusory world, is the world of the spirit. Its inhabitants perceive Lucifer's world as a fraud and disgraceful temptation. In Christianity, the unity of matter and spirit was destroyed, and this rift is still felt keenly by every Christian.

It is therefore unsurprising that Einstein finds a hint of cosmic religiousness only in the so-called Eastern philosophies, mainly in Buddhism. "The beginnings of cosmic religious feeling," he writes, "already appear in earlier stages of development—e.g., in many of the Psalms of David and in some of the Prophets. Buddhism, as we have learnt from the wonderful writings of Schopenhauer especially, contains a much stronger element of it."

The transmigration of the soul, on the other hand, a central concept in Buddhism, does not appeal to Einstein at all. An individual "who should survive his physical death is beyond my comprehension, nor do I wish it otherwise," Einstein says. And he goes on: "Such notions are for the fears or absurd egoism of feeble souls. Enough for me the mystery of the eternity of life, and the inkling of the marvellous structure of reality, together with the single-hearted endeavour to comprehend a portion, be it never so tiny, of the reason that manifests itself in nature."

Even a cursory glossing of Eastern philosophies reveals that the obvious candidate for association with Einstein's cosmic religiousness is less Buddhism and rather a religion that is referred to as "Chinese universalism." It is divided into two main currents: Confucianism and Taoism. At the center of both philosophies is the universe with all its manifold elements and aspects. Everything is linked to everything else in universal harmony.

Both philosophies strive to lead the human being toward perception of this harmony, but the paths they take are different, even contradictory. Whereas Confucian universalism forms the basis of a strict moral and political philosophy, it is employed by Lao-tzu, the founding father of Taoism, as the foundation for a mysticism and worldly wisdom that applies entirely to the individual. He set down his philosophy in the *Tao Te Ching*, the *Holy Book of the Way and Virtue*, or, in a different translation, the *Holy Book of the World Principle and Its Effects*.

Researchers have not been able to determine whether Lao-tzu really lived or whether he is merely a legend. This, however, is only of minor importance. For a book of oracular pronouncements like the *Tao Te Ching*, it seems appropriate that both its history and the biography of its author should vanish in the darkness of Chinese antiquity. As a legendary figure, we know Lao-tzu only from a few Taoist sources, mainly the speeches and parables of his (hypothetical) scholar Chuang-tzu who, living in the fourth century B.C., was a contemporary of Aristotle. In him, Lao-tzu finds a most eloquent interpreter.

Where Lao-tzu presents his philosophy in an earnest, ascetic manner, Chuang-tzu indulges in allegories. He sets the profound, sometimes extremely abstract and oracular texts of the old master in poetic parables, giving them a popular quality. Chuang-tzu is the poet among the Taoist sages. He did not develop the original philosophy further but freed it, brilliantly, of its solemnity and strictness, making it buoyant and amusing with his irony, wit, and roguish humor.

But what does Taoism mean? What entitles us to associate Einstein's concept of cosmic religiousness with this ancient Chinese philosophy of wisdom? It would be a rather presumptuous attempt to try and present Taoism in all its complexity in a short intermediate chapter. This chapter merely intends to show to what an extraordinary extent the Taoist philosophy intuitively anticipated many of the things that modern science much later discovered empirically. This is, of course, also true for Buddhism, which has much in common with Taoism. One is inclined to say that both religions are identical in their main propositions. This is also why the fusion of Buddhism and Taoism, which took place after Buddhism had been brought from India to China in the first half of the sixth century, presented no ideological problems whatsoever. This fusion gave rise to Zen Buddhism. It may therefore be justified to interpret Einstein's cosmic religiousness as a concept akin to the basic worldview characteristic of Buddhism, Taoism, and Zen alike.

TAO—THE ESSENCE OF EVERYTHING,
THE ESSENCE IN EVERYTHING

Tao is the central concept of this cosmic-religious worldview. It can easily be identified with the last, unspeakable truth of Buddhism, the Buddha-hood of all things. This ultimate truth is not communicable; it can only be paraphrased and hinted at. The attempt to understand Tao is as nonsensical as the attempt to understand God. As there can be no definition of God, there can also be no definition of Tao. The ultimate truth is beyond all opposites; even concepts like holy and unholy, good and evil just lead one away from the essence that must remain inexpressible; otherwise it would not be the essence. We are familiar with this problem from the chapter on Nicholas of Cusa.

Let us take a look, with all due humility, at the concept of Tao, conscious of the fact that its ultimate truth can never be named. Perhaps it is best to place one of Chuang-tzu's little stories at the beginning. It is entitled *Tao's Place:*

> Master Tung-kuo asked Chuang-tzu, "This thing called the Way—where does it exist?" Chuang-tzu said, "There's no place it doesn't exist." "Come," said Master Tung-kuo, "you must be more specific!" "It is in the ant." "As low a thing as that?" "It is in the panic grass." "But that's lower still!" "It is in the tiles and shards." "How can it be so low?" "It is in the piss and shit!" Master Tung-kuo made no reply. Chuang-tzu said, "Sir, your questions simply don't get at the substance of the matter.... Why

don't you try wandering with me to the Palace of Not-Even-Anything—identity and concord will be the basis of our discussions and they will never come to an end, never reach exhaustion. Why not join with me in inaction, in tranquil quietude, in hushed purity, in harmony and leisure? ... That which treats things as things is not limited by things. Things have their limits—the so-called limits of things. The unlimited moves to the realm of limits; the limited moves to the unlimited realm. We speak of the filling and emptying, the withering and decay of things. The Way makes them full and empty without itself filling or emptying; it makes them wither and decay without itself withering and decaying. It establishes root and branch but knows no root and branch itself; it determines when to store up or scatter but knows no scattering itself."

This is very similar to Nicholas of Cusa's intellectual effort to conceive of an inconceivable God via the reconciliation of an infinite number of opposites existing in human life.

Tao is not a concept like others. It is reality itself, the eternal formation and perishing of all things, and therefore the "inner harmony of our world" of which Einstein speaks. Our human existence is a part of this inner harmony in the universe. Taoism sees the cosmos as eternal flow. Everything in the cosmos, whether living or dead, is a part of this eternal flow. Life changes into death; from death emerges new life. The flow itself is the meaning of everything, an uninterrupted cycle consisting of an infinite number of bigger and smaller subcycles, emerging, existing, and decaying. Unity becomes profusion, and profusion is transformed back into unity. The cosmos does not appear as a linear system striving for a general and ultimate goal.

In the Taoist cosmos, an infinite number of variable quantities are cyclically related. In this interaction of everything with everything hides what is called Tao. That Tao itself has to remain unnameable is obvious for this reason alone; for even an exact itemization of all the events taking place in a village pond at a given moment, from the movement of living beings to every last atom, would require an eternity. Thus, Lao-tzu begins the *Tao Te Ching* with the enigmatic words that the Tao that can be named is not the eternal, the true Tao: "The way that can be spoken of/Is not the constant way;/The name that can be named/Is not the constant name." (Remember the words of St Augustine: "If you conceive of God, it is not God.")

The intangible Tao is perhaps best described as a principle of cosmic order. Taoist writers, in trying to paraphrase Tao as closely as possible, prefer to use terms like *order, the whole, maturity,* and *active force,* insisting, however, upon ridding these terms of every social aspect that might still be attached to them. If Tao is an active force it cannot be compared to others but is an entirely undefined force that nevertheless provides the basis for every conceivable action in the universe. Taoist masters have always appended the suffix *te* to the word *Tao,* expressing the realization of the active force in concrete single events.

In his book on Chinese philosophy, Marcel Granet states: "In everyday language, the double term *tao-te* was used to transfer the concept of 'virtue' *(virtus)* but not in its exclusively moral meaning. *Tao-te* means 'prestige,' 'noble influence,' 'active authority.' In mythical language, *te* refers to the nature of the most perfect and royal spirits."

The word *Tao* is usually translated as "path" or "way," sometimes as "reason" or "logos." Depending on which philosophy was currently in vogue in the West, *Tao* was also interpreted as "divine reason" or "nature"; recently, "energy" has been quite popular. These choices reveal a fundamentally wrong-headed occidental attitude toward Taoism, for they contain the assumption that Tao intends to be a world explanation. That, however, is exactly what Tao does *not* want to be. Tao requires no explanation of the world. Such an explanation ultimately strives toward a meaning—and that is absurd.

Just as the basic purpose of a river is to flow and not to carry ships or to drive power plants, the basic purpose of the world is that it constantly changes but always remains the world. By asking about the meaning of the flow, we want to remove ourselves from it, although we are—whether we want to be or not—always a part of the flow. And by asking about the meaning of the world, we want to distance ourselves from the world. For the Taoist, however, this wish, like everything else, is part of the flow. Whatever we do or fail to do, whatever we think or do not think, we are always carried along by the great watercourse that is the world. Tao is just a tag for everything that happens.

Our Western thinking, dependent as it is on precise information, cannot content itself with such a statement. It is not able to accept the idea that the world simply exists and is forever changing. We long for a meaning that we can understand or, better, grasp. At such an unreasonable request, the Taoist can only wag his head or burst out laughing. If everything forms an inextricable unity, the whole does not have more meaning than every single part of it. It is possible to say that Tao is the reason for everything, the primary force of being and nonbeing, but it is useless trying to grasp this force or to possess it. Strictly speaking, this would mean trying to find something outside ourselves that is contained within ourselves.

The Taoist regards Western mysticism's "other reality," its attempts to "reach the other shore," as just another form of delusion. Taoism aims at a radical disillusioning of man's hope for a meaning outside human existence. Taoism does not want to offer a meaning of life, particularly not an otherworldly one, but merely intends to show that the meaning is much closer than we think, that we do not have to look for unity because it is already there. "In the world everyone knows enough to pursue what he does not know, but no one knows enough to pursue what he already knows," as Chuang-tzu puts it.

Tao acts as an absolute and superior category that includes the categories of power, unity, and order. It affects the interaction of all forces in the universe without being itself a force or even a substance. Tao does not create but governs the infinite variety of action between everything that is. Nothing is created in the world, not even the world itself. It does not have a beginning and it will not have an end. The world is an eternal cycle.

If Tao creates anything at all, it is the rhythm of this infinitely polymorphic change that is the sum total of all the events in the cosmic space-time structure. Tao is immanent in every event, even the "event" represented by every human being. Tao is the rhythm of the space-time continuum, to use the terminology of modern cosmology for a change. Of course, it would not make sense to search for Tao as a primary force, as modern physics does so doggedly. For if physics should ever find this "primary force," it would be measurable and describable in mathematical terms.

But Tao cannot be measured. The *Tao of Physics* is not *the* Tao. Taoism only deals with the changing aspects of the one. Light and shadow, for example, would be two aspects of the one, the same as sound and echo. Taoism is not in the least interested in the succession of events, and therefore neither in the relationship of cause and effect. Measuring phenomena and the relationship between them is equally unimportant to the Taoist. What are measurable quantities good for if everything is constantly changing? "We deal," Granet writes, "only with signals, and a quantitative assessment of their size or the frequency of their occurrence does not say much about them. The weakest, most unusual, and fleeting signs reveal the most.... Therefore the most insignificant are worth recording, and the most unusual are of greater value than the more common ones."

It is in the smallest, most inconspicuous, and trivial phenomena that we detect the most significant information. Single events can be read as tokens of the universality of all things. For the Chinese of antiquity, the interpretation of these signals was less the task of the scientist than that of the historian.

But it would be wrong to conclude that the Taoist picture of the universe is a monistic one. Beyond the fact that they are rarely very helpful, terms like *monistic, dualistic,* or *pluralistic* have no significance at all here. At the most, one could say that in the Taoist world-picture the whole is always fully contained in every single part of it. Groups of events differ only in the intensity of their inherent active force and tension. The Taoist cosmos is hierarchically ordered, divided into different levels of order according to efficacy and responsibility. The Taoist directs his attention to the fleeting, unique, constantly changing forms, but only in order to understand the relationship between every single part, however small, and the cosmic whole. Only in this sense is the single part of interest at all. The deepest conviction of universal structure is gained via the part.

And still Tao can be searched for and found but not as something that might be named *Tao*. If one finds it at all, one will not be able to say what it is. Of course, one might be wrong. Only a Taoist master can provide certainty, but how do we know that somebody calling himself a master actually is one? Most suspicious are those "masters" who call themselves masters. The search for Tao is not an intellectual one; it does not manifest itself in the study of erudite writings but in intuitive, sensual, practical life and experience. Taoism is practical metaphysics. Tao is not conceived and known but lived and enacted. It can be felt but not thought. It can be suspected but not explained.

Einstein, too, said with regard to his scientific work that intuition, rather than strictly logical thinking, had been "of real value" to him. Lieh-tsu has the following to say about the nature of Tao: "Only he who gains it quietly and perfects it spiritually has it." But "to have" does not mean "to own" here; he cannot take credit for possessing it. After all, he already had it before he knew that he had it. To know Tao means to know it as the unity of the world. In one of his stories, Chuang-tzu has the master Lao-tzu say: "Heaven cannot help but be high, earth cannot help but be broad, the sun and moon cannot help but revolve, the ten thousand things cannot help but flourish. Is this not the Way?"

CYCLICAL EXPERIENCE

Now we are just as wise or foolish as before. But implanting wisdom is not a Taoist objective anyway. Terms like *foolish* and *wise* are foreign to Taoist thinking because such opposites exist only as attributes of wholeness. The foolish one is wise, and the wise one is quite often foolish. Wholeness is everywhere; it is divided into the two primary principles, yang and yin. From the infinitely manifold combinations of yin and yang, everything emerges that it may, finally, disappear again. Birth is not a beginning, however, nor death an end. They do not affect existence in space and time or the unity of all things.

Taoist thinking is rooted in the principle of polarity expressed in the antonyms yin and yang. Their opposition does not indicate conflict and mutual destruction but rather harmonious completion. The traditional symbol for Tao and for the yin-yang principle is the double spiral entwined into a circle (double helix). In a practical context, it is also interpreted as the symbol for sexual communication. For the astronomers, it was a symbol for double-spiral galaxies knotted into a circle. And, of course, one immediately thinks of the basic element of life, DNA (deoxyribonucleic acid), which stores the genetic information for every living being and appears, in three-dimensional representation, as a double helix as well. This sign would also be excellently suited as a symbol for the atom in which the positively charged nucleus and the negatively charged electrons form a unity.

According to Chinese tradition, the concept of yin and yang goes back to the first astronomers and not, as is often thought, to the old Chinese oracle makers. Yin and yang are primarily metaphysical rather than astronomical terms. Of course, ancient Chinese astronomy, like geography, was closely bound to religious concepts. With time, yin and yang became general terms used by theoreticians in nearly all disciplines. They have turned into the definitive Chinese universal concepts.

To merge and to separate, this is the way of nature's eternal change. *Yin* stands for the female, conception, the calm and soothing, darkness and coldness. *Yang* represents the male, procreation, the moved and moving, light and warmth. To play one side off against the other, to evaluate, to accept one and refuse the other is absolutely unthinkable in Taoism. There is no light without darkness, no good without evil, no life without death. There is no reason to be in favor of light and against darkness, in favor of life and against death, in favor of good and against evil. In Taoist philosophy, such differentiations and evaluations make no more sense than to ask for electricity but accept only the positive pole.

In this example, the equality of the two poles is obvious, but we are taken aback whenever the Taoist principle apparently denies any possibility of support and commitment for a particular side and negates the possibility of development and progress. How can there be improvements; how can righteousness be triumphant if it is inextricably linked to evil? This does not square with our linear understanding of time and history. It is even harder to reconcile with the Christian message of salvation that promises the victory of good over evil without noticing that Christianity itself more often than not has taken sides with evil—in the name of the good.

At least we seem, slowly, to recognize that our linear thinking, our deep-rooted belief in continuous progress, is a dangerous fallacy. The supposedly better is invariably followed by the worse. From one problem solved, two new, even bigger, problems emerge. Western thinking expresses an incredible arrogance. Man thinks he can place himself outside nature simply because he is able to understand nature. A delusion, the Taoist would say, wrong because it is one-sided and linear where nature is many-sided and cyclical.

In Western thought, especially in science and technology, its practical manifestations, the world is understood as something that is separated and different from one's own self. The world is a completely transparent system of external objects that must be manipulated according to current demand. Such a way of thinking refuses to realize that a manipulation of nature necessarily results in self-manipulation. Our so-called civilization has never been anything but progressive self-manipulation.

But if one takes a look at the origins of Western thought—that is, the beginnings of classical Greek philosophy—it becomes apparent that here, as well, the concept of cyclical change resulting from the polarity of natural forces is of central importance. Anaximander (ca. 610 B.C. to ca. 546 B.C.), for example, claimed that there was an infinite and unchangeable primary substance. All forms and phenomena are just transmutations of this substance. He supposedly said: "And into that from which existing things come-to-be they also pass away according to necessity; for they suffer punishment and pay retribution to one another for their wrongdoing in accordance with the ordinance of Time."

Here, as well, everything emerges from the conflict of opposites. The victory of one side over the other is always just temporary and will be annulled and atoned for "with the ordinance of time." The concepts of *becoming* and *change* are of particular importance in the philosophy of Heraclitus of Ephesus (ca. 550 B.C. to ca. 480 B.C.). He regards the eternal conflict of opposites as a prerequisite for universal harmony. No matter to what extent the world disintegrates into multitudinousness, it always remains a unity. Heraclitus says: "We must know that war is common to all and strife is justice, and that all things come into being and pass away through strife." For Heraclitus, the "imperishable change that renovates the world" is represented by the universal moving force of fire.

In his book *Physics and Philosophy,* Werner Heisenberg has pointed out that "modern physics is in some points extremely close to the doctrines of Heraclitus. If we replace the word fire by the word energy we can almost repeat his statements word for word from our modern point of view." Energy can be regarded as a "primary substance" underlying all change. Its essential characteristic is that its quantity in the universe is unchangeable. Elementary particles originate from energy and can be reconverted into energy—in fact, they *are* energy.

The conversion of one energy form into another can be compared to Heraclitus's struggle between the opposites. Perhaps the most elementary opposition in physics is that of the positive and the negative, of matter and antimatter, expressed by +1 and −1, the basic mathematical formula, so to speak, of an energetic primary substance. "All things are numbers," Pythagoras (ca. 570 B.C. to ca. 480 B.C.) supposedly said. This is what makes it possible to describe the physical universe in a mathematically exact manner.

Peter W. Atkins, professor of physical chemistry at the University of Oxford, has the following to say:

> At heart the basis of the universe must be as simple as the difference symbolized by 1 and −1, or by yes and no, or (more prosaically) by true and false. The fundamental building blocks of the whole of creation must have this simple binary form. Nothing simpler has properties. Only the difference symbolized by 1 and −1, by one and not one, or point and no point, is sufficiently simple to be creatable, but rich enough when sufficiently concatenated (as in mathematics and logic) to lead to properties. At root the universe is a dust of binary forms. That is the dust of space-time.

It seems appropriate to establish a relationship between the Taoist antonyms yin and yang with the basic physical difference of +1 and −1, but in doing so we would lose a metaphysical dimension inherent in the Taoist concepts. They should neither be interpreted as purely logical factors nor simply regarded as cosmological principles. They are inevitably both, but more than this, too. They are symbols that can never be fully materialized as is possible with symbols for natural forces or substances. No more can they be fully transcended, that is, be turned into purely philosophical and mathematical abstractions. It would therefore be wrong to describe Taoist thinking as irrational or mystic. Nor can it be accused of hostility toward science or technology. The only attitude it would oppose is the view that man occupies a superior position in the universe merely on account of his creative power.

No matter what great deeds he will do in the future, man will always be a part of the same cosmic principles as any kind of object. Just as every single human being exists in order to perish some day, mankind as a whole will disappear as well as the planet it inhabits, the Sun around which this planet orbits, even the galaxy in which this Sun is located. But cosmic unity will survive.

RELATIVITY IN A PRIMORDIAL STATE

Of course, it is hard to reconcile oneself with such a philosophy as it apparently renders our existence even less meaningful. To distinguish between meaning and meaninglessness, however, is just another consequence of a thinking that wants to separate the self from the universe, that wants to remove itself and sneak out of the unity of all things. We live in a world of distinctions, of details taken out of their contexts, of specialization, isolation, demarcation, and limitation. Our thinking is schooled in the examination and analysis of details, and we take this as a basis for our lives.

To see things from a Taoist point of view would mean to look at their eternal and universal aspects, the cyclical interconnection of everything with everything. Or, poetically speaking: "To see a World in a grain of sand/And a Heaven in a wild flower." But we are not able to do that. And perhaps this is the reason for our overwhelming fear of nothingness. Even if we understand intellectually that being and nonbeing are two necessary poles of a unity, our deepest emotions rebel against it. To be here is fine, but the knowledge that we have to disappear seems outrageous. At the same time, we forget that we already have been "there" and will merely return. For how, the Taoist might ask, would you know that you are alive unless you had once been dead?

Formed reality is also emptiness, and emptiness is, at the same time, formed. Perhaps these words lose their paradoxical quality if we quote one of Lao-tzu's allegories: "Shape clay into a vessel;/It is the space within that makes it useful./Cut doors and windows for a room;/ It is the holes which make it useful./Therefore profit comes from what is there;/Usefulness from what is not there." Only nothingness imparts a meaning to something.

Taoism develops its cyclical cosmology from yin and yang, the two poles of the cosmic source. Everything that is comes from the interaction of these primary principles, even the five primary elements that should rather be referred to as substances of force or forms of energy. They do not represent the static elements we know from chemistry but variable states of matter that may be specified in arbitrary order. One can emerge from the other; one can also destroy the other.

Everything that exists can, ultimately, be related dynamically to one of the primary elements. These elements or substances of force are symbolized as follows: The first element is wood, which as fuel gives rise to the second element: fire. Fire produces ashes and thus the third element: earth. Earth, in turn, contains the fourth element: metal. This element—as on the surface of a metallic mirror, for example—attracts dew, thus giving rise to the fifth element: water. And, since water nourishes the growing wood, things come full circle.

One could imagine an infinite number of such cycles, representing the whole of cosmic growth and decay. In Taoism, the interaction betwen these substances of force is referred to as *hsiang sheng*, which could be translated as a "mutually dependent order of forces." In this cosmic system, the principle of causality, which is so familiar to us, has lost its validity inasmuch as everything is cause and effect simultaneously. Another interaction of these primary elements is referred to as the "order of mutual conquest." In this system, wood, in the form of a plough, overcomes earth. Earth, in turn, thrown up in a dike, collects and conquers water. Water overcomes fire, and fire liquefies metal, thus rendering it malleable. And finally, metal, in the form of a saw, conquers wood by cutting down the tree. This reminds one of the children's game of paper, scissors, and stone, which is based on the same cyclical principle.

Thus, Taoism describes the universe as an infinite reference system in which the smallest is of the same importance as the biggest. Nothing can be omitted since then the whole system would collapse. It is not a mechanistic but a dynamic world-picture. What is more, it is a relativistic world-picture as defined by Einstein's theory.

Fa-tsang (653–712), for example, developed a very nice model of the universe. He regards it as a multidimensional network consisting of an infinite number of jewels, each jewel containing the reflections of all the others ad infinitum. Each jewel is a *shih*, a "thing-event." Here, the comparison with a point in space-time— an "event" in the theory of relativity—is obvious: a point determined by space and time. Every *shih* is subject to the principle of *shih shih wu ai* ("between one thing-event and another there is no obstruction"). Every "thing-event" is only what it is in relation to every other "thing-event." This principle, reduced to its essentials, is included in the theory of relativity.

Tao as the source will always defy human knowledge just as the human eye can never directly perceive its own face; it can do so only indirectly, as a reflection in the mirror or a projection. In fact, Taoism anticipates the entire problem of observation in modern science. In nuclear physics, for example, no observation of an elementary particle can be made without influencing its behavior. It is therefore impossible to make an absolute observation that is independent of the observer.

In astrophysics we have to face the problem that no matter how far we look into the universe, there are always even larger spaces unfolding. The farther we penetrate into the biggest and smallest things, the more they seem to elude us. The Taoist might claim that what eludes us is Tao. Or, in other words, it is man himself who stubbornly escapes the pursuit of man's observational mania. Our subjectivity is the greatest obstacle for ultimate and objective knowledge. Man cannot get beyond the limitations of a human frame of reference.

Exaggerating a bit, one could say that Taoism is a theory of relativity in religious garb. There is no absolute perception in space because we cannot conceive of absolute dimensions, only of relative dimensions. Every quantity, every measure is relative. As Chuang-tzu says:

"Nothing under the sky is greater than the tip of a leaf of grass."

Einstein claimed that one would have explored the entire universe if one succeeded in tracing every single characteristic of a grain of sand. For providing a complete scientific explanation of the sand grain would only be possible if one knows the exact laws governing all space-time events in the cosmos. Every grain of sand, every tip of a leaf, even an atom contains the entire universe. Conversely, the universe can be perceived as the tip of a leaf. Who knows, there might be an infinite number of universes!

The same goes for time: There is no perception in time because duration is always relative. Chuang-tzu says: "No being reaches a greater age than that of a child that died in the crib." To a day-fly, the duration of our lives must seem like an eternity while our life-span, relative to cosmic periods, shrinks to almost nothing. The Taoist, however, would dismiss this conception as well since there is no real difference between the universe as a whole and an individual being or object. Every one of us is the universe, or, in Chuang-tzu's words: "The universe came into being with us together; with us, all things are one."

What does this mean for everyday life? In fact, almost nothing. For we do not even know whether what we regard as our life is more than a mere delusion. After all, we do not have an absolute criterion for determining whether this life, which we consider the real one, is perhaps just a kind of sleep from which we will have to awaken into a real state of being (the Buddhist would speak of existence after enlightenment). Chuang-tzu poeticized this concept of life in his famous butterfly parable:

> Once upon a time, I, Chuang-tzu, dreamed that I was a butterfly, a butterfly flying about, enjoying itself. It did not know that it was Chuang-tzu. Suddenly I awoke, and veritably was Chuang-tzu again. But I do not know whether it was I dreaming that I was a butterfly, or whether I am a butterfly dreaming that I am Chuang-tzu. Between man and butterfly there must be *some* distinction! This is called the Transformation of Things.

We cannot be certain of values regarding our existence because, again, we have no absolute measure with which to determine what is good or evil, beautiful or ugly. For the Taoist, the conflicts of life are of minor importance; they merely express the universal and cyclical process of creation and destruction. The biological world in which every species is the prey of another appears—at first glance—anything but harmonious. Nevertheless, it is in accordance with cosmic harmony; it does not disturb it but contributes to its expression.

The picture is slightly different with regard to the disharmony and destruction caused by man among his own kind and in nature. For he has the opportunity to act differently, to lead a different life. If every human being followed what the Taoist calls *li*—which means "organic order" as opposed to mechanic, regular orders imposed from outside—then everybody would live in harmony, not because they were forced to do so but simply due to their alternating resonance and interdependence. In the original sense, *li* denotes the markings in jade or the grain in wood. It is the principle of flowing water, drifting clouds, and trees moving in the wind. Flowing water is therefore Chuang-tzu's favorite image for poetically paraphrasing Tao in order to show the path man has to follow to find Tao:

> The fluidity of water is not the result of any effort on the part of the water, but is its natural property. And the virtue of the perfect man is such that even without cultivation there is nothing which can withdraw from his sway. Heaven is naturally high, the earth is naturally solid, the sun and moon are naturally bright. Do they cultivate these attributes?

And, in a different context:

> When water is still, it is like a mirror, reflecting the beard and the eyebrows. It gives the accuracy of the water-level, and the philosopher makes it his model. And if water thus derives lucidity from stillness, how much more the faculties of the mind? The

mind of the Sage being in repose becomes the mirror of the universe, the speculum of all creation.

For the Taoist, this would be the only true form of knowledge: not to distinguish between subject and object, between the observer and the observed but to be one with the universe. This knowledge could no longer be questioned because it would include all questions. It would not be knowledge gained through research and thinking and would be free of the obsession to know. Such a knowledge, the Taoist says, does not understand the world; it has the world.

Martin Buber, the great Jewish philosopher, writes about the Taoist concept of true knowledge:

> This knowledge is action. Action is the only reference, the eternal criterium, the absolute, the unspeakable, and the unchangeable. Perfection is glimpsed not in contemplation but in action. What man calls action is not action. It is not an activity of the entire mind but a gradual penetration of single insights into the fabric of Tao, the interventions of single actions in the nature and order of things. It is bound up with necessities. Insofar as they approve of it, human beings call it virtue. What they call virtue is not virtue. It is limited to "human kindness" and "justice."... It is wrong because it appears as an obligation, as the object of a commandment. But love cannot be commanded. Love commanded only brings about evil and misery.... That is why those who preach love spend their days complaining about the world's malice.... That is why Lao-tzu says to Kung-fu-tse: "Just as biting flies keep you awake all night, I am plagued by all this talk about human kindness and justice. Strive to return the world to its original innocence."

But how? one wants to ask.

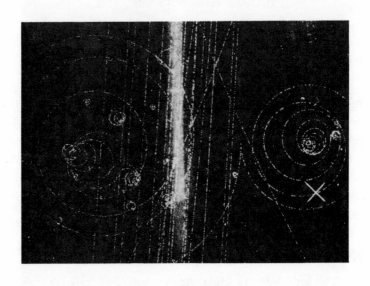

Traces of Charged Particles
in the Bubble Chamber
Somehow, somewhere, a microphysical particle
has moved within the area of a
macrophysical cloud trail.

{ 4 }

THE RENUNCIATION
OF SUBSTANCE AND CAUSALITY

Quantum Mechanics

The atomic theory used by physicists and chemists of the nineteenth century did not fundamentally differ from that formulated by the Greek philosopher Democritus (ca. 470 B.C. to ca. 380 B.C.). According to this theory, the atom should be imagined as an extremely small, smooth, and shiny globule that is impenetrably hard and unchangeable. Additionally, Democritus argued that not only matter but also the soul consisted of atoms, and that these "soul atoms" caused different reactions in the various organs of the human body, such as reason in the brain and emotions in the heart.

For Democritus, not all atoms were the same; material dissimilarities were the result of differences in the size and arrangement of atoms. In this respect, at least, the atomic theory of the nineteenth century was more differentiated. Different kinds of atoms were classified according to their mass or weight relative to the lightest atom, that of hydrogen. Its mass was indicated as 1. As the oxygen atom has approximately sixteen times the mass of the hydrogen atom, it was assigned an atomic weight of 16. The other known elements were classified accordingly and grouped in the periodic table.

On this basis, the molecular arrangement of atoms could be examined. Finally, one could even design molecules on paper and develop chemical substances not found in nature. It was also possible to predict the existence of elements that had not yet been discovered. The atomic theory seemed to be complete, and it was believed that there would be no further surprises.

In 1896, however, the French physicist Antoine Henri Becquerel accidentally discovered that a certain substance had characteristics that could not be explained by the current atomic theory. He was working with a substance containing traces of uranium in the course of experiments with X-rays—which had been discovered by W. C. Roentgen (1845–1923) the previous year. If one shone light on this substance, it started emitting light as well. Becquerel assumed that this light should also contain X-rays. His assumption turned out to be wrong, but he noticed instead that the light contained another mysterious kind of radiation that passed through black paper and clouded a photographic film behind it.

Further investigations revealed that this radiation was caused by the uranium atoms that constantly gave off particles as if they were exploding. Since *explosion* is a misleading term, a new term was invented: Uranium was said to be *radioactive*. The fact that uranium atoms could emit particles rendered the concept of the atom as a hard, indivisible globule invalid. It obviously consisted of several even smaller particles that were constantly emitted by radioactive substances.

THE ATOM AS A
MINIATURE PLANETARY SYSTEM

The development of this phenomenon is inextricably linked to the name of the New Zealand–born physicist Ernest Rutherford. For his experiments, he used specific subatomic particles emitted by a variety of naturally radioactive elements, the so-called alpha particles. These particles are identical with the helium nucleus, that is, they are the remainders of helium atoms that have lost—for whatever reason—both their electrons. Alpha particles are therefore helium nuclei carrying a double positive charge. Such a mutilated atom, deprived of its electrons, is called an ion.

In the beginning of his experiments, Rutherford examined the alpha particles themselves by exposing them to strong electric and magnetic fields and observing their behavior, but later he turned them into observational "tools." Alpha particles became a most appropriate key to the hidden world of atoms. They were used as an extremely potent probe with which one penetrated, rather violently, the atomic structure of a substance and watched what happened. Rutherford let alpha particles impinge, in the manner of extremely fast projectiles, on thin metallic foils and observed the effects.

Here we should first explain how it was possible to observe particles that are invisible to the human eye. In this case, atomic physics benefited from Scotch mist. As a Scottish meteorologist, one does well to specialize in fog and cloud formation, which is what C. T. R. Wilson (1869–1959) did. He discovered that moisture condenses particularly fast on electrically charged dust particles. In order to examine this phenomenon more thoroughly, Wilson developed the so-called cloud chamber, which could be filled with moist air. If a charged particle travels through this otherwise absolutely dust-free chamber, one can follow its path via the trail of condensed water droplets it leaves behind. For what is true for charged dust particles also applies to charged subatomic particles.

With the help of such a cloud chamber, Rutherford observed that almost all of the alpha particles hitting the metallic foil passed through undisturbed. Matter therefore had to be incredibly grainy, with lots of space between tiny accumulations of matter. Consequently, atoms were not hard globules, arranged one immediately next to the other, but seemed to consist mainly of empty space.

Nevertheless the cloud chamber experiments showed that once in a while an alpha particle passing through the metallic foil was deflected and hurled off its path at a large angle. Such a particle had apparently been subject to a very strong force or had collided with something very small and dense. The law describing this deflection is called Rutherford's law. It makes a very simple statement: The force acting on the alpha particle is the electric repulsion between its own double positive charge and the positive charge of an atomic nucleus in its vicinity. It is the same force that causes two positively charged metal balls to repel each other, a phenomenon described by Coulomb's law, which basically corresponds to Newton's law of gravitation: The repulsive force is inversely proportional to the square of the distance between the charges. The closer an alpha particle gets to an atomic nucleus, the stronger it is repelled by it.

In 1911, Rutherford proposed an extended atomic model. The center of the atom is a tiny core in which nearly all the mass is concentrated. Charge and mass are therefore concentrated in a minimum of space. The nucleus is so extremely small that one would have to place about one hundred thousand nuclei side by side to arrive at the diameter of the atom itself. The space around the nucleus is occupied by a certain number of electrons that differs according to the type of atom concerned. The hydrogen atom, for example, has only one electron, the oxygen atom eight, and the uranium atom ninety-two. All electrons are identical regardless of the type of atom they belong to; they all have the same negative charge that is indicated by the number -1.

In every atom, the positive charge of the nucleus and the negative charge of electrons neutralize each other, which means that the atom itself does not carry an electrical charge. Since a hydrogen atom has one electron with a charge of -1, the nucleus must carry a charge of $+1$. The oxygen atom has eight electrons with a combined charge of -8; the nucleus must therefore carry a charge of $+8$.

But Rutherford discovered even more, showing that if an alpha particle collides with a nucleus, something other than an alpha particle is emitted. He was thus the first to induce a nuclear transmutation. Rutherford let alpha particles hit nitrogen nuclei and observed that hydrogen nuclei were emitted. He called these particles protons. Since, by bombarding an atomic nucleus with subatomic particles, one could turn it into the nucleus of a different type of atom, atomic nuclei had to consist of even smaller particles (protons). Only the nuclei of hydrogen atoms seemed to consist of just a single particle, for all of Rutherford's efforts to break it down failed. Hydrogen nucleus and proton are identical.

The fact that nuclei of different atoms consisted of a different number of protons gave rise to a new problem that was to be the main concern of nuclear physicists in the 1920s. It turned out that the mass of atomic nuclei was twice as high as the number of their protons permitted. The oxygen nucleus, which carries a charge of +8, should have consisted of eight protons, but in fact its mass was not eight times but sixteen times that of a single proton. Where, physicists asked themselves, did the additional mass come from?

All kinds of theories were developed—all of them unsatisfactory—until the idea came up that the nucleus might contain other particles with the same mass as protons but no electrical charge. These particles would add to the mass of the nucleus but not to its charge. But how to detect uncharged particles? In the cloud chamber, for all its earlier value, one could only locate charged particles. Maybe, scientists thought, it might be possible to detect them indirectly. This was achieved by the British physicist James Chadwick (1891–1974) in 1932.

Chadwick observed that beryllium, when exposed to bombardment by alpha particles, released radiation. This beryllium radiation ejected protons from a layer of paraffin close to the beryllium, and these protons could be detected in the cloud chamber. Chadwick concluded that the protons had to have been released by some kind of subatomic particle, and called this particle the neutron.

Thus, another step toward an exact description of the atomic structure had been taken. The atomic nucleus now consists of protons and neutrons; together they make up the mass of the nucleus, the neutron having a slightly larger mass than the proton. The oxygen nucleus, for example, which carries a charge of +8 (atomic number) and has the mass 16 (atomic weight), consists of 8 protons and 8 neutrons. Correspondingly, the uranium nucleus, with a charge of +92 and a mass of 238, consists of 92 protons and 146 neutrons.

PULSING IN QUANTUM JUMPS

Rutherford's atomic model had resembled a planetary model on the basis of Newton's law of gravitation, where electrons orbit the nucleus like satellites on arbitrary elliptical paths. Unfortunately, the laws of mechanics and electricity predicted that such an atom would be unstable since a charge that does not move in a straight line becomes weaker by constantly emitting electromagnetic radiation. Electrons moving on elliptical paths would therefore continuously release energy in the form of radiation, become slower, and finally collide with the nucleus. This, however, is not the case.

As long as the electrons are not exposed to an external force, they do not emit light or any other kind of electromagnetic radiation. According to Newton's classical physics, the stability of the electron orbits was totally inexplicable. This contradiction was resolved by the Danish physicist Niels Bohr (1885–1962) who suggested that the electrons were limited to a series of allowed orbits; they may jump from one path or shell to another, but only if they release a certain amount of energy in the form of a quantum of light. The light's color corresponds to its energy, which is precisely the same as the difference in energy between the two shells. The energy differences for such electron or quantum "jumps" are therefore not arbitrary but fixed or "discrete." Here we had better stop for a while and begin a new train of thought.

Having introduced the term *quantum*, it becomes necessary to present a theory of atomic systems—if that is at all possible in everyday language—that is referred to as *quantum theory*. It was developed alongside and in close interaction with the experimental investigation of the atom outlined above. Max Planck (1858–1947) is generally regarded as the originator of the quantum theory, although he worked in a sphere that does not really belong to the central fields of nuclear physics. Planck dealt with the well-known phenomenon that matter that is heated up eventually starts glowing until it is red or white hot.

Since, in the case of a black object, the color of the emitted radiation is dependent only on the temperature, it is particularly suited for a physical investigation of this phenomenon. A simple fact, but the physicists of the nineteenth century had had no end of trouble explaining it. Consequent application of the natural laws known at the time did not lead to significant results. Planck's ingenious idea consisted of shifting the entire problem from the radiation itself to the radiating atom.

By studying measurements of the spectrum of heat radiation, which were made at the same time, in the summer of 1900, by Curlbaum and Rubens in Berlin, Planck found a formula that provided an exact explanation for these measurements. The formula was based on the assumption that the radiating body—or, more precisely, the radiating atom—cannot absorb and emit energy continuously but only in separate indivisible amounts, elementary "energy packets" that Planck called quanta.

Thus, the radiating atom can only exist in certain states that the physicist calls discrete energy states. In the atomic sphere, the emission and absorption of energy occurs in finite and separate quanta of energy. This contradicted the classical theory that described radiation as something uninterrupted and flowing, in short, a wave. Planck's formula shook the foundations upon which the physical description of nature rested.

Five years after Planck's quantum hypothesis, the young Einstein gave a fresh impetus to this field of physics as well. With the sure instinct of the scientific genius, he applied Planck's theories to a couple of problems which, until then, had caused many headaches among physicists. The first one was the so-called photoelectric effect, which is the ejection of electrons from a metal that is exposed to light. This effect provided the basis for the development of the photographic plate.

Experiments had shown that the energy of the emitted electrons does not depend on the intensity of the light but only on its color, that is, its frequency or wave length. With the help of Planck's quantum hypothesis, Einstein could now explain this phenomenon. Visible light should no longer be regarded as a wave but as consisting of quanta of light or energy that move in space like subatomic particles. It is these quanta that stimulate the nerve cells in the eye or are registered as heat by the nerve ends of the skin.

The energy of a single quantum, Einstein concluded in agreement with Planck's hypothesis, must be the frequency of light (v) times Planck's constant (h): $E = vh$. Planck's constant h is a universal constant that is of central importance in quantum mechanics: $h = 6.626196 \times 10^{-34}$ Js, where J denotes energy (Joule) and s stands for time (seconds). Since Planck's constant has the dimension of an action (energy times time), it is also referred to as Planck's quantum of action.

The other physical problem that Einstein solved using Planck's quantum hypothesis was the specific heat of solid bodies. The specific heat values calculated on the basis of the classical theory corresponded nicely with measurements taken in the range of very high temperatures, but were significantly greater than the measured values in the range of very low temperatures. If one applied Planck's theory instead, this heat phenomenon could be definitively explained by attributing it to the elastic vibrations of the atoms in the respective body.

Einstein's calculation corresponded exactly to all measurements, even those taken at extreme temperatures. Both results were of significant importance for the development of the quantum theory. It had become apparent that Planck's constant could not only be applied to the range of heat radiation but also to the range of visible light. Now, however, physics was confronted with an entirely new and very confusing problem. Light could be interpreted as an uninterrupted electromagnetic wave but also as a shower of individual light quanta traveling through space at the speed of light. The photoelectric effect, for example, can only be explained by the quantum theory whereas the wavelike nature of light has been proven by a variety of other experiments, such as the diffraction of light by transmission through a grating.

This phenomenon can only be explained by the wave theory of light. If one imagines light as being composed of quanta, then a hair held between a source of light and a projection screen should cast a sharply defined shadow. The fact that such a shadow does not appear suggests that the light rays have been diffracted, in the same way as waves of water wash around a rock. In this case, light must be described as a wave. A similar phenomenon is called interference. If we send light through two narrow parallel slits in a partition, what we see on the screen are not two corresponding bright points but a uniform pattern of parallel fringes. This is analogous to the effect created by the collision of two wave systems on the water surface. They reinforce each other where two wave crests coincide, and they cancel each other out where a crest of one wave coincides with a trough of the other. In the light pattern on the screen, light fringes appear where both light waves reinforce each other, and dark fringes appear where they cancel each other out.

The obvious question is: How can light have two different characteristics at the same time? Must it not be either one or the other? Well, physics still has to live with this contradiction that perhaps will be resolved one day by an entirely new approach. This paradox, it transpired, was not to be limited to light. When physicists applied the quantum theory to Rutherford's atomic model, examining the electron orbits, they were confronted with the same dualism.

According to quantum mechanics, electrons could be described as particles moving on paths but also as waves, or, more precisely, as "waves of matter." Quantum mechanics might therefore also be referred to as wave mechanics. Depending on the kind of experiment carried out, electrons should be regarded as particles whenever they move freely in space and as a system of waves surrounding the nucleus whenever we deal with atoms. One might even regard the entire atom as a system of overlapping waves or claim that all matter is composed of waves and that we live in a cosmos of waves.

THE ATOMIC COSMOS—INDISTINCT,
INDEFINITE, AND UNPREDICTABLE

At the beginning of the 1920s, many physicists already agreed that these apparent contradictions were not attributable to an inadequate theory but represented one aspect of reality in the atomic sphere. In this sphere, nature is no longer unequivocal. Physicists therefore attempted to reconcile the ambiguity of nuclear physics with a precise mathematical system. The physical problem to be discussed here is basically very simple. One has to realize that just as Newton's classical mechanics are not appropriate for describing the world of extremely large things, they can no longer be applied to the world of extremely small things either.

On the basis of the classical laws of mechanics we can, for example, calculate the precise path of a body if we know its position, speed, and the external forces acting on it. In the world of atoms this is no longer possible, not because the measuring devices employed are too inaccurate but because nature itself seems to have established a limit here. One is tempted to say that nature has drawn a veil over its deepest secrets, making events in the atomic and subatomic range "blurred," indistinct, and indefinite. To demonstrate that this is an obstacle set by nature herself and not due to imperfections of the observational methods employed, Werner Heisenberg envisaged a microscope that could make electrons visible. Of course, one would first have to solve the problem posed by the fact that electrons are smaller than the wavelength of visible light and can be observed only by illumination with radiation of a much shorter wavelength. Even the wavelength of hard X-rays would be too long.

Electrons could only be made "visible" by means of extremely short-wave gamma radiation. The photoelectric effect, however, shows that even the photons of visible light can destroy the stability of electrons and eject them from the atomic structure. If we tried to determine the exact position of an electron by illuminating it with gamma rays, we would immediately change its speed and, consequently, its path. We would therefore never be able to ascertain both the position and the speed of an electron. The path of the electron would remain undeterminable and obscure even with a gamma-ray microscope.

This obscurity is of no importance in the sphere of everyday mechanics because Planck's quantum of action is extremely small; it lies in the range of 10^{-34}. The position and speed of particles that are bigger than atoms can therefore be calculated quite accurately with the laws of classical mechanics. If, for example, we have determined the position of a moving body with a mass of 1 gram accurate within 10^{-9} centimeters, we can still give its speed accurate within 10^{-17} cm/sec.

But if we deal with particles of the size of a single atom, this is no longer possible. In this sphere, we would have to apply the laws of quantum mechanics but, since these laws only provide information about probabilities, they are of a purely statistical nature. They do not describe the behavior of individual particles but provide statistics—that is, a list of probable states—for a collection of similar particles. To clarify the proceedings in quantum mechanics, Einstein and Infeld use radioactive disintegration as an example:

> Radioactive disintegration is one of the many processes which quantum mechanics strives to describe in laws; in this case, laws that describe the spontaneous transmutation of one element into another. We know, for example, that of one gram of radium, half a gram will have decayed after 1,600 years while the other half will be still unchanged. We can give an approximate prediction of how many atoms will decay in the next half hour but not even in theoretical descriptions would we be able to explain why precisely these and no other atoms are affected. The current state of our knowledge does not allow us to determine which atoms are bound to disintegrate. The fate of an atom has nothing to do with its age. We do not have the slightest trace of a law from

which we could draw conclusions regarding the behaviour of single atoms. We can only formulate statistical laws, laws which are valid for great masses of atoms.

The behavior of individual elementary particles, such as electrons, cannot be described according to the law of cause and effect that applies in classical physics. Consequently, we can no longer speak of the path on which this or that electron moves because in order to determine a path we would have to know the position and speed of an electron at every single moment. That we can follow the trails of particles in the cloud chamber just appears to be a contradiction.

These trails are phenomena in the macrophysical range; we can observe them with the naked eye. Compared to the size of the respective particle, such a trail is incredibly large. It does not reflect the exact movement of the particle but represents only a rough estimate. The only thing one can say is that somewhere, sometime, a microphysical particle has moved in the area of the macrophysical cloud trail.

Elementary particles are no longer described according to their paths but according to certain states which, in some instances and under specific conditions, have the characteristics of paths. We can at best observe two states of a particle, but we will never be able to determine which path the particle moved on between those states. It is impossible to illustrate the transition along the lines of matter traveling in space. Subatomic particles do not have positions and speeds that could be accurately determined, but take up imprecise and indefinite states that could be described as a combination of position and speed.

These so-called quantum states of particles are stable or almost stable but can quite easily be disturbed by other elementary particles. In this case, a particle may change from one state to another. Such transitions, however, cannot be predicted; they are entirely accidental. The cause of an individual transition remains obscure.

Something unknown does something, but we do not know what it does. At best, we know how many transitions are likely to occur in a given period of time.

Thus, in the atomic sphere it is no longer possible to imagine pictures or provide graphs. The physicist, measuring and observing events in the microphysical range, is confronted with the confusing fact that these events lack all causality. He cannot measure every quantity of an observed microphysical system simultaneously, which would be the prerequisite for establishing laws of cause and effect. If I can accurately determine the position of a particle, I cannot determine its energy or impulse at the same time. There is always an either-or.

Niels Bohr referred to this fact as *complementarity*. Complementarity is present in the fact that light must be described as a wave at one time or as a shower of light quanta at another, and electrons either as a wave of matter or as particles. In both cases, the concepts complement each other. The one concept precludes the other since a given thing—in this example, the electron—cannot be particle and wave at the same time. In a certain sense, the physicist plays with both concepts that are, anyway, just mental crutches and not representations of the "real" electron.

Depending on the kind of observation he makes, the physicist changes from one picture to the other and back again. Every measurement taken is therefore also complementary to every other measurement because both cannot be taken at the same time. Quantum mechanics, however, manages to describe even this paradoxical situation, which renders any kind of observation indefinite and indistinct, with a strict mathematical law. This law is closely linked to the name of Werner Heisenberg. It states that specific complementary quantities such as the position or the impulse of an electron are subject to Heisenberg's indeterminacy or uncertainty principle.

This principle says that the product of the two uncertainties can never be smaller than Planck's constant, divided by the mass of the particle observed. This law is typical for the quantum theory: It limits the range of possible results of a microphysical experiment, but it cannot determine an exact result, which means that every observation of a microphysical system produces a unique knowledge about this system: a knowledge newly gained that could neither have been acquired by analysis nor calculations.

In the world of atoms, nothing repeats itself and everything happens by accident. And this is true in spite of the universal order which, after all, is based on atomic structures. Quantum mechanics simply states that natural phenomena are indeterminable and that the future cannot be predicted because it is not within the scope of causal predetermination. Any scientific definition of existence has to include *freedom* as an essential existential characteristic. We see the world as through a clouded window pane. Actual reality (whatever that may be) cannot be "purely" perceived by us.

In his book about Einstein, Lincoln Barnett says:

> Whenever [man] attempts to penetrate and spy on the "real" objective world, he changes and distorts its workings by the very process of his observations. And when he tries to divorce this "real" world from his sense perceptions he is left with nothing but a mathematical scheme. He is indeed somewhat in the position of a blind man trying to discern the shape and texture of a snowflake. As soon as it touches his fingers or his tongue it dissolves. A wave electron, a photon, a wave of probability cannot be visualized; they are simply symbols useful in expressing the mathematical relationships of the microcosm.

And Einstein himself once said: "One gets the impression that modern physics is based on assumptions which somehow resemble the smile of a cat that is not there." But it is not only the microphysical world that seems to be obscured as if seen through a veil; our everyday world, too, is full of improbabilities and uncertainties. Even with the most accurate measuring devices, for example, physicists would never be able to precisely determine how a tree will lose its leaves in autumn. Not even the flight path of a single leaf could be accurately precalculated. Here, again, we could at best prepare rough statistics and probabilities.

In the preface to his book on the cultural history of Egypt, Egon Friedell writes:

> All our experiences and perceptions, actions and theorems are surrounded by a dim aureole of uncertainty. Between ourselves and the objects, a veil is put up, as in the theatre when they try to express "vision." Everything that occurs carries the stigma of the transitional, the ruse, and the hiatus. It is at the pinnacles of our existence, in the moments of the most profound emotion, caused by the power of nature, the power of love, our own power, that this feeling seizes us most strongly. Everything is, as Seneca says, "only borrowed tableware," and, according to Marcus Aurelius' gloomy wisdom, "our time [is] a moment, what belongs to the body, a river, what belongs to the soul, a dream, life a journey in foreign countries, and posthumous fame oblivion." Who dares say "no" to existence? All the villages in this world are Potemkin's. There is a tacit agreement among all of us just to play the game, and, at the same time, an arrangement not to be a spoilsport, never to talk about this secret rule. Even "wild" or "primitive" man (and he in particular since, close to nature, he sees through it) does not believe in the solidity of the scenery and machinery surrounding him; he takes them for magic, maybe even humbug. But we know as well as he does that we are living in a vast haunted house. Nobody, even if he tries to dampen or hiss down the voice of doubt, is really so stupid as to trust his reason and its tale-spinning. Everything is just fog and frenzy, wisps of cloud and the dance of veils, fifteen minutes of rainbow; "and even dreams are a dream."

In less poetic terms: The uncertainty principle is a basic fact of life and experience, an essential designation of our existence.

Quantum mechanics is distinguished by yet another important assumption. It claims that a macrophysical system—a table, for example—consisting of many microphysical subsystems (nuclei and electrons) may have characteristics that cannot be compared with the characteristics of the subsystems. Thus, if one tries to measure the characteristics of the microphysical subsystems, this leads unavoidably toward the destruction of the characteristics of the macrophysical system. A characteristic of the table, for example, would be its solidity. Such characteristics are referred to as *integral*.

A characteristic of the electrons and nuclei that the table is composed of would be, for example, their position. If one tried to measure the position of these "table electrons" and "table nuclei," one would have to examine the table, as we have mentioned before, with a gamma-ray microscope. These measurements, however, would turn the table into a chaotic jumble of nuclei and electrons, thus destroying its integral characteristic: solidity. Even if it was possible to reassemble all the electrons and nuclei and to rebuild the table, it would never be exactly the table that we started to examine. The whole is more than just the sum of its parts.

THE OLD MAN DOES PLAY DICE

Even though classical physics and quantum physics are two very different disciplines, the boundaries between them are indefinite. Necessarily so. There has to be a connection between the visible world in which we live, governed as it is by the deterministic cause-and-effect laws of Newtonian mechanics, and the invisible, noncausal world of the atoms. For everything that exists is composed of atoms. One has to accept the paradox that a more or less causal macroworld is based on a noncausal microworld. The transition between both worlds is fluid.

The physicist would say that quantum physics and classical physics are linked by a principle of correspondence. The further we approach our perceptible world from the viewpoint of the atomic world, the more the laws of quantum mechanics correspond to those we know from our world; they dissolve into them, so to speak. The statistical probabilities of nuclear physics turn into certainties as we leave the world of individual atoms. We have encountered something similar in connection with Einstein's theory of relativity which, too, does not render Newton's mechanics invalid but acquires importance only in the range of cosmic dimensions. Nevertheless, the theory of relativity is still a classical theory in that it is strictly deterministic; it establishes laws that predict every single event in four-dimensional space-time according to the principle of cause and effect.

It is therefore understandable that throughout his life Einstein kept a critical distance to the quantum theory, although he had contributed strongly to its development. After all, he did not get the Nobel prize in 1921 for his theory of relativity but for his theoretical work on quantum physics. Yet he continued to regard the quantum theory as a provisional solution because it represented a statistical rather than strictly deterministic description of nature.

Einstein's scientific genius could not accept the idea that the atomic world was ruled by chance. He expressed his dissatisfaction in the famous words "God does not play dice!" or "The old man does not play dice!" Though one should not ignore the irony in this statement, Einstein certainly had his doubts about the quantum theory, from both scientific and religious points of view. Scientifically, his main argument was that no scientific theory can claim to be definitive. It is always possible that we are simply not yet able to discern the whole truth about the behavior of elementary particles. Perhaps this apparently accidental behavior conceals a complex and mathematically decipherable system to which we simply lack the key.

What speaks against Einstein's objection is the fact that quantum mechanics completely agrees with experimental data. After all, it has been the basis for the development of nearly all modern technologies. Although quantum mechanics is not entirely objective, it is nevertheless an exact science and an incredibly versatile and successful one to boot. It is not only a prerequisite for the work of the physicist; chemists and biologists trying to understand the microstructure of chemical bonding, and astronomers trying to comprehend what happens inside stars, cannot manage without quantum mechanics either.

With the help of quantum physics it became possible to determine the behavior of transistors and integrated circuits, an indispensable requirement for the development of modern microelectronics. Without quantum mechanics there would be no computer, and even our pet hate, "the tube," would not have been invented.

It is slightly ironical that the computer should contribute to the development of a new, very strange branch of mathematics: chaos theory. One could also call it a theory of chance. Basically, it is nothing but a scientific investigation into Einstein's objection against chance in nature. It seeks to find out whether seemingly random and unpredictable events in nature might yet be based on laws so complex that they can only be determined by computers. One could hardly find a more paradoxical development.

On the basis of quantum mechanics—which, after all, integrates chance—computers are developed and employed in the search for a natural law of chance, the logic of the unpredictable. For more and more natural phenomena that hitherto seemed to obey only the strict laws of cause and effect or the laws of strictly periodical recurrence have been found to be influenced by chaos. What seems to demonstrate a rigid order on the surface, may be based, in deeper layers, on a kind of "orderly disorder." It looks as if chance itself participates in microphysical events, like a microphysical quantum, that is, like something that might one day be calculated and represented in a mathematical model.

It is therefore not at all contradictory to attribute orderly and harmonious phenomena in the perceptible world to chance and chaos in the microphysical sphere. These "accidents" might obey "metamathematical" laws that we simply cannot understand yet. Maybe we need a new, extended mathematics anyway. Neuroscientists have discovered, for example, that in a normal brain, one that functions properly, brain waves follow an irregular pattern that is not yet mathematically decipherable.

The brain wave patterns of epileptics and normal test subjects have been shown to differ in that the irregularities are more pronounced in the normal brain. The EEG (electroencephalogram) patterns of a healthy person are more chaotic. One would automatically expect the contrary to be true. During an epileptic fit, the brain wave patterns are particularly regular and periodic, suggesting that, in nature, order and harmony can arise from chaos and disorder. The quantum theory even seems to prove that order in the macroworld would not be possible without chaos and atrophy in the microworld. "Even in chaos, nature cannot help but proceed in an orderly and regular fashion," as Immanuel Kant has remarked.

Einstein's scientific doubts about the nonobjective character of the quantum theory are understandable. Perhaps science will be able in the near future to prove that the accidental, too, reveals mathematically describable regularities. It is surprising, though, that Einstein employs God in his argumentation. We have encountered this before in connection with the theory of relativity. Einstein could not get used to the concept of an expanding universe—for religious reasons—although it was suggested by his equations. As if divine creation had to be entirely and eternally static to be truly divine. Why should this be the case?

What is more, Einstein calls upon God, although he had clearly rejected the concept of a personal God. After all, he regarded "cosmic religiousness" as the only acceptable form of religion. The absence of strict determinism in quantum physics, however, is not contradictory to cosmic religiousness. On the contrary! It is almost typical for such a religious worldview that it can only be defined in "uncertainty principles," at least where the so-called ultimate truths are concerned.

A Buddhist or Taoist should be enthusiastic about quantum theory because it leaves certain things undefined. And this indefiniteness also appears in religion whenever it wrestles with God or the divine. Every conception of God must necessarily be indistinct and recondite. Cosmic religiousness virtually breathes in the rarefied atmosphere of the indefinite. God has to play dice to ensure that

He and His creation will never be fully grasped by human reason. Only thus can God keep on being God.

There is a certain similarity between the way quantum physicists occupy their minds with the smallest building blocks of matter and the way great religious philosophers once contemplated the divine. One is inclined to say that the teachings of Buddha and Taoism, the philosophy of Nicholas of Cusa, and the mysticism of Meister Eckhart are all quantum theories of religion or quantum metaphysics. J. R. Oppenheimer said, with respect to the nonobjective nature of quantum physics:

> To what appeared to be the simplest questions, we will tend to give either no answer or an answer which will at first sight be reminiscent more of a strange catechism than of the straightforward affirmatives of physical science. If we ask, for instance, whether the position of the electron remains the same, we must say "no"; if we ask whether the electron's position changes with time, we must say "no"; if we ask whether the electron is at rest, we must say "no"; if we ask whether it is in motion, we must say "no." The Buddha has given such answers when interrogated as to the conditions of a man's self after his death.

Or, in the language of Taoism: The Tao that can be named is not the real Tao. The quantum physicist would add: And an electron that can be exactly defined is not a real electron.

ELEMENTARY PARTICLES,
ELEMENTARY PARTICLES,
ELEMENTARY PARTICLES...

The quantum theory was completed in the 1930s, and its basic foundations have remained sound. The harmony and inner coherence of this theory made modifications neither necessary nor possible. Let us return to the experimental examination of the atom and its components. The discovery of the neutron by the British physicist James Chadwick in 1932 heralded a new phase in nuclear physics. Now the neutron itself was used as a projectile in the examination of the atomic nucleus. Since it carries no electrical charge and is therefore not repelled by positively charged nuclei, it was better suited for this purpose than the alpha particle.

On January 6, 1939, two German physicists, Otto Hahn (1879–1968) and Fritz Strassmann (1902–1980), informed professional circles, via an article in a technical journal, that they had succeeded in splitting uranium nuclei by bombarding them with neutrons. Physicists soon began to realize that the ground had been prepared for artificial release of the energy dormant in atomic nuclei. For the time being, however, they were occupied with other problems resulting from this newly acquired knowledge. Of particular concern was the fact that the positively charged protons in the nucleus should, in fact, repel each other with a very strong force, causing the nucleus to disintegrate immediately.

There had to be a force balancing the strong electromagnetic force of repulsion and holding the protons together. And it had to be a force that acts only across very small distances since protons located outside of nuclei—free protons—repel each other if they come too close together. This very powerful attractive force, which exists only within atomic nuclei, is called *nuclear force* or *strong force*. But where does it come from? physicists asked themselves. It was finally assumed that it must result from a continuous exchange of particles between protons and neutrons which, however, only takes place if protons and neutrons sit right next to each other. (In general, every physical force is due to an exchange of particles. The electromagnetic force between electrically charged particles, for example, results from an exchange of photons or quanta of light.)

From this assumption, it followed that the mysterious carrier particles should have a mass lying between that of protons and electrons. Without having experimentally proved their existence, physicists called these particles *mesons*. But how to detect them? Perhaps it was possible to release them from the nuclear structure by bombarding nuclei with particularly energy-rich, that is, strongly accelerated, particles. Physicists began to devise machines which, utilizing strong electromagnetic forces, would accelerate subatomic particles to such a degree that they could knock mesons out of nuclei. With the "accelerators" developed in the 1930s and 1940s, however, the experiment was not successful. The achieved acceleration rates were still too low.

In the end it was nature herself who released the physicists from their dilemma. The Earth is constantly bombarded with a natural radiation called cosmic radiation. It is composed of subatomic particles of varying energy; some of these particles have a considerably higher energy than could be produced in accelerators at the time. Cosmic radiation hits the Earth randomly, and cannot be concentrated on a specific spot, and this proves problematic for experimental purposes. One has to wait patiently until such a high-energy particle accidentally hits a nucleus in the desired manner, and, of course, at that very moment a physicist has to be present with a measuring device.

In 1936 a particle was discovered that fulfilled the requirements of the theory: It was heavier than an electron and lighter than a proton or neutron. Unfortunately, it was also lighter than it should have been according to the calculations.

Ten more years had to pass until finally, in 1947, the British physicist C. F. Powell (1903–1969), who studied cosmic radiation in the Bolivian Andes, discovered a particle that exactly matched the calculated characteristics. The lighter meson discovered before was called *mu-meson* (or *muon*) and the one discovered by Powell *pi-meson* (or *pion*). The latter is a very unstable particle; a pion exists only about twenty-five billionths of a second and changes then into a muon. Although it is of very short duration, it can nevertheless be detected; it is so fast that within this extremely short period it travels a distance of several centimeters, leaving a trail of corresponding length in the cloud chamber. The lighter muon survives slightly longer, a few millionths of a second, before it changes into a stable electron.

With the help of increasingly powerful accelerators, new particles were discovered in rapid succession in the 1950s and 1960s. What is more, for every particle, physicists detected an antiparticle. The counterparts of the electron and proton, for example, were the positron (an electron carrying the charge +1) and the antiproton (with a charge of –1). If an antiproton comes near a proton, the proton turns into a neutron and the antiproton into an antineutron.

Since both neutron and antineutron do not carry an electrical charge, they can only be distinguished by a property that physicists refer to as autorotation or spin. Spin, however, is not a property exclusive to neutrons and antineutrons but characterizes all elementary particles. To illustrate this, one should imagine particles as whipping tops that can rotate about their axis in two directions. Such an image, however, can only serve as a mental aid since, according to the laws of quantum mechanics, elementary particles do not have a precisely definable axis.

If there is an antiparticle for every particle, there has to be an antinucleus for every nucleus, too. Antinuclei were first detected in 1965. It became evident that there had to be matter consisting not of normal particles but of antiparticles—antimatter, that is. In our world, however, there are hardly any traces of antimatter. It can only be detected in extremely small and very unstable quantities; it can be artificially created in the laboratory, but does not survive for long.

Once in a while, the particles in cosmic radiation produce a few antielectrons, but these disappear quickly because in our material world they hit one of the innumerable "normal" electrons within fractions of a second. Particles and antiparticles are absolute opposites. If they meet, they destroy each other; their respective mass is completely converted into radiation energy, that is, into light quanta or mesons. As we know from quantum mechanics, light quanta are treated like elementary particles in nuclear physics. They are called photons. A photon, however, is a special kind of particle because it does not have an antiphoton as an opposite. The photon is its own antiparticle.

The transformation processes of particles and antiparticles must, of course, also be possible in reverse: If enough energy is concentrated on a minimum of space, elementary particles may be produced from "pure" radiation, but only together with their respective antiparticles, never individually. Since both immediately annihilate each other and are converted back into energy, this is an endless and meaningless cycle. One might conclude from this that there are perhaps areas in the universe that consist only of antimatter. What speaks against this hypothesis is that in this case large and therefore measurable amounts of radiation should be constantly emitted from the border areas of matter and antimatter; this, however, is not the case.

One thing at least seems to be quite certain: The Milky Way consists only of matter. But this is, ultimately, just a question of algebraic signs anyway, a matter of + or –. Furthermore, it seems a pretty safe bet to assume that at the beginning of the universe—if there was a beginning—there must have been far more matter particles than antimatter particles. For if there had been an equal amount of both kinds of particles, they would all have destroyed each other. Consequently, the universe would have consisted solely of radiation, or rather its composition would have been determined by an eternal cycle of radiation-producing matter and matter decaying into radiation.

In the course of this discussion, we have moved from the very small to the very big, and the latter is a topic reserved for later chapters. But the reader may have begun to feel that this maze of particles can be wearying. One gets the impression that every newly discovered particle just opens the door to another world of particles. By now, about two hundred elementary particles have been discovered, and most of them are not really elementary; they can still be split up into even more elementary particles, the only restriction being the energy available in the accelerator.

One more enigmatic particle, however, should be mentioned here: the neutrino. Although its existence had been suggested by the electron observations of Austrian physicist Wolfgang Pauli (1900–1958) as early as 1931, it was not detected until 1956. In most cases, the existence of an elementary particle is first suggested by a theory and then proved by experimental physicists in the laboratory. The neutrino has, of course, a counterpart, the antineutrino, although for the layman this seems slightly absurd since the neutrino consists basically of nothing.

It does not carry a charge and nobody has as yet succeeded in quantifying its mass. Although it seems to be more of spiritual than of material nature, it has one physically determinable property: It has spin. In many respects, it is similar to the photon; in fact, they seem to differ only in the size of their spins. Neutrinos, innumerable as photons, travel through space and nothing can deflect them from their paths. They could effortlessly pass through lead walls as thick as our planetary system because they do not interact with other particles. Neutrinos and photons are created, for example, by nuclear reactions in the interior of the sun. Every square centimeter of the Earth is hit by about 65 billion neutrinos per second—by day and night—because neutrinos can also pass through the globe.

THE SEARCH FOR THE
PRIMARY COSMIC FORCE

Scientists strive to systemize knowledge gained from experiments and to explain it, if possible, by a single and universal law. Nuclear physicists became dissatisfied with merely discovering, naming, and classifying new particles. A vast expenditure of labor and resources had been absorbed in the attempt to record the structure of matter, not only quantitatively but also qualitatively, that is, to codify this jumble of particles into a system that served to explain, definitively, not only the structure of the atomic world but also the universe and its origins.

It was important to develop laws to show which particle transmutations are possible and which are not. Of course, these laws had to incorporate the classical properties of particle transmutations:

energy, impulse, electric charge, and spin. But very soon the conservation laws of classical physics proved inadequate to explain all the observed transmutations of subatomic particles. Physicists therefore devised new conservation laws that complied with the experimental data but could not, for the time being, explain them.

The strangest of the new properties has been aptly named *strangeness*. Every particle is attributed a strangeness number, and whenever a particle transmutes into another, the total strangeness number has to remain unchanged. For the layman, all this is completely impenetrable and, in fact, not very relevant. In any case, research on strangeness revealed that not only one kind of nuclear force acts in particle transmutations but two. Apart from the strong force mentioned above that holds protons and neutrons together, there is a weak nuclear force (or simply *weak* force) that amounts to only one hundred quintillionth of the strong force.

The various known particles can be roughly grouped, according to their mass, into three categories, depending on whether they are subject to the strong or the weak nuclear force: *light, intermediate,* and *heavy* particles. The name attributed to intermediate particles we know already; they are called mesons. Light particles are referred to as leptons; this group includes the electron, the neutrino, and their antiparticles. The muon, which was at first also considered to be a meson, finally turned out to be a lepton. Heavy particles are called baryons; they include the building blocks of the nucleus, that is, the proton, the neutron, and their antiparticles. The photon is a special case, but can be classed with the light particles. The strong nuclear force is active in the interaction between mesons and baryons. The weak nuclear force is active in the interaction between leptons and leptons, leptons and mesons, and leptons and baryons.

Apart from the strong and the weak nuclear force, there are two other elementary forces that should be mentioned here. The first one is the electromagnetic force already discussed. It is the second strongest force, about a hundred times weaker than the strong nuclear force. The electromagnetic force acts between electrically charged particles and can therefore be either attractive or repulsive. That electrons are not subject to the strong nuclear force is of fundamental importance for the "functioning" of the universe since it is due to this fact that atoms can integrate into loose molecular structures. If electrons were subject to the strong force, chemical bonding would not be possible; there would be no crystallization and no development of organic elements. Nature would consist only of atomic nuclei, and the only physical reactions would be nuclear reactions.

The fourth elementary force has already been discussed in the chapter on relativity: It is gravitation, by far the weakest of the four basic forces. The force of gravitation between individual particles is so small that it is negligible in comparison with the other elementary forces and does not affect the physical properties of the particles. Whereas the strong and weak nuclear forces are only effective at very small distances, the electromagnetic force and the force of gravitation are infinitely long-range. More precisely, they are both inversely proportional to the square of the distance involved.

Gravity is always an attractive force. Even though gravity between subatomic particles is practically zero, in the case of massive bodies, such as the planets, it adds up to a significant force. Now the problem for quantum mechanics which, as we know, describes every force as an exchange of elementary particles is to find appropriate force-carrying particles for gravity and to accurately define their effects, that is, to explain in mathematical terms how, for example, gravitational quanta are exchanged between the elementary building blocks of the Sun and the Earth. These gravitational quanta which, for the time being, exist only in theory are called gravitons. If these particles exist at all, they must have the same mysterious qualities as photons or neutrinos, that is, no charge and no mass. But, although there are experiments that undeniably prove the existence of photons or neutrinos, there is so far no such experiment for the graviton. The graviton therefore is the only elementary particle that the quantum theory demands but cannot as yet describe in mathematical terms.

Einstein's general theory of relativity remains, so far, the only theory to describe the force of gravitation. Physicists, however, strive to describe all elementary forces in a single theory. A quantum theory of gravitation is needed. Just as it became possible in the nineteenth century to unify electricity and magnetism—which had been regarded as separate phenomena until then—into a single electromagnetic force, the central concern of today's physicists is to describe the four basic forces as different aspects of a primary force. This, however, can only be achieved if the four elementary forces are first united under a single theoretical umbrella.

It is quite certain that this umbrella will be quantum mechanics since it already provides a unified description of three of the four basic forces. Gravity is still holding out, but it seems to be only a matter of time until it will become definable in terms of quantum mechanics. Or it might be that everything is completely, unimaginably different. The problem could also be further increased by the discovery of a fifth elementary force, an antigravitational force. If such a force exists, it would have to be even weaker than gravitation. Its range would be limited to a few hundred meters at the most. To detect such a weak force is extremely difficult. Nevertheless, scientists are busily carrying out experiments to prove its existence. If they succeed, it would indicate that the cosmos does not have four dimensions—as in Einstein's theory—but five. And why should five dimensions be the limit?

WHERE DOES EVERYTHING COME FROM?
WHEN DID IT START?

In the 1960s nuclear physicists had at least succeeded in establishing some degree of congruence between the many subatomic particles. Nevertheless, it remained unclear why there was such a great variety of particles. The profusion of particles seemed to lead away from the concept of unity of matter. That, however, would be a misleading interpretation. After all, experiments had shown that particles could be produced from other particles and transmute into still other particles, indicating that matter is completely transformable, that something more universal must be hidden behind the variety of particles. Werner Heisenberg writes:

> All the elementary particles can, at sufficiently high energies, be transmuted into other particles, or they can simply be created from kinetic energy and can be annihilated into energy, for instance, into radiation. Therefore, we have here actually the final proof for the unity of matter. All the elementary particles are made of the same substance, which we may call energy or universal matter; they are just different forms in which matter can appear.

This variety of particles could, of course, be grouped into more fundamental categories. The only question was: How? In the long history of the sciences, it has often been the case that a tangle of different observations, which at first seemed merely confusing, was ultimately simplified by a fundamental discovery or a hypothesis. Chemistry, for example, was at first confronted with an endless variety of substances until it was finally discovered that they can all be traced back to ninety-two elements whose inner structure basically derives from the hydrogen atom which, in turn, consists of a positive proton and a negative electron.

From science's origins in Greek philosophy onward, every form of research has been informed by the dialectic between singularity and multiplicity. Science is grounded on the demand for simplicity. This demand derives from the self-image of science as economy of thought. It aims at explaining a maximum of observations with a minimum of symbols. Scientists search for a fundamental order that they may find common characteristics in the profusion of things. Order means standardization. From this arises science's belief in a basic principle underlying all phenomena, something like a primary force. And this is the point where physics and metaphysics meet: Both disciplines are concerned with the source. For if we know of the source, we know also of the nature of the world, and can determine what awaits this world.

So, in the 1960s, nuclear physicists started looking for "particle families" in which to group the almost two hundred different particles known at the time. Their objective was to bring the confusing variety of particle properties into a system more fundamental than the vague classification into light, intermediate, and heavy particles. The efforts of the American physicist Murray Gell-Mann turned out to be particularly successful. He developed a system of eight different properties and named it the *eightfold way*, after a Buddhist term. Physicists obviously lean heavily toward metaphysics when they advance into the borderlands of the perceptible.

Even though Gell-Mann's system made it possible to integrate all known elementary particles into a single family of first eight and later ten "superior particles," it did not make the physicists— including Gell-Mann himself—very happy. The question of whether the elementary particles might not be made from yet smaller particles became ever more pressing. Gell-Mann succeeded in working out theoretically which properties would have to be attributed to the building blocks of protons and neutrons. He called these hypothetical particles quarks. If they were to be integrated into the current atomic model, heavy particles such as protons and neutrons would have to be made up of three such quarks. Their most striking property would be that they would carry only fractions of electrical charges contrary to the then known particles that had either no charge at all or carried a positive or negative integer charge. Fractions of charges had so far never been measured. Gell-Mann claimed that quarks would carry charges of $-1/3$ or $+2/3$, for example.

Finally, at the end of the 1960s, the advanced state of particle accelerators permitted the collision of protons with other protons or electrons at a speed sufficient for breaking up protons, if that was at all feasible. Now questions concerning the existence of quarks could be dealt with experimentally. The results showed that protons were indeed composed of even more elementary particles or at least that phenomena occurred that might be attributed to real particles resembling the hypothetical quarks.

If quarks really exist, one would have to conclude from the experiments that there are six types of them. Each type comes in three different "colors" or "color charges." Color is, of course, a purely arbitrary and symbolic term; instead of "red," "green," and "blue" quarks one might as well speak of "striped," "spotted," and "tiger" quarks. Again, each quark has an antiparticle: the antiquark.

Heavy particles (hadrons) are made up of quarks. The proton consists of three quarks, two with a charge of +2/3 and one with a charge of –1/3, resulting in the total proton charge of +1. A neutron consists of two quarks with a charge of –1/3 and one quark with a charge of +1/3, resulting in the total neutron charge of 0. A combination of quarks is only energetically permissible if their colors add up to "white," that is, if their color charges cancel each other out.

Even the quarks that make up protons and neutrons must be held together by the strong nuclear force. Since quantum mechanics defines every force or interaction as an exchange of particles, a new class of force-carrying particles must be responsible for the interaction between quarks. The interactive particles that are exchanged between quarks and provide for the integrity of the quarks in heavy particles are called gluons. The quarks that make up protons and neutrons are linked, so to speak, by a string of gluons. These gluons in turn...

...But no, that's enough of elementary particles! Even our most modest goal—to get at least a partial idea of the findings that inspire and excite scientists—has evaporated into thin air. Knowledge has given way to confusion, intermittent understanding to chronic headache. As a layman, one probably never gets further than the image of the globule anyway since one is forced to interpret the unimaginable as something that can be visualized. In the layman's imagination, neutrons look exactly like protons or electrons: little round balls with differing masses that we translate into differing sizes, which is nonsense, of course. In our imagination, these balls somehow stick to each other or move past each other. And if two such balls collide with a sufficiently high energy, the result is a flash of light and a number of new particles which, again, look like little balls. Nuclear physics as a game of pool.

Of course, we understand that the building blocks of matter become more enigmatic the more elementary they are, but this mysterious—or, better, spiritual—quality can no longer be differentiated in pictures. For the nonspecialist, the scientific results gained in many years of hard work take on an absurd quality from a certain point of research onward. It seems to be a never-ending story. Whenever specialists rejoice at the start of a new phase of scientific knowledge, it becomes harder for the layman to distinguish this phase from the previous one. In the layman's skull, only Democritian globules whirl around anyway.

The quark theory does not simplify matters for the nonspecialist either, but merely shifts comprehension problems onto a different level, a different "elementary level" so to speak. To know that a proton is made up of three quarks does not really give us a better understanding of the structure of the microworld. Strictly speaking, everything is just a matter of the speed at which different particles collide with each other. Who says that quarks should not be composed of other, even more elementary particles? After all, the energy with which particles are forced to collide can be, at least theoretically, increased infinitely. It is just a question of feasibility.

The development of the accelerator would consequently end with a plant the size of the universe in which different particles would impact upon each other at infinite speeds. Well, such thoughts are less than sensible. Yet a measure of senselessness is apparent in the attempts to build ever-more gigantic accelerators, as if scientists refuse to accept that they will never reach a point that represents ultimate knowledge. For acute as experimental conditions may be, there can always be conditions more acute and thus a possibility of unpredictable results. Human knowledge, no matter how much it may expand in the future, will always remain limited since man himself is limited by nature.

Why should the answer to the supposedly final questions of nuclear physics be provided by a 27-kilometer accelerator tunnel like the one put into operation in the summer of 1989 in the European Center for Nuclear Research (CERN) near Geneva? In America, physicists already toy with the idea of an 80-kilometer tunnel, a "superconducting super collider," costing some fourteen billion dollars. A veritable cost-accelerating plant. Where all this is leading to is a question that even scientists cannot answer at the moment.

Physicists, of course, consider these questions much more matter-of-factly and practically. For example, the new CERN plant, called LEP (large electron-positron collider), will, for the time being, be used primarily for detecting a single type of particle, the so-called Z^0 boson that is produced from the collision of electrons and positrons at 90 GeV. If the kinetic energy of the particles is below 90 GeV, the result of such a collision would be "only" a photon. CERN physicists plan to produce one such Z^0 boson every second. And each instance has to be analyzed individually. A truly Sisyphean task!

At the moment nobody can say what the results will look like, but physicists generally tend to look for phenomena deviating from the currently valid theory. "Of particular interest," a technical journal says, "is the proof of the existence of a sixth quark named top (or truth) in which everybody fiercely believes." As one can see, even physicists believe in things. From a less passionate viewpoint, one might ask where, in today's world, the difference lies between believing in something unimaginable that is called *God* and believing in something unimaginable that is called *truth*. If God is truth, then it must be contained in everything, even in the "truth quark." In other words, by studying the nature of the quark we might get closer to the nature of God than we imagine.

Andromeda Nebula M 31
The deity the religious man tries to understand
by means of symbols and images is identical in nature
with the power represented by natural laws.
[MAX PLANCK]

{ 5 }

A QUANTUM THEORY OF RELIGION?

*Planck, Heisenberg, and Other
Nuclear Scientists on the Relationship
of Science and Religion*

On November 11, 1930, the *Berliner Tageblatt* published a short essay by Albert Einstein entitled *Religion and Science*. It was his first public statement on this topic. After a general introduction in which Einstein presents the two forms of religion he regards as dominant—the religion of fear and moral religion, incorporating also their transitional forms—he addresses the only kind of religious belief with which he himself can identify and he terms it "cosmic religious feeling" or "cosmic religiousness."

To seek shelter with a God out of fear, misery, lack of orientation, or other wordly troubles has, for Einstein, very little to do with true religiousness. God's function here is simply to relieve one's soul. God as an antidepressant. Also, man's ethical behavior does not require a religious basis; it should be derived from human existence itself and based on "sympathy, education, and social ties." Man would be in a poor way, Einstein writes, if he would only be able to show sympathy for fear of God's punishment and in the hope of divine reward. History has revealed to a frightening extent—and the present still proves it, daily—how hatefully human beings attack each other under the banner of religion, and not only those with different religions but also those who share the same faith.

Cosmic religiousness, Einstein claims, is common to people who do not need dogma or the concept of a personal God to be able to believe in something superior, universal, and meaningful. Many distinguished personalities, whether philosophers, scientists, or artists, were filled with this "highest kind of religious feeling." And Einstein goes even further by suggesting that "cosmic religious feeling is the strongest and noblest incitement to scientific research." It is not easy to accept this notion today. One rather feels that the only driving force for science is a terrible pressure for technological progress, and that in modern science religion is exemplified only in the belief that everything is possible. But perhaps the great scientists of earlier times were truly inspired by this feeling, as Einstein contended. The work of a few modern scientists, among them Carl Friedrich von Weizsäcker, is certainly distinguished by this religious dimension.

At the end of his essay, Einstein suggests that only the religious—or rather "cosmic-religious"—scientist is a true and serious scientist. He writes:

> Only those who realize the immense efforts and, above all, the devotion which pioneer work in theoretical science demands, can grasp the strength of the emotion out of which alone such work, remote as it is from the immediate realities of life, can issue. What a deep conviction of the rationality of the universe and what a yearning to understand, were it but a feeble reflection of the mind revealed in this world, Kepler and Newton must have had to enable them to spend years of solitary labour in disentangling the principles of celestial mechanics!... Only one who has devoted his life to similar ends can have a vivid realization of what has inspired these men and given them the strength to remain true to their purpose in spite of countless failures. It is cosmic religious feeling that gives a man strength of this sort. A contemporary has said, not unjustly, that in this materialistic age

of ours the serious scientific workers are the only profoundly religious people.

The passion in Einstein's words is suprising since he rarely allowed himself to get carried away. Perhaps this shows how dry and dispassionate our relationship to science and scientists has become. Somewhere, people undertake research in innumerable laboratories, and once a year, when Nobel prizes are distributed, we listen with half an ear. But what they are awarded for does not interest us, for we would not understand it anyway. Names of scientists pop up and vanish just as quickly from public consciousness. Who could even name a great living physicist or chemist! After all, what they have to say, or choose to say, is only relevant for their respective disciplines.

On the other hand, a lot of people would certainly lend their ears to a great scientist if he chose to speak about the questions afflicting every one of us, not least questions of a religious or ethical nature. For it is particularly the scientist, who has reached the frontiers of the imaginable and continues to push back these borders through new observations, whom we secretly expect to answer the metaphysical questions, as if science provided him with a special, direct "line" to the transcendental. That may be naive, but it is an understandable naivete.

Essentially, everybody can babble about the transcendental, which is why it has become the favorite topic of self-proclaimed prophets, gurus, and "masters" in our time. If a great scientist should choose to speak about God, one is inclined to think his comments should have a special authority. Such a man would not simply say what crosses his mind; he would certainly use his words and terms with the seriousness characteristic of his scientific work. In fact, nearly all the great scientists of our century have frequently commented on religious questions in public. This confirms Einstein's thesis that to search seriously for knowledge means to search equally seriously for faith. And it is also a confirmation of the fact that modern physics has penetrated deeply into spiritual areas that were traditionally the habitat of religion.

MAX PLANCK'S
SCIENTIFIC GOD

Let us start with Max Planck, the originator of modern physics. He is the author of a lecture entitled *Religion and Natural Science*. At the outset, Max Planck points out that it is not his intention to attack or even ridicule anybody's beliefs, whatever they may be. Only one kind of belief, he claims, has exiled itself into the realm of the ridiculous: the naive belief in miracles. He maintains it would be impossible for the scientifically educated, even those with only a superficial knowledge, to believe in phenomena contradicting the laws of nature.

And Planck risks the prediction that, with the progress of science and the dissemination of an increasingly broad knowledge, the last vestiges of miracle belief will disappear automatically. "Even young people growing up today...refuse to be spiritually tied by teachings which they regard as unnatural," Planck says. In this prediction he was unfortunately utterly mistaken. He would have been shocked to see what an incredible attraction the belief in the miracle and its manifold variants has again today, particularly for young people. Occultism, spiritism, pagan cults, even black masses with their chilling rituals are booming. The trade in superstition does not merely thrive; it proliferates.

Especially in Catholicism, superstition and miracle belief have again become frighteningly popular. News of weeping or bleeding statues of Mary abounds, attracting thousands of salvation-seekers. Planck's equation "more science = less superstition" does not seem to come out even. He left an important factor out of his calculation. An enlightened time, governed by knowledge and its technological by-products, can give rise to a strong need for unreason seeking to work itself off in cultic circles that strike us as almost medieval. Irresponsibility and lunacy disport themselves in religious garment.

After all, even the most dispassionate realist cannot deny that the whole "world of reason" has turned out to be terribly mad, even suicidal, in the interim. Knowledge, where it obeys only the laws of power and profits, has become a danger for mankind. And so the occult boom with which we have been living for so many years—it has proved more than a passing fad—also represents disgust and protest against a cold world, governed and ruined by unfeeling reason, in which the individual has lost his spiritual support. The old and institutionalized denominations no longer seem to be of any help.

But we should not blame Max Planck too much for not having anticipated this development. For he himself found spiritual support in two equally strong roots: exact sciences and what he called "true religious thinking." He regarded science and religion as two parallel paths leading to the same destination. That this was so simple for Planck is surprising since his concept of God was not very sophisticated. Planck's God is the one that Einstein rejects because he cannot reconcile him with modern scientific knowledge: God as a supernatural yet somehow manlike being.

Einstein would probably have regarded Planck's religious concept as a mixture of religion of fear and moral religion. Planck felt "the reverent awe of a supernatural power governing human existence and controlling our weal and woe. To be in accord with this power and to maintain its favour is the continuous aspiration and the highest goal of the religious being." Here we have once again the concept of God as Father superior, authority, and provider of spiritual relief.

Nevertheless, it would be wrong to suspect Max Planck of religious dogmatism. For him, it is a characteristic of the deeply religious person that he does not cling to his concept of God, which can only be symbolic anyway, but uses it conscious of the fact that there may be other possible concepts or symbols of God. And if all

symbols for God are valid, then all religions are valid because, ultimately, they must all be concerned with the one God even though
they try to approach him with different symbolic and cultic lan-
guages. At the end of this train of thought, Planck risks a definition
of true religiousness, proceeds by asking what the irrefutable scientific truths are, and finally inquires, in a third step, if the demands of
science can be reconciled with his definition of true religiousness.

Planck's definition of the truly religious man, in accordance with
his divine symbolism, seems slightly childish and old-fashioned. The
religious man's answer, he says, to the question of whether God
lives only in the soul of the faithful or independent from human
faith would be "that God existed before there were human beings
on Earth, that He holds the entire world, believers and nonbeliev-
ers, in His omnipotent hand for eternity, and that He will remain
enthroned on a level inaccessible to human comprehension long
after the Earth and everything that is on it has gone to ruins. Those
who profess to this faith and who, inspired by it, in veneration and
complete confidence, feel secure from the dangers of life under the
protection of the Almighty, only those may number themselves
among the truly religious." This reads a bit like a quote from the
catechism. It contains even a whiff of dreary ecclesiastical dogma.

The belief in God's protection works only as long as one applies
it, quite egoistically, to oneself. If we survive danger, we feel confirmed in our naive faith; if we perish, we can no longer doubt it.
However, if we apply it to others who believed equally in God's
protection and nevertheless suffered the most appalling fates, then
such a naive faith easily acquires a touch of cynicism.

But we should not dive deeper into the whirlpools of theological
sophistry. Max Planck starts being convincing when he deals with
the question of religious belief from a scientific point of view:

> The most differing measurements have unanimously led to
> the conclusion that all physical events can, without exception, be
> traced back to mechanical and electrical phenomena, triggered
> by the movements of certain elementary particles such as elec-

trons, positrons, protons, and neutrons. The mass and charge of a particle are indicated by a specific and very small number which can be specified more precisely the further measuring techniques are developed. These small numbers, the so-called universal constants, are the unchangeable building blocks, so to speak, making up the entire system of doctrines of theoretical physics.

Planck uses the universal natural constants to build a bridge between physics and metaphysics. He asks about the essential meaning of these constants: "Are they ultimately inventions of man's inquiring mind, or do they possess a real meaning which is independent of human intelligence?" Planck regards the existence of natural constants as the fundamental proof of the existence of "a reality in nature which is independent from human measurements." These constants governed natural phenomena long before man entered the scene to discover and describe them. Physics therefore forces us to assume a real world, independent from us, which we can never perceive in a direct and unrefracted manner but only as conveyed by the limited scope of our sensory perception that marks the limits of every measurement.

That alone, Planck concludes, should be reason enough for man to assign himself a very modest position in the infinity of the universe, in spite of his considerable intellectual capacities. But the miraculous quality that physics detects in nature is not limited to the existence of universal constants indicating "that all natural phenomena are governed by a universal law which we can conceive of to a certain degree." Another proof for the miraculous is, according to Planck, the principle of energy conservation. Energy may be converted from one form into another, but it can never be destroyed. "If you take all the existing energy, that is the world's energy supply. This supply is unchangeable, and no phenomenon in nature can increase or decrease it.... The energy principle extends its reign over every discipline of physics, according to the classical theory as well as the quantum theory."

Planck gives a third example indicating the existence of a superior reason in nature: the principle of least action. To explain it, Planck takes light as an example:

> As is generally known, a ray of light falling diagonally onto the surface of a transparent body such as a water surface is diffracted upon penetrating the body. This diffraction is caused by the fact that light propagates more slowly in water than in air. Such a diffraction or change of direction also occurs in the atmosphere because light propagates more slowly in the lower and denser atmospheric layers than in the higher ones. If a ray of light emitted by a bright star which is not in the zenith reaches the eye of an observer, its path will be curved to a certain degree as a result of various diffractions in the different atmospheric layers. This curvature is perfectly determined by the following simple law: Of all possible paths between the star and the observer's eye, light always uses that which can be covered in the shortest time span, taking into account different propagation speeds in different atmospheric layers. The photons making up the beam of light therefore behave like intelligent beings. Among all possible routes they choose the one which leads them to their destination most quickly.

Of course, by his choice of words, Planck suggests that a ray of light would be conscious of its destination, that it wants to reach the eye of this and no other observer and therefore looks for the shortest path leading to it. Light, however, is deflected from this ideal path by matter. It is diffracted at the borders of different media such as atmospheric layers of differing density. One could say: Light always takes the least time-consuming path, and in a homogeneous medium that would be a straight line. But, since light propagates in different substances at different speeds, the straight line is no longer the least time-consuming path when it comes to a transition from one substance to another. It is therefore not necessary to claim that light is in any way "reasonable" or "determined."

The principle of least action, however, is not only valid for light. In general, one can say that for every physical object or system there is a number of possible events that may transfer it, within a certain period of time, from one state into another. But of all these hypothetical events only the one with the smallest "action value"—that is, the one that requires the least energy—will actually take place. It was Leibniz who discovered this natural principle and interpreted it as a solid proof for the work of a higher, divine reason in nature.

In this context, one is also reminded of the way in which atoms combine into molecules. Atoms always seek to reach, either by releasing electrons or by absorbing them, an energetically more favorable and stable state, that is, to develop the stable electron shell of an inert gas. One could therefore refer to the principle of least action as nature's "principle of laziness." A lazy person, when censured, can always plead his disposition; he merely obeys a universal law of nature; he is the perfect incarnation of divine reason.

Even God Himself, if He really created the world, must have been an extremely lazy creator; He devised a cosmos that did not require any further divine intervention in order to work. For this reason alone, our performance-oriented society is unnatural. Perhaps one could relate the central importance of contemplation and "not-doing" in Taoism and Buddhism to this elementary physical law. "The Tao does nothing and yet nothing remains undone," Lao-tzu says. On the other hand, one must not interpret the Eastern principle of "not-doing" as laziness or indolence, or even as mere passivity since it refers to an inner stability that might best be described as "walking along the line" or "floating with the current." The physical principle of least action is represented here as a "principle of the greatest effect with the least expenditure." Just as physical systems changing their state take the way of least resistance, so does man if he follows the Tao. Taoism refers to such a principle of life as *wu-wei*.

Of course, these thoughts are not from Planck. They came to me impulsively as I contemplated the term *laziness*. Unfortunately, I have a strong inclination toward laziness, which is accompanied by the constant wish to transfer myself into the pleasant, since won-derfully stable, noble-gas state of sleep. With the progress of sci-ence, Planck claims, man will continue to approach the unattain-able goal of absolute perception of nature and will recognize ever-more clearly the essential and, for Planck, divine nature of the world order.

God's reason would therefore, in principle, not be different from human reason. In this case, however, God turns into some-thing provable, and a religiousness based on this assumption would require proofs for the existence of God to hold its ground. Thus, it would come dangerously close to superstition, and superstition is, after all, a religiousness marked by the desire for solid proof and the constant attempt to look for and—no matter what the cost—to find it.

"If faith contends with science, trying to use its criteria, it is doomed to become a pseudo-science whose efforts are bound to be constantly frustrated and whose claims must be contradicted in every single step," the Polish philosopher Leszek Kolakowski writes. Planck's undoubtedly honest attempt to derive the existence of God from physics, thereby providing a scientific basis for reli-gion, does not clarify religious questions but leads instead to con-fusion between rational knowledge and intuitive belief that has nothing in common with knowledge. This compulsion to prove God empirically implies, in fact, an un-Christian attitude: I believe in God because I know that He exists. True faith, however, demands the contrary: I believe in God because I cannot know whether He exists. This inability to know includes permanent doubt. Krishnamurti even claimed that doubt, not faith, is the most important aspect of religion.

Max Planck, on the other hand, seems to regard doubt—together with dogma—as faith's arch-enemy. For him, science becomes a brother-in-arms to faith in the struggle against doubt, which is surprising since science is generally accused of promoting doubts about the existence of God. For Planck, science's world order can be perfectly reconciled with the religious God. He states: "The deity which man tries to approach by means of symbols and images is identical in nature with the power represented by natural laws." From this it follows that "religion and science do not exclude each other, as some people believe or fear today but complement and require each other." God, Planck believes, "is at the beginning of religion and at the end of science."

PHYSICISTS DISCUSS THE DIVINE

Werner Heisenberg has commented on the relationship of science, philosophy, and religion in various essays and lectures, above all in his famous autobiographical volume *Physics and Beyond*. This book represents the attempt to reconstruct conversations held over the years with colleagues and friends on all kinds of questions from the realm of nuclear physics, in order to allow the reader to participate in them in retrospect.

One of these conversations took place in 1927 on the occasion of a scientific conference in a hotel in Brussels. One of the participants had asked the following question: "Einstein talks so much about God. What does that mean? It is hard to imagine that a scientist like Einstein feels strongly committed to a religious tradition." Nobody seemed able to answer the question—unfortunately Einstein himself was not present—and therefore the subject was quickly switched from Einstein to Max Planck whose views on religion and science were obviously familiar to everybody.

It was generally agreed that his opinions were deeply rooted in nineteenth-century thinking, that is, in the strict separation between objective and subjective reality: here the material world, there the spiritual world. Science is concerned with what is right and what is wrong; religion with what is good and what is evil. Science and religion are compatible because they keep to themselves and restrict their statements to their own spheres. Werner Heisenberg stated that, with all due respect for Planck's traditional Christian view, he did not feel comfortable with this neat separation.

Wolfgang Pauli agreed with Heisenberg. He regarded the separation of science and faith as a temporary and makeshift solution. After all, this separation could also be dangerous if religion—for whatever reasons—lost its persuasiveness and, consequently, its function as an ethical and moral force.

In this case, "things might happen which are so terrible that we cannot even imagine them now." A decade later they did happen. Pauli admitted candidly that Planck's philosophy did not appeal to him even though it was logical in itself, and that he felt more comfortable with Einstein's views. Although Einstein frequently speaks of "our Lord," it is obvious that to him the concept of a personal God was entirely alien and that he was not tied to a religious tradition. Einstein simply had a feeling for the central order of things, and this feeling represented his religiousness. "He senses this order in the simplicity of the natural laws. One can assume that he felt this simplicity strongly and directly when he discovered the theory of relativity." For Einstein, there could be no separation between science and religion because this central order was at the same time objective and subjective.

In the meantime, Heisenberg recounts, the British physicist Paul Dirac, then still very young, had joined them. He stated categorically that "religion makes a lot of incorrect claims which are in no way justified by reality. To begin with, the term 'God' is a product of human imagination.... I cannot see that to assume the existence of an omnipotent God gets us any further." Continuing his argumentation, Dirac made use of the well-known thesis of religion being opium for the people: Man finds solace in God and waits for a "real life" after death while putting up with all kinds of injustice in his earthly existence and doing his duties calmly and nicely. Of course, the young Dirac failed to see that many people fight against injustice and oppression on account of their religious convictions. It all depends on the nature of your religiousness.

Heisenberg objected to Dirac's statements as well, claiming that it would be wrong to reject religion per se just because it may be administered wrongly and abused politically. There is nothing that might not be abused, and science is no exception. Heisenberg suggested that Dirac should not think of a religion worshiping a personal God. Perhaps he would be more convinced by a religion that knows no God, such as the ancient Chinese religion. But Dirac would not hear of it. He could not come to terms with religious myths in general. And he went on by saying:

> I can only believe what is true. How I should act I can deduce purely rationally from the situation that I live in a community with others to whom I have to grant the same rights for living that I claim for myself.... All this talk about God's will, about sin and repentance, about a hereafter by which we have to orientate our actions only serves to disguise the rough and austere reality.... Even the talk of the universality of things and suchlike I find disgusting. It is the same in life as in science: We are confronted with problems and must try to solve them. And we can only solve one problem at a time, not several. To talk of universality is just an intellectual superstructure erected after the fact.

Heisenberg writes that the discussion continued in this vein for quite a while. That is not suprising. Discussions of such complex matters follow a standard pattern; each argument is solid in itself and contains a certain measure of truth, yet remains somehow unsatisfactory. For one wants to know only one thing finally and definitively: Does God exist or not? But since there can be no objective answer to this question, only subjective ones, such debates will be held again and again without yielding a generally satisfactory answer.

The discussion at the Brussels Hotel, Heisenberg tells us, had a humorous conclusion. Wolfgang Pauli, hardly older than Dirac, had remained silent for a long time, looking disgruntled and, occasionally, grinning sardonically. Finally he was asked about his opinion of Dirac's view. "Well, well," said Pauli, "our friend Dirac has a religion, and its guiding principle is: 'There is no God, and Dirac is His prophet.'"

Heisenberg reports that some time later he told his friend and great colleague Niels Bohr of this conversation. According to Heisenberg, Bohr immediately defended the young Dirac for standing uncompromisingly for logic. For Bohr, this was a prerequisite for scientific thinking. What can be spoken about at all must be expressed clearly, and if it cannot be expressed clearly one should remain silent about it. It seems that the great religious minds felt much the same.

Buddhists, for example, like to relate the story of how the Buddha, instead of delivering the expected *sutra,* quietly showed his disciples a flower. Only one of the disciples spontaneously understood this gesture, responding with a smile. The legend's irony lies in the fact that the message has been handed down by means of words. To remain silent about God may be an adequate form of dealing with the inexpressible for the enlightened.

For us "average mortals," however, feeling a need for communication with others, particularly as regards metaphysical questions, language remains the only possibility, at least if one regards esoteric forms of communication such as séances or group ecstasy as humbug. Of course, one cannot speak about God as one speaks of physical phenomena. That is why Bohr says that for him, as for Paul Dirac, the concept of a personal God is completely foreign. Yet, on the other hand, he would admit that one cannot expect religion to address its subject with a clarity comparable to that of science. Nevertheless, since every religion claims universality—that is, claims to communicate a universal and therefore objective truth—one should expect that scientific criteria be applicable to this truth.

"But," as Niels Bohr is supposed to have said, "to me the world's separation into an objective and a subjective side seems much too drastic. The fact that religions, at all times, have spoken in images and allegories and paradoxes can hardly mean anything else than that there is no other way to grasp the reality to which we refer here. But that does not mean that it is not a true reality." In this respect, modern physics is confronted with similar problems where the vantage point is concerned. Bohr, however, considers these problems liberating. The term *objectivity* no longer possesses absolute validity in modern physics.

The theory of relativity, for example, has done away with the simultaneity of two events, something that had been regarded as objective and precisely determinable. It introduced a subjective element to the term *simultaneity* so that two events that a static observer perceives as simultaneous do not necessarily have to be simultaneous for an observer moving at a very high speed.

In quantum mechanics, the subjective factor becomes even more obvious. Niels Bohr said:

> The objectifying language of earlier physics can only convey statements about the factual. For example: Here the photographic plate has darkened, or: Here cloud droplets have formed. Atoms are not mentioned. The predictions concluded from this statement, however, depend on the formulation of the question to be answered experimentally which the observer can freely decide upon. Of course it does not matter whether the observer is a human being, an animal, or a machine. But predictions concerning future events cannot be made without referencing the observer or the observational medium. In this respect, all physical facts dealt with in modern science acquire objective and subjective characteristics. The objective world of the sciences of the previous century was, as we know today, an ideally demarcated world but it did not represent reality.

For this reason alone it is unjustifiable to damn religion for its lack of an objectifying language. Or, for that matter, because individual religions employ very different symbols, images, and rites. One could regard them, just as in quantum mechanics, as complementary descriptions that "exclude each other but only in their entirety convey an impression of the variety of relationships mankind has established with the universal." As for the different religious cults, one could compare them with the different measuring techniques in physics—here masses, there measures. Their strictness and accuracy make these rites actually resemble the fastidiousness of religious ceremony.

Heisenberg countered Bohr's contention by arguing that religious statements like "There is a living God" or "There is an immortal soul" were not legitimate and suggested that one might at least ask for the meaning of the phrase "there is." He wanted to know whether one could not interpret this religious "there is" as "rising to a higher level of abstraction" similar to the introduction of an imaginary mathematical unit such as the square root of -1, which is attributed the letter i. Mathematics states: There is $\sqrt{-1}$. Complex analysis and other important branches of mathematics are based on this imaginary unit.

At the same time, the relationships that can be formulated on the basis of $\sqrt{-1}$ have not been artificially created by $\sqrt{-1}$. They exist independently of man's introduction of imaginary numbers, which is proven by the fact that this "imaginary" mathematics can be excellently applied in sciences and technology, making things describable that objectively exist in nature.

A similar case is the mathematical concept of infinity, which does not have an equivalent in nature but serves to give us an understanding of a variety of natural phenomena. If mathematics says "There is a square root of -1" or "There is a thing like infinity," this might be compared with the religious statements "There is a God" or "There is an immortal soul."

Niels Bohr agreed to this comparison, but only as long as one looked at the problem from a purely epistemological point of view. On an emotional level, the comparison becomes unsatisfactory. Bohr said:

> In mathematics we can mentally disassociate ourselves from the contents of these claims. It remains, strictly speaking, a play of thoughts which we can participate in or stay out of. Religion, however, concerns ourselves, our life, our death. Its doctrines

determine our actions and belong, at least indirectly, to our existential foundation. We cannot be indifferent spectators.

For Bohr, the comparisons given by Heisenberg are, finally, nothing but theoretical sophistry. He finished the conversation, Heisenberg recounts, with a typical Niels Bohr story. It is well known, but since it is so engaging it is worth repeating:

> Near our summerhouse in Tisvilde lives a man who has put up a horseshoe, which—according to old folk wisdom—is a good-luck charm, at the front door of his house. When an acquaintance asked him: "Are you really that superstitious? Do you really believe that it will bring luck?" he answered: "Of course not; but they say it helps even if one does not believe in it."

Horsehead Nebula
in the Orion Constellation
The meaning of life
is that it makes no sense to say
that life has no meaning.
[NIELS BOHR]

LETTING
THE MIND THINK
AS IT WILL

A curious sensation: The more one gets to know about the smallest units of matter or about the unfathomable dimensions of cosmic structure, the more hollow it all seems. Why is this so? Because everything we regard as important—the pleasing trifles that comprise human experience—are absolutely insignificant in this world-picture. If our planet Earth is nothing but an indistinguishable speck of dust, what are we, roaming on its surface? No more than a rapidly multiplying colony of bacteria.

Nevertheless we regard ourselves as incredibly, even cosmically, important. We think of the Earth as the cosmos. We inhabit the world; *we are the world*. Science, however, tells us with brutal directness: You are nothing special, earthling! From a cosmic point of view, you and your cosy little planet are supremely unimportant, the product of a mere coincidence. You are a carbon-based biological structure, a rather unstable conglomeration of protons, neutrons, and electrons. That is what you are composed of, and that is all that will remain of you after your death.

But this is not the only disillusionment one has to endure when reckoning with modern science. Even though one learns to understand the world's individual phenomena more completely and becomes able to join the conversation on this or that topic to a limited degree—because one knows the key terms and has at

least a vague idea of all those things one will never fully comprehend, even if one squeezes the maximum from one's brain cells—
when all is said and done, one is not a lot wiser than before.
There is still no inkling of the wisdom necessary to master life in
a better way.

For the wish behind all these questions remains unfulfilled: the
wish to understand the meaning of the great cosmic spectacle and,
consequently, the meaning of one's own existence in this temporally and spatially inconceivable event. One knows that even if one
were the greatest physicist and astronomer and chemist and biologist and philosopher and so forth, all in one person, one would
nevertheless—or perhaps precisely for this reason—not be able to
grasp the meaning of life. But how could it be otherwise! If there
were a definition of the meaning of life, it would have to be a general, objective one. But is there a more meaningless life than one
whose meaning is available, so to speak, in black and white, on
paper?

SENSE—
SENSELESSNESS—
SENSUALITY

No, if there is a single "meaning of life" in this world, then it
must be a meaning refracted by billions of individual minds. To
occupy oneself with modern science can be helpful for finding an
individual meaning, not least for its disillusioning value. Science
makes it harder to deceive oneself, to live a lie. I believe that this
personal meaning has, in fact, more to do with an unfolding of the
senses, generally referred to as sensuality: to become conscious of
oneself as a temporally and spatially limited, living unity, as a
unique and sensual embodiment of a superior, temporally, and spatially boundless universality.

But this, again, gives rise to a feeling of discomfort. The vocabulary is redolent of pew and incense. One can already feel it, the

unpleasant tug into the currents of empty sermonizing. This shallow babble about meaning! Let us forget about it. This mode of inquiry into *the* meaning of life is suspect for it aims at a measurable, clearly defined quantity derived from linear thought processes. It is the attempt to catch *the* meaning with a fly swat.

Niels Bohr has given the meaning-seekers a cunning answer: "The meaning of life is that it makes no sense to say that life has no meaning." To look for a meaning theoretically and not, at the same time, practically seems to me too glib. But how could a practical search for meaning be conducted? How does one look for the inconceivable? How does one notice when one has found one's meaning? How can one be sure that it is not yet another one of those ingenious self-deceptions? So much of what constitutes *the* meaning for others appears absolutely meaningless to us.

After all, there is a rich supply of practical "how to find a meaning" solutions, an immense meaning market. One person does this; the other does that. All these attempts perhaps relieve the dreariness of everyday life, but they do not help to provide *the* meaning. I assume that the one indisputable meaning of existence has to be something very simple, simple and yet unnameable. But it is very easy to write that down. If we are honest, we have to admit that this one meaning is not so important to us.

Who is prepared to be truly radical in grasping the meaning of existence, to grab at the roots of our life, and sever it from daily routine, security, insurances, and conventions? "To leave the home for homelessness," as Buddha has done, for example. Others have done it as well. Buddha held out for total asceticism, and it led him to the brink of death. That was his necessary, individual path at the end of which he realized that such radicalism would not help him reach his goal but would kill him. He finally found his meaning, the central fire of his enlightenment via a "middle passage" between abundance and asceticism.

Of course, it would be wrong, even ridiculous, to claim that the meaning of life only reveals itself to those who "leave their homes" and abandon family, occupation, possession, and habits. For that would be to objectify the search for a meaning which, as we have discovered, can only be subjective. It would be a dogmatization of meaning. Recipes for finding meanings are meaningless. A Taoist might say that one can conceive of the whole world, including its hidden meaning, without leaving the house, for the world is identical with one's own self.

That is probably why I like Taoist thinking so much. The strenuous search for a meaning is the best way not to find it. The scholar asks: "What is the Tao?" The master replies: "Your ordinary consciousness is the Tao." Question: "How can one return into accord with it?" Answer: "By intending to accord, you immediately deviate." Question: "But without intention, how can one know the Tao?" Answer: "The Tao belongs neither to knowing nor to not knowing. Knowing is false understanding; not knowing is blind ignorance. If you really understand the Tao beyond doubt, it's like the empty sky."

Like the empty sky. Like the empty, starlit night sky. There is hardly a more exalted and exalting sight in nature except, maybe, the sea or the mountains. It is the impression of majestic greatness and unchangeable duration that makes one feel small and transient, although this sense of insignificance can be calming, provided one is more or less at peace with oneself and the world.

If a human being is content and perhaps even happy, he does not care how fleeting his existence is. For if it is real happiness, it is as unlimited as the universe and of eternal duration. To feel like this is identical with happiness. For the happy man, the stars are nothing but stars, sparkling lights arrayed exclusively for him and his happiness. Of course, even the happy person knows about the ephemerality of his happiness and his life but...he does not really believe in it. This attitude makes happy people so intolerable and tedious. They are no longer interested in the world as it is; their world is not of this world.

But just as the starry sky reflects the happy man's happiness as a warm sparkle, it reflects all the dilemma of a miserable life. The unhappy person, lonely and forlorn, shudders at the sight of the infinite spaces above. How absurd it appears to him to relate himself and his minute life span to this infinity. And yet he does it all the time, seeing not only his own life but the entire history of mankind consumed by the inconceivable dimensions. For him, the stars are not warm and consoling. He sees less the twinkling lights than the void behind the glitter.

Nevertheless, both viewpoints converge in one decisive respect: Man always relates himself to the night sky. The sky is a magical mirror reflecting his own frame of mind. But it is more than that, too. Those who are neither happy nor unhappy because they are constantly lost in thought—an occupation that can make one unhappy, too, but rarely happy—prefer to follow their thoughts, which lead them so mercilessly beyond all limits, to places where there are no boundaries. As if the question about the inconceivable could only be answered by the inconceivable itself.

I have studied the night sky so often and yet each time feels like the first in spite of its familiarity. Since it is always the same sky, it must be me, or rather my view, that is changing. That is a truism, of course. Everybody changes and his worldview changes accordingly. And the stars are part of the world. As banal as all this is, it has far-reaching consequences for the exact definition of terms like *objectivity* or *truth*. For it means that there is no such thing as the night sky *per se*. The night sky exists only *per me*, that is, as my eyes and mind perceive it.

Now it is easy to dismiss such an attitude as pure sophistry, pointing out that there is, after all, an objective view of the world and, therefore, of the night sky, the view provided by exact science.

Everybody can retain his conception of the night sky, if he wants to, but only science tells us what the night sky *per se* is. Unfortunately, this argument originates from the eighteenth and nineteenth centuries, and it overlooks an important factor.

Even physics, the most exact of all sciences, is a product of the human mind and not something that has been added to the world "machine" like instructions-for-use issued by a superior authority. Physics represents an interpretation of the world by the human mind. It is objective, but this objectivity is interchangeable with human objectivity. Science does not describe nature as it is but is itself a part of the interaction between nature and ourselves. Even man is just nature, and his mind as well is just nature. The Austrian physicist Erwin Schrödinger has expressed this thought as follows:

> The reason why our sentient, percipient, and thinking ego is met nowhere within our scientific world-picture can easily be indicated in seven words: because it is itself that world picture. It is identical with the whole and therefore cannot be contained in it as a part of it. But, of course, here we knock against the arithmetical paradox; there appears to be a great multitude of these conscious egos, the world however is only one.

The word *appears* in the last sentence suggests what Schrödinger is driving at: to risk the leap from human awareness of the universe to a single and universal consciousness. But before we try to follow this daring leap into the realm of metaphysics, let us once more return to the night sky. On the one hand, I am certain that the sky has existed for an infinitely long time, at least long before there was even the slightest trace of life on Earth. From this it follows that there must be a night sky *per se*, independent of the perceptions of the human mind.

At this point, however, I must accept the verdict from, of all places, the physicists' corner, that one cannot speak of *per se* anyway. Even though science demands objectivity of itself, it does not mean objectivity toward nature but objectivity toward the world observed and observable by man. Whatever can be said about nature, summing up all scientific observations, describes the "real world" only insofar as these statements are the common denominator of all human minds.

Physics therefore represents an exact language that can be used to express the general consent of all individual human minds. That works pretty nicely, as long as science only describes that part of nature that can be sensually perceived by humans. Modern science, however, penetrates into parts of nature that remain inaccessible to human senses. Here the question arises whether the world of the physicist is still my world, whether what is created and examined in highly complex laboratory experiments and under extremely artificial conditions has anything to do with my world. The physicist would say "yes." He would argue that these extreme laboratory conditions represent the normal state of the universe at a very early time. In this case, his observations naturally—in the literal sense of the word—affect me. For my existence can be traced back to this early state of the cosmos: Every single atom that I am composed of was generated at that time.

It becomes obvious that here thinking starts to move in circles. Is there such a thing as the world *per se*? Or can we only speak of our individual perception of the world, which is, however, not separated from it but identical with it? We will have to accept that there is no answer to this question. The paradox is that there is a world, but it consists of as many worlds as there are individual minds; where those minds agree, one deals with the world described by science.

MODERN PHYSICS—
A METAPHYSICAL VENTURE

It was modern physics itself that made this perceptual dilemma apparent, and for many it came as a shock. Since Einstein's theory of relativity, physics—and therefore, potentially, every human mind—recognizes that the world has a dimension inaccessible to the human senses. More precisely, physics discovered a structure of the world that is objectively present but does not belong to man's "real" world. It would only turn into a subjective, real world if we were able to move in the universe at speeds approaching the velocity of light. As long as we cannot do that, four-dimensionality is of no relevance in our lives; for us, it does not exist, although we know that it exists.

Physics has made the phrase "real world" questionable. Our three-dimensional world, the temporal environment of human existence, suddenly acquires the character of a shadow play. We are like those figures in Plato's famous parable, shackled in a cave, regarding the silhouettes on the walls—their own as well as those of the things in the cave—as the only real world. They do not know of the fire burning behind their backs for, being bound, they can only look in one direction. With respect to this parable, one could compare relativity to a loosening of the bonds. Man still cannot look directly at the fire, but he knows at least that it exists. He continues to see only shadows, but begins to be aware of the fact that they are only shadows, mere reflections of a more complex reality.

Quantum mechanics has loosened the shackles of human consciousness even further. Now, one could say, the cave dweller can at last look directly at the fire in the cave's center. And, by looking at the fire, he suddenly recognizes the limitations of his world. He starts to observe and explore it thoroughly, scrutinizing it for its ultimate building blocks, thus enlarging it without being able to change its cavelike character. Above all, he does not know where the fire comes from or what feeds it. He does not know its origins. Finally he is forced to realize that his liberated consciousness and his explorations of the cave world affect the cave's appearance. In other words, he can never perceive the cave alone, but only the cave housing the observer, and by observing it—tapping its walls, for example—he changes its characteristics.

Such images possess, admittedly, a strong metaphysical hue. But they also convey the plight into which quantum physics has plunged the human mind. In quantum mechanics, the physical and the metaphysical meet—on the basis of exact science. Once man has realized that his cave-world is a delusion, that is, just a cave *in* the world but not *the* world, he feels forced to leave it, to find a way out. This way out, however, cannot be found solely by physics, which has already admitted its nonobjectivity in the microworld.

It is therefore not surprising that a quantum physicist of such distinction as Erwin Schrödinger does not fear the leap from exact physics to vague metaphysics. Indeed, he undertakes it, and in a truly hazardous manner. He makes an attempt to leap beyond the cave itself, using a host of very different ancient Eastern philosophies as safety ropes, mainly the old Indian teachings of the *Upanishads*. These are the holy scriptures of the old Vedic religion that preceded Hinduism and was later assimilated by it.

But to speak of "safety ropes" is unsound, for to engage in mystical philosophies means to abandon the basis of definite facts. It would be more appropriate to compare mysticism to a swaying tightrope leading out of the cave with no indication of whether it merely leads into another cave with an even more delusory shadow world. In that case, at least one would bring to it one's experience from the first cave. Who knows, perhaps the whole universe is nothing but a grotto curved in on itself.

Schrödinger insists on not playing off or even exchanging exact scientific observations against mystical ideas. He writes: "We do not wish to lose the logical precision that our scientific thought has reached, and that is unparalleled anywhere at any epoch."

The axiomatic statement of the *Upanishads* says that there is only one consciousness; the multitude of consciousnesses is a mere delusion. Perhaps the meaning of this statement becomes more obvious in a nice parable by the thirteenth-century Persian mystic Aziz Nasafi whom Schrödinger quotes in this context:

> On the death of any living creature the spirit returns to the spiritual world, the body to the bodily world. In this however only the bodies are subject to change. The spiritual world is one single spirit who stands like unto a light behind the bodily world and who, when any single creature comes into being, shines through it as through a window. According to the kind and size of the window less or more light enters the world. The light itself however remains unchanged.

Schrödinger admits that such a philosophy is rather alien to our Western thinking, and we are inclined to dismiss it as extravagant and unscientific. That the mystical concept of a spirit shining through every individual existence seems strange indicates not only that Eastern thinking is foreign to us—that is only natural—but also that, generally, we do no longer know what to make of religious symbolic language. After all, Christianity also speaks of spiritual unity. The above quote might as well have come from one of the great Christian mystics. Wherever religions get rid of their rigid theological corsets, they end up with the same mystical images.

The traditionally atheistic attitude of science results from its view of the spiritual as something that has originated from matter in the course of evolution. This means that consciousness only exists where it is moderately warm and where the long-term environmental conditions are more or less stable, that is, where no significant climatic changes occur. In short, spirit in the universe requires the existence of Earth-like planets and will disappear if its material foundations disappear.

Science should not be blamed for this scientific view, however. Its worldview is based on space-time—it has to be!—whereas spirit is not subject to the laws of space and time. What is spirit, then? The astrophysicist A. S. Eddington has provided a sly answer:

"Mind is—but you know what mind is like, so why should I say more about its nature?" By questioning the classical laws of space and time and shaking its own seemingly unshakable foundations, physics has opened up to the spiritual to a certain degree. An elementary particle, for example, must appear, at least to the layman, to be located somewhere between matter and spirit, a mysterious "something" that consists mainly of kinetic energy. The same is true for concepts like *field of force* or *wave*.

Ultimately one always deals with a form of energy. Energy, however, is something that one tends to class with the spiritual rather than the material. The boundaries have become fluid, and they are no longer of real interest to the modern scientist; he has long since overtaken them with his abstract language of formulas. In the term *energy*, the age-old dualism of matter and spirit has dissolved into a "primary force" that still remains to be found.

If modern physics has abolished the boundaries between matter and spirit, why is it still so difficult for us to integrate the mystical concept of a single consciousness into our worldview? The main reason is probably that our thinking is traditionally rooted in Greek philosophy, which has always demanded objectivity. The "one spirit" and the "one consciousness," however, cannot be objectified. They cannot be reached logically but only intuitively. In our thinking, intuition does not rank very high and in many respects has atrophied anyway.

Nevertheless, in extreme situations, in moments of danger or misery, it reappears. When there is no time left for analyses, one intuitively does the right thing—or the wrong. In the old Eastern philosophies, on the other hand, intuition is of central importance; it represents an ideal mode of seeing and perceiving. Here, wisdom has nothing to do with the network of words and numbers with which we try to snare the world. It is a specific kind of intuition that enables man to plunge into the "primary source of reality." That is, to arrive at a point where, perhaps, the "primary force" acts, which modern physics seeks on its complex logical path. What matters is a truth beyond all proof, which need not be a truth of the beyond.

Each of us probably feels uncomfortable with the thought that consciousness should exist only as a human attribute. Intuitively, we sense the incredible presumption of such a claim. Not only does it deny the animals any form of consciousness but it also draws an arbitrary demarcation line within the history of human evolution; it presumes that man—and therefore a human consciousness— emerged at a specific point in history. But there is no such point, not even in the evolutionary history of an individual being. Who can say when nascent human life starts possessing consciousness?

Equally arbitrary is the way in which spirit is assigned to a specific organ: the human brain. Spirit can only be located in a functioning brain. Every one of us will probably realize how problematic such a narrow concept of spirit and consciousness is, if only because in nature, particularly in the history of nature, there are only fluid transitions. From which point on can one speak of a brain, or of a human brain? What gives us the right to deny plants a plantlike form of consciousness, and therefore a spirit, if everybody can see, for example, that plants are distinctly conscious of day and night, or heat and cold.

But even if we agreed that consciousness exists wherever organic life exists, it would be difficult to draw the line between organic and dead matter. Nobody will doubt that a piece of iron does not have a consciousness, but nobody could say for sure that the DNA molecule, the carrier of genetic information in living cells, does not have a consciousness.

And behind this problem that we can still more or less comprehend arises another that leads us straight into the foggy swirl of metaphysics. Can we truly believe that spirit and consciousness originated in the universe with the appearance of life on Earth? And that, up to that point, the great world theater played to an empty house? Again, intuition detects a hole in this argument. Compared to the age of the world, consciousness would be a very young product, more or less randomly created by certain chemical and biological conditions and perhaps gone again tomorrow. This idea has an absurd, even ridiculous quality.

Schrödinger asks: "Does a world which nobody can perceive really merit this name?" The classical and materialistic science would have answered "yes": The world does not have to be conscious of itself in order to exist. Modern science would not be so sure about that since it is no longer a materialistic science. George Berkeley, Newton's opponent and the arch-enemy of materialism, already stated: "All the choir of heaven and furniture of earth, in a word all those bodies which compose the mighty frame of the world, have not any substance without the mind.... So long as they are not actually perceived by me, or do not exist in my mind, or that of any other created spirit, they must either have no existence at all, or else subsist in the mind of some Eternal Spirit."

In the final consequence, Einstein's theory of relativity claims the same: Space and time are "pure conceptions," as inseparable from the observer as the concepts of color, shape, or size. To speak of "space" only makes sense if we are referring to the order of things contained within it. Time is not an independent quantity outside the order of events that we experience and use for measuring, or rather imagining, time. One could dismiss this as philosophical sophistry if modern science did not take exactly that view. Science has mathematically established the limitations of the human senses that had hitherto been discussed only by philosophers. Where there is a world, there must also be a consciousness of the world. And that is exactly what the intuitive knowledge of religion claims as well: Spirit and consciousness did not gradually emerge but were born with the world.

Logical thinking gets us no further here. All these issues are, ultimately, a matter of faith. At least the physicist Erwin

Schrödinger was convinced that the teachings of the *Upanishads* and other religious scriptures may, after all, hit upon a profound truth. He tried to approach this truth by means of very simple questions similar to those that all of us will have asked ourselves at one time or another:

> What is it that all of a sudden called you from nothingness, to enjoy this spectacle which pays you no heed? ... What is your self? What conditions were necessary for this creation to become *you*, exactly *you*, and not—somebody else? Which clearly defined *scientific* meaning could this "somebody else" have? ... What makes you detect such a wilful difference—the difference between you and somebody else—when, objectively, both are the same?

We will not find answers to these questions either. Even Schrödinger did not find them, or at least he did not tell us about them. These questions are like bubbles thrown up by the gray "primary soup" itself. What remains are the old traditional answers, equivocal oracles from the dark depths of human history: "You, along with every other conscious and individual being, are everything and everything is you. The life that you are living is therefore not only a part of the world-event but, in a certain sense, the *whole* world-event. This whole, however, cannot be viewed at a single glance." It seems as if the world contains something that has to remain a secret. Perhaps this secret is even contained in man himself; for man is always the greatest mystery to himself.

Whatever one may think of these metaphysical speculations, one aspect should puzzle even the most hard-boiled materialist: the way in which Eastern philosophy slots perfectly into a modern physics based on the theory of relativity and quantum mechanics. If modern physics focuses more and more on the ultimate, absolute, and universal, then the idea of a universal and eternal consciousness, filtered through the windows of our human minds, no longer seems alien. Physics itself demands it.

Of course, there are other ways of perceiving or at least sensing a physical-metaphysical unity. For such a perception or notion must not be restricted to physicists, philosophers, or great religious spirits. Basho, the celebrated Japanese haiku master, is said to have advised his students who were still too deeply entangled in abstract concepts: It is better you think about why the two halves of a watermelon are so alike.

Sirius Accompanied by a White Dwarf
If there was a big bang the universe must have consisted of an
infinite amount of energy concentrated in a single point.
God knows where that came from.

{ 6 }

EVEN
STARS ARE BORN

The Expanding
Universe

The world is not a watermelon; it is a self-inflating soap bubble. This discovery was made in 1929 by the American astronomer Edwin O. Hubble. He noticed that the observable galaxies were rapidly moving away from us. Hubble owed his discovery to the so-called spectrograph, an astronomical device used for analyzing the spectrum of light emitted by single stars or whole galaxies. With the help of the spectrograph, Hubble found out that light spectra originating from faraway galaxies are shifted toward the red end of the spectrum, which means that the frequency of the light emitted by these galaxies is lower when it arrives at the Earth. Additionally, he noticed that the size of the red shift is directly proportional to the distance of the respective galaxy. The explanation for this phenomenon is that the source of light is moving away from the observer, and the greater the size of the red shift, the faster it moves.

This so-called Doppler effect is an everyday experience with respect to sound waves. If a car is approaching us, the sound of its engine is at a higher pitch that corresponds to a higher frequency of sound waves. If it moves away from us, the pitch is lower. Today, the speed at which the universe is expanding is estimated at approximately 15 kilometers per second per one million light-years. The remotest galaxies still within the range of radio telescopes, the so-called quasars—they are about three to eighteen billion light-years away from us—move at speeds of up to 270,000 kilometers per second, almost the speed of light.

Since all the galaxies that can be observed from Earth move away from us, one might think that we are at the center of the universe. That would suit us, wouldn't it? But it is not like that. In fact, all galaxies are moving away from all other galaxies, similar to the way dots painted on a balloon move apart when the balloon is inflated. In this analogy, as well, the speed at which the dots move away from each other is proportional to the distance between them. Years before Hubble's discovery, the Russian physicist Alexander Friedmann had already mathematically derived this expansion tendency from Einstein's general theory of relativity. Einstein himself, as we have mentioned before, clung steadfastly to the idea of a static universe.

BIG BANG AND ETERNAL PULSING

If the galaxies are moving away from each other rapidly, it should be only logical that the distance between them must have been zero at one time, which means that the universe was concentrated in a single point where the density of matter and the curvature of space-time was infinite. This point in time, or rather, the point where time began, is called the "big bang." According to the big bang theory, the universe was generated from the explosion of an infinitely dense matter packet. Instead of a "matter packet" we could also speak of an "energy packet," since in the unimaginable primary state of the universe where all natural laws break down, a conceptual separation between matter and energy has no meaning. Mathematicians call such a state, determined by infinite quantities, a *singularity*. Singularities cannot be described mathematically.

The age of the universe can be roughly estimated from the relative expansion speed of the galaxies, established by Hubble, and the assumption that the universe was created in the big bang. It must be about ten to twenty billion years old. Whether the universe really began with a big bang has not yet been proved, however. It might be that this point x only represented the transition of one cosmic phase of development to another. The big bang theory, however, is supported by the discovery of background radiation in the microwave range by the American physicists Arno Penzias and Robert Wilson in 1965. This weak radiation that we receive evenly from all directions can only be interpreted as the remaining radiation from an extremely hot initial state of the universe. It represents what we can still "hear" of the big bang.

If one assumes that there has been a big bang and accepts that the universe is expanding, the question arises whether the cosmos will continue to expand forever or whether the expansion will eventually stop and be followed by a phase of contraction. In this case, the universe would recollapse into its initial state. To answer this question, astronomers would have to know the average density of the matter contained in the universe since only matter can counterbalance the expansion through the gravitational forces acting between material objects.

The current state of knowledge suggests that the density of cosmic matter is too small to prevent expansion. It might be possible, however, that the future exploration of the cosmos will uncover as yet undiscovered forms of matter, and the critical density necessary for expansion to stop in the far future would be reached after all. For us humans this is quite irrelevant. Long before the universe would recollapse—in ten billion years, at the earliest—our Sun and with it all life forms on Earth would have died.

For astronomical minds, however, the theory of a pulsing universe is tantalizing. For example, one could imagine the development of the cosmos as a film which, at the point where expansion stops and the universe begins to contract, starts runnning backward at an increasing speed until it arrives at the big bang singularity and everything starts anew. Apart from the fact that the reversal of natural phenomena would mean that nature stops being nature, this idea would imply the periodic recurrence of the same cosmic events. In other words, everything, including humanity, would return after the next big bang, at an interval of about eighty to one hundred billion years.

Should we be glad about such a rebirth? Well, to enthuse about an absurdity is absurd in itself. Many of us will recall Nietzsche's famous theory of "Eternal Recurrence" that, in fact, is not Nietzsche's invention but can be found in a lot of old myths, even in pre-Socratic philosophies and Christianity's mystical slipstream. What distinguishes the old philosophies of cyclic recurrence from Nietzsche's philosophy is their resigned character, a world-weariness that Nietzsche does not share. He gives a new interpretation to the meaninglessness of eternally recurring time. Precisely because every moment recurs, the here and now acquires the dignity of eternity. Eternal recurrence does not render life empty but concentrates it. It forces us, Nietzsche claims, to live each moment so that the thought of its return will not evoke horror. Nietzsche's tragedy was that he could not live up to his own demand for an ecstatic, playful, creative, and wholly centered existence. He must have been horror-stricken by the idea of a rerun of his life.

Eternal recurrence or not, these mind games have a slightly ridiculous character. Somehow they even lag behind naive religious fantasies of rebirth that have never implied precise repetition but a return to a different level of existence. In any case, it is pointless to imagine a rebirth we can never experience as such. The reborn ego would certainly not remember the previous one. Therefore, it would not be a rebirth.

The philosophy of eternal recurrence is also contradicted by quantum physics. In a lecture on Nietzsche, Carl F. von Weizsäcker stated:

There are of course cosmological models claiming that the universe will contract after a finite period of time, which admit the concept of periodic recurrence. However, they are not convincing with regard to the identical recurrence of individual events, in two respects. First of all, these models neglect the irreversible thermodynamic processes; if these processes were included, contraction would probably not be a mirror-image of expansion, and recurrence would not be periodical in a strict cosmological sense. Furthermore, the quantum theory suggests that individual processes—such as the conception of a Zarathustra or even the development of an Earth with all its current characteristics—are subject to statistical laws and would not recur in exactly the same manner, not even in a large, strictly periodical universe.

From the indeterminacy principle of quantum mechanics alone it follows that the elementary particles generated by the next big bang would not behave exactly like the ones that make up our world.

As Weizsäcker points out, the laws of thermodynamics or, more precisely, the second law of thermodynamics speaks against a reversal of natural processes in a contracting universe. The first law states that the energy content of an isolated system—and current knowledge regards the cosmos as such—does not change. The overall energy content of the universe remains constant. It is neither possible to create energy nor to destroy it. All that can be changed is the energy form. The first law of thermodynamics is therefore a conservation law.

The second law postulates that the processes within an isolated thermodynamic system (in this case, the universe) are, to a certain degree, irreversible. The conversion of kinetic energy into heat energy, for example, can be reversed only to a certain extent. It is possible to convert the entire kinetic energy of an object into heat—this is what happens if a body decelerates to zero, and all of its kinetic energy is converted into frictional heat—but a body can never convert its entire heat content into kinetic energy. A steam engine running out of steam, for example, still contains a certain amount of heat that is too small to be converted into kinetic energy.

The generation of heat is a process that cannot be completely reversed. Heat is a form of energy that cannot be converted one hundred percent into other forms of energy. Wherever heat is generated, this process entails the loss of available convertible energy; this energy can no longer be used for any kind of work. Physics refers to this phenomenon as *entropy*. Entropy is, in fact, a unit of measure: the amount of energy that can no longer be converted into work.

COSMIC LAW:
NOTHING CAN BE REVERSED;
NOTHING REPEATS ITSELF

For the universe, strictly speaking, every natural process is irreversible inasmuch as every process generates heat, however small the amount. Even the movement of the planets is slightly decelerated by the gas and dust particles in the universe, and thus a tiny amount of kinetic energy, converted into heat energy, is doomed to remain heat energy for eternity, which implies that no natural process is exactly repeatable. Even the planetary orbits are never precisely the same.

Nature as a whole, the entire cosmic scenario, represents an irreversible process. This process has the natural tendency to move toward a state of maximum disorder until, finally, only heat energy—distributed evenly in the cosmos—will remain. This will be the state of maximum entropy. In this context, however, *heat* is a slightly misleading term. According to quantum mechanics, the heat of a body is merely the disordered movement of its atoms. Heat energy is, strictly speaking, just a less-ordered form of kinetic energy.

In a very distant future, the universe will be a universe without natural processes and with a uniform temperature. At that point, the energy content of the cosmos can no longer be used for chemical-physical processes since they demand different energy concentrations or, put simply, different temperatures. It will be an absolutely stagnant universe in an eternal state of balance, a cosmos killed by heat. In the state of maximum entropy there will be no time either. Time is, so to speak, just a function of the increasing entropy in the universe, reflecting the gradual transition of energy from order to disorder.

"Entropy," as Lincoln Barnett writes, "points the direction of time. Entropy is the measure of randomness. When all system and order in the universe have vanished, when randomness is at its maximum, and entropy cannot be increased, when there no longer is any sequence of cause and effect, in short when the universe has run down, there will be no direction to time—there will be no time." In fact, time remains, since the atoms continue to pulse like minuscule clocks, providing a measure for speed and duration, but it has lost its directional arrow. Time no longer passes, although it has expanded with the universe. The cosmos cannot escape this fate, which is absolute disorder. At its core, the universe is incessantly driven by the decay of its original order.

Our everyday concept of order and disorder tempts us to take the opposite view: that the universe is changing toward order and that its primary state, probably consisting merely of high-energy radiation and, later, gaseous clouds, represents the quintessence of disorder and chaos. This concept can also be found in all creation myths. In the beginning, there was always disorder, primary chaos, which gave rise to order, that is, the cosmos. *Cosmos* is the Greek word for order, decency, and decoration. However, we first have to rid ourselves of our habitual understanding of order and disorder to understand how these terms are used in thermodynamics.

Primary chaos, consisting exclusively of radiation, represented a state of order. If physics speaks of *order* it refers to energy processes. Indeed, our planetary system is a highly ordered system; but it is only an island of relative order within a universe which, as a whole, drifts toward disorder. Whenever we burn a piece of wood, say, or eat a carrot, which our body partly converts into heat, we contribute to an increasing cosmic disorder by converting ordered matter into disordered heat.

Nevertheless, it remains very difficult to regard the initial state of the universe, as far as it has been hypothetically described, as a state of order. The more convincing cosmogenetic hypotheses assume that fluctuations of density in the rapidly expanding universe did not occur right at the beginning but began later, prompting the development of areas of varied matter densities. Since gravity was strongest in those areas with the highest density, these areas expanded and finally collapsed, giving rise to galaxies. Even this crude model shows that our everyday idea of order is contrary to the physicist's definition.

We would instinctively claim that the gathering of dispersed matter represents the establishment of order. A galaxy must surely be more ordered than a gaseous cloud in which particles buzz around randomly. But this contradiction is only apparent. One should not be misled by the development of a shape such as a star. From a physical point of view, the visible shape is not the only form of order; with respect to the second law of thermodynamics it is even of rather small importance.

The terms *order* and *disorder* refer to energetic conditions, not outward form. Every star, even if its form implies a certain degree of order, will contribute much more to the disorder in the universe, due to the production of heat inside it, than it has added to cosmic order by the development of its shape. Stars are islands of limited order that ultimately only increase energetic disorder or entropy by producing heat, most of which is not reusable. The universe began in a uniform and ordered state but then became lumpy and disordered, even though individual "lumps" such as stars tend toward order.

Our planetary system and the Earth, too, are temporally limited islands of relative order in the cosmic sea of continuously encroaching disorder. Even human beings represent small islands of order. Such an island, however, can be maintained only at the expense of increasing overall disorder by converting utilizable energy into energy that can no longer be used. If this process is interrupted, the island sinks, and the human being dies. The ordered "unity" called man dissolves into molecular chaos.

NO BEGINNING?
NO END?

The hypothesis of a collapsing universe would suggest that during the phase of contraction previous physical processes are reversed and cosmic order increases. In this case, one of the basic natural laws, the second law of thermodynamics, would be repealed. During this phase, nature, as we know it, would no longer exist. Heat energy could be completely converted into kinetic energy, but kinetic energy would be converted only partly into heat. The time arrow would no longer point into the future but into the past. Organic life would be unthinkable in the phase of contraction unless one imagines a life that begins with death and progresses toward conception. A nugatory notion.

The British astrophysicist Stephen Hawking therefore suggests that, if there should be a contracting universe, the phase of recollapse would have to be essentially different from the phase of expansion. Even during contraction, disorder would increase. Unfortunately, he does not tell us how he arrived at this conclusion. Hawking merely points out that his model is a rather complex one. In other words, he does not want to bother us nonspecialists with it. Hawking belongs to an astrophysical lobby increasingly inclined to the thesis that the universe has neither a beginning nor end in time. Such a statement, however, does not get us much further either.

Hawking surmises that physics is only confronted with the problem "big bang—yes or no?" because it has not yet managed to combine Einstein's theory of gravity and quantum mechanics in a quantum mechanics of gravitation. If physics succeeds in this—and Hawking is confident it will—then it will be mathematically possible to describe a universe without singularities. For us laymen, however, this would not make things any easier. If we cannot imagine the universe "exploding" from a single point of mass with infinite density, we will certainly not be able to imagine a universe without a beginning.

The big bang, as inconceivable as it is, has something familiar about it: It is the perfect starting point for a linear development of the universe. And our thinking has always felt most at home with linearity. This start-finish thinking also dominates our religious concepts. For example, the big bang can be perfectly reconciled with a God as creator. In the beginning there was the big bang. In the beginning was the Word. Here, physics and the Bible say the same thing—just in other words.

The credence afforded the big bang theory by the Catholic church is apparent, for example, in Pope Pius XII's public declaration in 1951 that the big bang model was in agreement with the Bible. A decade before, he had remained silent about the persecution of the Jews by the Nazis, which was certainly not in agreement with the Bible. Stephen Hawking tells of a lecture tour to Rome in 1981. Jesuits in the Vatican had invited him to a conference on modern cosmology:

> At the end of the conference the participants were granted an audience with the Pope. He told us that it was all right to study the evolution of the universe after the big bang, but we should not enquire into the big bang itself because that was the moment of Creation and therefore the work of God. I was glad then that he did not know the subject of the talk I had just given at the conference—the possibility that space-time was finite but had no boundary, which means that it had no beginning, no moment of Creation. I had no desire to share the fate of Galileo, with whom

I felt a strong sense of identity, partly because of the coincidence of having been born exactly 300 years after his death!

THE BIRTH OF THE UNIVERSE

Until Hawking and his colleagues provide proof for their theory that there was no big bang, or prove that everything proceeds in an altogether different manner, we have to put up with a model that the majority of astrophysicists currently regard as the most convincing. It is known as the standard model and enables physics to describe the development of the universe from a very early phase until today more or less logically and without gaps (although, of course, innumerable detailed questions remain unanswered or are answered very differently). For the time being, however, nothing can be said about the cosmos at point zero.

From the three universal constants used in quantum mechanics (speed of light, gravitational constant, and Planck's quantum of action) a smallest theoretical length is derived: the limit for mathematical calculations. This "characteristic length" is 2.6×10^{-33} cm. As a comparison, the average diameter of an atom is approximately 10^{-8} cm (1 divided by a 1 with eight zeros). If the theory of an expanding universe is correct, physics can conclude from quantum mechanical calculations that 10^{-43} seconds after the big bang the universe had a diameter of 2.6×10^{-33} cm, a density of 5×10^{93} g per cubic centimeter—which is of course absurd since there were no cubic centimeters—and a temperature of 10^{33} degrees Kelvin. Quite mysterious quantities. These numbers mark the limits to which the presumed first moments of the universe can be traced back physically.

However, to speak of a "first moment" makes as little sense as speaking of seconds or centimeters. These data tempt us to believe that in such an extreme state of the universe there could have been absolutely measurable time and absolutely measurable space. They suggest the existence of a "timer" outside of this initial state. Above all, they suggest a clock that can measure an interval of 10^{-43} seconds. Even using the atom as a clock would not make sense since this hypothetical early cosmos did not yet contain atoms—it would have been unimaginably smaller than the already incredibly small atom.

In an abstract, quantum-mechanical sense, these numbers may work, but for the human mind they belong to physical areas ruled by laws that exclude measures and clocks. Space and time become abstract constructions. One might ask whether it is scientifically correct to use the universe as we see it now as a basis for projecting its point zero. Of course, physicists know very well that this is only a makeshift solution. It is better to describe something with huge question marks than not at all—such is their motto.

The explosionlike expansion of the universe caused its density and therefore its temperature to decrease. Terms like *expansion* and *density*, however, are in fact misrepresentations. Whatever took place immediately after the big bang—if it took place at all—should not be imagined as an explosion in three-dimensional space since such an explosion has a center from which it expands more or less evenly in all directions.

During the "big bang explosion," each elementary particle must have been moving away from all other particles and was therefore simultaneously the center and the periphery of the "explosion." If there was a big bang, the universe must have consisted of an infinite amount of energy concentrated in a single point. God knows where that came from. In a certain sense, the big bang is a reversal of the process that is artificially created, on a miniature scale, in modern high-energy plants. There, for example, protons and antiprotons collide at very high speeds and annihilate each other in a flash of light. In other words, they are converted into photons.

In the extreme big bang state the reverse must have happened: Elementary particles and their antiparticles were generated from pure energy, mainly electrons and positrons as well as an equal number of the mysterious neutrinos and antineutrinos—and, of course, plenty of photons. If the quantum theory is correct, this "primary soup" of electrons, positrons, neutrinos, antineutrinos, and photons, which developed approximately one hundreth of a second after the big bang, must have been preceded by an extremely short "quark soup" phase.

Since atoms disintegrate into nuclei and electrons at temperatures of several thousand degrees Kelvin, and nuclei into protons and neutrons at several billion degrees Kelvin, these particles might, at even higher temperatures of several trillion degrees Kelvin, decay into quarks, provided that free quarks can exist at all. But this phase of the universe would certainly not have lasted longer than a hundredth of a second. This does not make cosmic beginnings any more comprehensible for the layman, but it may show what scientists in high-energy plants are working at: nothing less than a big bang simulation, the search for the absolute. That is the scientists' way, obliged always to verify, down to the final details. It seems that man cannot be at peace with open questions; he cannot enjoy mysteries, in particular the deepest ones; they provoke him; he has to unravel them. It is not God he wants to find but an ultimate, all-encompassing world formula, a physically describable absolute.

Whether it is "quark soup" or any other "primary soup" makes no real difference to us. We have enough problems with the concept that, although these elementary particles were rapidly moving away from each other after the big bang, they were at the same time constantly colliding so that, in continuously alternating processes of creation and destruction, they managed to establish a kind of "primary soup" balance between them. That particles collided with each other at incredibly high speeds, constantly generated from energy and decaying into energy—in fact they *are* energy— while moving apart, may become more plausible if we keep in mind that a hundredth of a second after the big bang, this "primary soup" had a temperature of 100 billion degrees Kelvin and a density four billion times greater than that of water.

Well, it does not make things more plausible, I'm afraid. How can particles move in such density? On the other hand, they cannot help but move at such extreme temperatures since their motion constitutes the temperature. A bottomless pit, or rather, a void composed of innumerable somethings. In any case, a pretty thick soup.

For physics' cosmic "recipe" to work, however, one has to assume that this "soup" contained a pinch of protons and neutrons, that is, heavy particles—the beef stock in the soup, so to speak. The ratio must have been about one proton or neutron per one billion light particles. In the earliest phase of the universe there was therefore a clear predominance of radiation over matter particles. But how could protons and neutrons survive the collision with lighter particles?

Well, they did not survive them but were demolished and newly created in the same instant, according to the following four (simplified) reactions: The collision of protons and antineutrinos produces positrons and neutrons (and vice versa). The collision of neutrons and neutrinos produces electrons and protons (and vice versa). It is hard to conceive of this confusion as the ordered state that it is according to the second law of thermodynamics. Perhaps terms like *order* and *disorder* are misleading in the early cosmic phase since this phase lasted only a few hundredths of a second anyway. Let us refer to the whole picture as "ordered disorder." Antonyms are probably the most appropriate way to describe the incomprehensible.

According to the standard model, the expanding universe has cooled down from 100 billion to about 30 billion degrees Kelvin after approximately one tenth of a second. That is still a rather abstract temperature. The structure of the universe has not changed much, but with the sinking temperatures it becomes easier for the neutrons to turn into the slightly lighter protons than vice versa. The ratio between these nuclear particles, until then more or less equal, has therefore shifted in favor of the protons. Heavy particles consist now of 62 percent protons and 38 percent neutrons.

After slightly more than a second, the universe still has a temperature of 10 billion degrees Kelvin. It is still much too hot for protons and neutrons to combine into nuclei. The percentage of protons has climbed to 76 percent. The temperature is low enough, however, for neutrinos and antineutrinos to step out of the thermic particle interaction; they start to behave like free particles and can spread unhindered. Electrons and their antiparticles (positrons) now annihilate each other faster than they are generated from radiation.

After approximately fourteen seconds, the universe has a temperature of 3 billion degrees Kelvin. This is already below the threshold temperature for electrons and positrons, which means that they merely annihilate each other. There is not sufficient radiation energy left for generating new electrons and positrons even though it is still incredibly high.

After the first three minutes, the universe has a temperature of 1 billion degrees Kelvin. This is "only" seventy times as hot as the center of the Sun. Electrons and positrons have annihilated each other almost completely, and the universe consists almost exclusively of photons (electromagnetic radiation), neutrinos, and antineutrinos. But now the temperature is low enough for protons and neutrons to combine into atomic nuclei, which had not been possible before in the high-energy particle confusion.

The first nucleus to be formed is that of heavy hydrogen (deuterium); it consists of one proton and one neutron. These nuclei integrate into the more stable helium nuclei that are made up of two protons and two neutrons. Simultaneously, the decay of free neutrons into protons continues until all neutrons have either been boiled down to helium nuclei or disintegrated into protons. At this point, the nuclear material of the universe is composed of about 26 percent helium nuclei and 74 percent protons or hydrogen nuclei.

However, the percentage of nuclear material relative to the overall energy volume of the universe is still very low. The main contributors to cosmic energy are photons, neutrinos, and antineutrinos. In addition, there is a small amount of electrons that has escaped the previous electron-positron annihilation. The number of surviving electrons corresponds to the number of protons either contained in helium nuclei or existing as free protons (hydrogen nuclei). Thus, the overall charge of the universe is zero. At this point, about 35 minutes have passed since the big bang. The temperature of the universe is approximately 300 million degrees Kelvin, and its energy density is only a tenth that of water.

Where "small amounts" of protons and neutrons or electrons have been mentioned, this is meant relative to the amount of photons, neutrinos, and antineutrinos. After all, this "small amount" of atomic material gave rise to all the matter contained in the cosmos. Only when radiation energy decreased in the further course of cosmic expansion was the energy balance increasingly dominated by matter. Of course, the number of photons in the cosmos has always remained constant; only its overall energy content has decreased. One assumes that for each nuclear particle there are about one billion photons. But these are reckless hypotheses that are constantly modified by scientists.

The predominance of matter over radiation started in a phase of cosmic development in which the temperature had become so low that photon energy was insufficient to prevent helium and hydrogen nuclei from capturing free electrons and forming stable atoms. This became possible about seven hundred thousand years after the first thirty-five minutes of the universe. An absurd time relation! For seven hundred thousand years the universe, although constantly cooling down, was still too hot to allow for the development of atoms. This process began only when the temperature of the universe was about 3,000 degrees Kelvin. Hydrogen and helium—in a ratio of about three to one—are therefore the two building blocks of all other elements.

One cannot stress strongly enough that this "hot big bang model" is merely a model. The American physicist Steven Weinberg, who was the first to write a popular book about the hypothetical first three minutes of the universe, does not deny that this model contains numerous elements of uncertainty. Above all, it proceeds from the assumption that the so-called cosmological principle is also valid for the hot early phase of the universe.

The cosmological principle states that all galaxies and other cosmic objects move away from each other homogeneously. In mathematical terms: The relative speed between any two galaxies is proportional to the distance between them. There is little doubt that this principle is valid from the point when matter and radiation started to separate. However, nothing indicates that this principle is also valid for the first seven hundred thousand years of the universe as the big bang model tacitly assumes.

"The appropriate response to such uncertainties," Steven Weinberg states, "is not (as some cosmologists might like) to scrap the standard model, but rather to take it very seriously and to work out its consequences thoroughly, if only in the hope of turning up a contradiction with observation." Weinberg himself admits that he had "a feeling of unreality" writing about the first three minutes of the world "as if we really know what we are talking about." But the standard model, Weinberg says, has at least one achievement to its credit. If some day "the standard model is replaced by a better theory, it will probably be because of observations that drew their motivation from the standard model."

Indeed, the validity of the big bang model has become questionable since November 17, 1989. On that day the American astronomers Margaret Geller and John Huchra discovered a galaxy cluster of hitherto unknown size. Like a wall made up of billions of suns, it stretches 500 million light-years across the universe. According to the big bang model, such a huge conglomeration of matter should not exist; gravity alone would not be sufficient to create it since the big bang model claims that galaxies are constantly moving away from each other.

Or, there are cosmic "vacuum cleaners" gathering matter into galaxy clusters in specific areas of the universe. What other reason could there be for this extremely uneven distribution of galaxies in the cosmos? Unfortunately there is no room for cosmic vacuum cleaners, whatever they might look like, in the standard model. So astronomers are looking for an extented big bang model with which to explain the formation of galactic superclusters.

In fact, this latest discovery seems to have rendered the universe more mysterious than ever. And the "great wall" detected by Geller and Huchra did not long remain the only one. In the interim, an Anglo-American group of astrophysicists has scanned the entire sky with an infrared astronomical satellite (IRAS), finding numerous examples of galaxy clusters and superclusters. After complex data analysis, the scientists compiled a galactic map of the universe indicating that the distribution of "matter islands" in the universe is very uneven. The cosmos contains immense voids, like huge bubbles, on which galaxies rest.

Once again it looks as if the rigorously constructed theoretical sky is about to crash around the astronomers' heads. Confusion reigns in the astronomical world. "There is not a single theory," British astrophysicist Will Saunders of the University of Oxford admits, "which might serve to explain the galactical structures." For more than a decade astrophysicists believed that the theory of dark matter—that is, nonradiating and therefore unmeasurable matter—had finally solved the mystery of galactic creation. Of course, dark matter is itself rather mysterious.

It has now become evident that the concept of dark matter in the universe can explain only the stability of individual galaxies but not the existence of galaxy clusters. According to the cold dark matter or CDM theory, 90 percent of cosmic matter would have to consist of mysterious dark substances. This invisible matter should generate the gravity necessary to prevent the rapidly rotating galaxies from disintegrating. Visible matter alone is not sufficient to hold galaxies together. But what kind of invisible matter could this be? Gases within the galaxies are out of the question; they would emit radiation of a characteristic wavelength. Theoretically, it could be matter in the form of comets, asteroids, and planets that do not emit radiation.

On further reflection, the astrophysicists surmised that such objects probably do not exist in large enough quantities as they consist of heavy elements that are rather scarce in the cosmos. The remaining candidates for dark matter are the so-called brown and white dwarfs, neutron stars, and black holes. That is, various final stages of burnt-out stars. It might be possible that huge black holes are concealed in the spherical and dense galactic centers. Unfortunately, the gravity of these black holes would affect neighboring objects to such a degree that their behavior would betray the existence of such holes. Massive neutrinos are another possibility, those mysterious elementary particles whose existence is certain but scientists have nevertheless not yet been able to detect. However, experiments have shown that if neutrinos have mass at all, it could, at the most, amount to a thousandth of the electron mass. Since neutrinos move at speeds close to the speed of light they are called "hot." They are therefore a "hot" variety of dark matter.

Astrophysics is caught in a cleft stick: The CDM theory is appropriate for explaining the development and stability of individual galaxies, but it fails to explain their accumulation into "great walls." Such galactic clusters, on the other hand, could quite nicely be explained by the concept of "hot dark matter" which, however, does not account for the emergence of individual galaxies. One model unhinges the other.

At the moment, astrophysicists are confronted with the problem of having to find a model that can explain two things satisfactorily: first, the development of "small-scale" cosmic structures such as galaxies and, second, the emergence of "large-scale" structures such as superclusters and gigantic black holes. When cosmology is perplexed, as it is now, scientists usually search for a possibility of forcing contradicting models into the framework of a new theory, or revive theoretical concepts discussed and abandoned at an earlier point. "We struggle with a great many ideas," says Dr. Alan Dressler, an astrophysicist at the Carnegie Institution of Washington. This, however, is the scientist's purpose, and should be no cause for complaint.

In their search for new solutions, some scientists have lighted upon an old favorite: the cosmological constant that Einstein, in 1917, introduced into the equations of his theory of relativity to save the static universe he favored for religious reasons. Einstein postulated an antigravitation quantity to which he assigned the Greek letter lambda. With the lambda constant, the cosmic expansion resulting from Einstein's original equations could be mathematically neutralized. When it became absolutely certain that the universe is expanding, lambda was dismissed from Einstein's equations, that is, set to zero. The predictions contained in the standard model of the big bang theory assume a zero value for lambda as well. Even a very small positive value would significantly change the dynamics of cosmic development.

A member of the IRAS group, G. Efstathiou of the University of Oxford, proved that the CDM model can be reconciled with IRAS observations if two conditions are fulfilled: Mass density in the cosmos must be only a fifth of the critical mass (so far it had been assumed that cosmic density is above the critical point, which would mean that the universe eventually stops expanding and enters a phase of contraction), and the cosmological constant must differ only marginally from zero. Wolfgang Priester of the Astrophysical Institute at the University of Bonn has long maintained that it is not legitimate to set lambda to zero. He has developed a computer model which, by using lambda as a natural constant, describes the development of the universe, including both large-scale and small-scale structures, without resorting to hypothetical dark matter.

In Priester's model, cosmic development takes place as follows: After a short phase of rapid inflation, cosmic expansion is gradually slowed under the influence of gravity and lambda until, about 5 billion years after the big bang, it comes to a quasi-standstill. This "period of rest," which lasts approximately 10 billion years, allows for the formation of galaxies. Subsequently, the cosmos continues to expand and, after about 30 billion years, smaller structures such as planets start to emerge. According to this model, the universe would be between 35 and 40 billion years old. Hitherto, scientists believed that it could not be older than 15 billion years. However, many recent astrophysical observations indicate that the cosmos might in fact be older. New types of telescopes have already detected quasars, early stages of galactic development, at distances of 18 billion light-years.

Of course, Priester's model is just one among many. Proof for its correctness—or the correctness of a different model—has yet to be provided. Even the classical cold dark matter and hot dark matter theories are far from being abandoned since they undergo constant modification and adaptation to new observational data. It looks as if the various theories will have to contend with each other a little longer. An ultimate explanation of the universe will never be delivered anyway. Perhaps science should finally rid itself of this fixation. Could it not be possible that the cosmos has several origins?

The theoretical turmoil currently characterizing modern cosmology should not be interpreted as an astrophysical crisis. The standard model, which lasted a decade, was probably too good to be true or, to put it another way, was marked by an overly simple linearity. Its basic precept, namely that the universe developed explosively from a single point of infinite density, has not yet been questioned. The big bang hypothesis holds its ground. This "divine" origin is still supported by the precise measurements of background radiation in the microwave range, the "echo" of the big bang.

Most astrophysicists refuse to surrender the idea of a cosmic beginning, although their theoretical edifice currently looks somewhat bizarre—a "baroque confusion." "Most scientists prefer to assume that God had a simpler creative masterplan," claims astrophysicist Edmund Bertschinger of the Massachusetts Institute of Technology. Scientists usually question everything until it has been experimentally proven beyond a shadow of doubt. God, apparently, they do not question.

But how, according to the standard model, did the development of the universe continue after the elementary materials helium and hydrogen had been generated? Casually, one could speak of "dumpling development." The weakest of the four elementary forces, gravity, finally started to act in the diffuse gaseous masses filling the universe. Until then, it had been of no importance whatsoever among the substantially stronger forces acting between the elementary particles. When these forces had done their creative job, so to speak, giving rise to stable atoms, it was gravity that made these atoms collect in gaseous clouds. In the course of millions of years, these loose clouds integrate into more and more dense formations.

This process, however, only functions if it incorporates unimaginably great masses of gas. Now the entire gaseous mass in the universe did not gather in a single dense material cluster but developed instead into innumerable individual systems that may or may not be part of bigger systems. Astronomy has not yet explained this phenomenon in detail. It certainly is connected with the fact that turbulences within gas clouds lead to the development of areas of varying density that pursued their own paths toward further compression.

It is also unclear whether individual galaxies developed that gathered, due to mutual attraction, in clusters and superclusters, or whether the development started with these clusters, and the individual galaxies were secondary products created by variations in density or collisions between galaxy clusters. In any case, the increasing pressure within the self-compressing cloud forces its temperature to rise. At first the compression proceeds slowly, but it becomes more and more rapid. A kind of gas core forms at the cloud's center.

This process probably took relatively little time. It is assumed that a dense gas cloud the size of our planetary system takes only a few hundred years to compress to the size of the Sun. Around this core a disk of matter assembles that can—but does not necessarily have to—develop into planets. In the interior of the central gas ball the temperature becomes so high that cyclical processes of nuclear fusion are triggered; the threshold temperature for these processes is several million degrees Kelvin.

The pressure of the heated gas inside the new star would theoretically reinflate it immediately, thus destroying what has been created only a moment before. The gravity between the matter particles, however, neutralizes this force and keeps the star in a stable balance—at least as long as nuclear fusion can be maintained. During the fusion of hydrogen nuclei into helium nuclei, part of the nuclear mass is converted into energy, according to Einstein's formula $E = mc^2$. The fusion of four hydrogen nuclei into one helium nucleus is described by the following calculation: A hydrogen nucleus has an atomic weight of 1.008; the atomic weight of a helium nucleus is 4.004. The weight of four hydrogen nuclei therefore exceeds the weight of one helium nucleus by 0.028 atomic weight units. The residual mass has been completely converted into radiation. In a single nuclear fusion of this kind, 25 million electron volts or 4×10^{-12} joules of energy are released.

In the case of our Sun, this process started about 4.5 billion years ago. A further 3.5 billion years had to pass before life began to emerge on one of the planets orbiting the Sun. The nuclear energy released by the Sun was a prerequisite for this development. It took another 999 million years before a creature that called itself "man" began looking further and further into the cosmos, contemplated its contents, and finally reconstructed the evolution of the universe back to its very beginnings—almost to the very beginnings! These are still shrouded by a veil, the veil of the first hundredth of a second.

To raise this veil, however, will be a theoretical affair, and so complex that whoever has made a God responsible for the creation of the world will be perfectly safe in clinging to that idea. That the beginning of the universe—if there was one—can be described in terms of quantum mechanics does not change the fact that it remains an event inconceivable for mankind. To exaggerate, the quantum-mechanical God that physics will call "primary force" does not lose any of its divinity.

The mathematical formula representing God would only be another abstract symbol replacing the innumerable symbols man has already created to have at least a name or an image for the incomprehensible. The British astrophysicist A. S. Eddington, however, argued that physics will never render the term *God* unnecessary, not even when it finds an all-encompassing "world formula." Eddington regarded the fear that physics might represent God by a system of differential equations, as it has done with all natural forces, as unwarranted:

> For the sphere of the differential equations of physics is the metrical cyclic scheme extracted out of the broader reality. However much the ramifications of the cycles may be extended by further scientific discovery, they cannot from their very nature trench on the background in which they have their being—their actuality. It is in this background, that our own mental consciousness lies; and here, if anywhere, we may find a Power greater than but akin to our consciousness. It is not possible for

the controlling laws of the spiritual substratum, which in so far as it is known to us in consciousness is essentially nonmetrical, to be analogous to the differential and other mathematical equations of physics which are meaningless unless they are fed with metrical quantities. So that the crudest anthropomorphic image of a spiritual deity can scarcely be so wide of the truth as one conceived in terms of metrical equations.

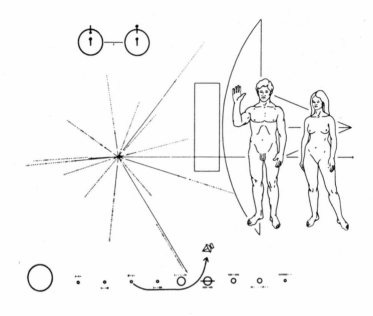

A Message to Extraterrestrials
Naked as Adam and Eve before the Fall—
a truly interstellar message in a bottle!
What would happen if alien guests from outer space
accepted this invitation?

{ 7 }

EVEN STARS MUST DIE

Red Giants, White Dwarfs, Black Holes

Even stars must die, and they do so when they run out of "fuel." Their fuel is hydrogen, as we already know, or, more precisely, hydrogen nuclei that are fused into helium nuclei. Helium is the ashes, so to speak, remaining in the "star oven." The Sun, for example, can only maintain its star status by converting 597 million tons of hydrogen into 593 million tons of helium per second; the remaining 4 million tons of mass turn into energy and are released into outer space. A minuscule part of this energy makes life on Earth possible.

The fuel supply of the Sun is so incredibly large that despite the high conversion rate it will be sufficient to "heat" for another 5 billion years. After all, that is what the Sun has been doing for the last 4.5 billion years. During this incredibly long period, only about 0.03 percent of the overall mass has been lost. Relative to the Earth, the Sun is a gigantic thermal power plant; relative to the Milky Way it is a tiny luminous point of medium brightness that would be hard to find in the outer arms of the spiral. And this point of light is circled by a blue speck, a million times smaller, on which a very strange species roams of late, regarding itself as very big and important.

Even though the Sun is probably going to shine for another 5 billion years, and homo sapiens will have made his exit from the stage of the cosmic theater long before that, astronomers nevertheless would like to know what will happen to the Sun and all the other stars when they run out of fuel. Roughly outlining a rather complex development process, one can say that the "helium ashes" produced in hydrogen fusion deposit in the center of the star. The density in this area is therefore constantly increasing.

The same thing happens, of course, to the temperature, which may climb to more than 100 million degrees Kelvin. At such temperatures, helium can be reconverted into the elements beryllium and carbon, and the latter, at a later point, into even heavier elements. In the case of giant stars with many times the mass of our Sun, the temperatures at the center can rise up to 1 billion degrees Kelvin. At these temperatures elements like calcium or even iron can be generated by nuclear fusion.

The enormous increase in pressure and temperature inside the star causes its outer layers to inflate, and so less and less of the radiation generated inside can get out. The inner balance of the star is disturbed. The outer layers are forced outside until a new state of balance is established. Astronomers call such an inflated star a "red giant." In approximately 3.5 billion years our Sun will become a red giant, too. According to calculations, its diameter will then grow about four hundred times. It size would reach far beyond the orbit of the planet Mercury. At this point, at the latest, life on Earth will end. Even though the overall energy production of the Sun will continue to increase, its luminosity will diminish with increasing size. When the new state of balance is established, it will glow only faintly red.

But even this balance will not be maintained forever. It will last only until the nuclear reactions inside stop for good, eliminating the pressure, which hitherto has prevented the gigantic amount of matter from falling in on itself due to the pull of its own gravity. At that point the red giant collapses. Massive stars—that is, those of more than one and a half times the mass of the Sun—have problems contracting. If the mass is above this critical limit the star throws off a major part of its mass in a huge explosion. While the star is collapsing, the temperature of the gases once more increases to such a degree that the entire remaining fuel is consumed instantly. In this case, one speaks of a supernova. The huge temperatures created in the explosion are sufficient even to generate the heaviest of elements such as uranium.

The first man to observe such a supernova was the Danish astronomer Tycho Brahe (1546–1601) on November 11, 1572. This observation, together with his sightings of comets, shook the belief in a divinely perfect universe at least as much as the theoretical argumentations of a Copernicus or Kepler. For here one could see with the naked eye that the sky was not perfect. If it had been, nothing new should have appeared. Of course, the church managed to interpret this observation as a sign from heaven, a warning from God to mankind, and it did the same with the comets. Yet another sign from heaven was observed in February 1987: the supernova "1987A" in the Large Magellanic Cloud.

Masses of matter hurled into space in a supernova can contribute to the development of new stars. Our Sun, too, has been generated from the material emitted by exploding stars and, along with it, the Earth, which is but a by-product of the Sun's birth. The heavier elements, such as carbon and oxygen, required by any kind of life form, were generated in the interior of stars. With the exception of hydrogen, all the atoms—or rather atomic nuclei—of which we are made were once located inside stars that subsequently exploded as supernovae.

The remainder of a collapsing star that is not hurled into space falls in on itself and settles down to a final state as a "white dwarf" with a radius of a few thousand kilometers and a density of hundreds of tons per cubic centimeter. In the far future, even the Sun will, although not via a supernova, collapse to a white dwarf that will eventually cool down and become a "black dwarf."

There are other final star states, however. In the case of very massive stars of fifty or more times the mass of the Sun, so much mass remains after the supernova explosion that the atomic structure preserved in white dwarfs is destroyed under the pressure of collapsing matter. The electrons on the atomic shell are compressed to such a density that they can no longer remain intact. They combine with the protons in the nucleus into further neutrons.

Gravity, the weakest force among the elementary forces, has squashed the atoms into some kind of neutron slush. The matter of the collapsed residual star consists exclusively of tightly compressed neutrons. Only the strong gravity acting between them can neutralize the incredible gravitational pressure of matter and maintain a final and stable balance. This kind of star is called a neutron star. It is, so to speak, an atomic nucleus consisting only of neutrons with a radius of only a few kilometers and a density of hundreds of billions of tons per cubic centimeter. If the Earth was compressed to its neutron mass, its radius would only be about 130 meters, but it would contain the entire mass of the Earth.

Astronomers had expected that the 1987 supernova mentioned above would definitely confirm their theory of neutron stars developing from supernova explosions. Until now, however, their expectations have not been completely satisfied. At the scene of the explosion where a neutron star should be located only dust clouds have been observed so far. Researchers at the European observatory ESO, however, noticed that the intensity of the heat radiation emitted by these clouds has remained nearly constant since mid-August 1989. This suggests the existence of an invisible "heater" that is hidden behind the dust clouds, heating them up and maintaining a uniform temperature. This "heater" might be—in agreement with the theory—a neutron star. Such a star, however, should emit a pulsing radiation corresponding to its strong self-rotation.

American scientists recently reported they had detected such a pulsing radiation at the site of the supernova, but unfortunately these measurements have so far not been confirmed by other astronomers. Whether supernova "1987A" really gave rise to a neutron star will probably only become apparent when the dust clouds have dispersed, providing a glimpse of what they currently conceal. But will we still be there to see it, considering the time it takes for earthly dust clouds to disperse?

IN THE FORECOURT
OF THE ABSOLUTE MYSTERY

Of course, the untiring astronomers asked themselves what would happen if a collapsing star still had sufficient mass for even stable neutron matter to be destroyed by gravitational attraction. The logical answer to this question initially sent a shudder down astronomy's spine: There would be nothing left to counterbalance gravity. The star would collapse to a "point of matter" with zero volume and infinite density. Even the strong nuclear force that neutralizes gravitational pressure in the neutron star and maintains its stability would eventually not be sufficient.

According to calculations, collapsing residual stars of more than 3.2 times the mass of the Sun would certainly settle down to this most extreme state. It would no longer be a "state," however, since it would be beyond all known natural laws. It would be a singularity, just as the big bang, a point in space-time that cannot yet be described mathematically. But there is a name for this amorphous, theoretically derived object: "black hole." Nobody has ever seen one—because it is invisible. Neither matter nor light nor any other kind of radiation can escape a black hole since the gravitational field surrounding its infinitely dense center is too strong.

Even though one cannot see a black hole one can at least calculate how big it would have to be if a given amount of mass was concentrated at its center. If we assume, for example, that the mass of our Sun would be concentrated pointlike at the center of a black hole, its radius would be about 6 kilometers. This "no man's land" around the center of the black hole would coincide with the paths of light rays that just fail to escape from the black hole.

As soon as a visible body enters the "no man's land" around the black hole, the light emitted by it can no longer escape; the photons are "sucked" into the center of the black hole and the body becomes invisible for an outside observer. The speed at which the photons are moving away from the body is too low compared with the force of the gravitational field attracting them. Astronomers call this "no man's land" the event horizon. It surrounds the black hole like an impenetrable veil preventing any glimpses inside.

It almost looks as if cosmic censorship exists. In this case, black holes must be particularly obscene objects that the creator has chosen to hide from outside view. What cannot be seen, however, attracts the imagination most strongly and arouses an especially urgent desire to expose it and view it in all its nakedness. Stephen Hawking says ironically: "God abhors a naked singularity." But what God abhors incites astrophysicists all the more.

Black holes have become virtual cult objects of theoretical research—understandably, since astrophysicists expect from their work no less than a final understanding of the beginnings of the universe. After all, a black hole represents a kind of inverted little big bang. For the physicist, a black hole is a practical example of a singularity, so to speak, and therefore it has acquired an almost mythical quality. It might harbor the answers to the supposedly ultimate questions of theoretical physics.

It is important, however, that the necessarily speculative theoretical work be confirmed by measurements and observations. The existence of black holes has been derived exclusively from physical calculations; so far they are only computer-real, which means that the astronomers have to start looking for black holes in the cosmos. But how can they be detected as they are invisible and do not emit signals in the form of radiation? It might seem like looking for a mousehole in pitch-black night.

Astrophysicists finally came to the conclusion that an indirect indication for the existence of a black hole might be provided by interstellar matter entering its gravitational field. Such matter would be attracted in a rapidly accelerating spiral motion, similar to water sucked down a bath's plughole. The matter particles would become so hot that they would emit X-rays even before reaching the event horizon.

At the beginning of the 1960s, radio telescopes made it possible to detect sources of X-rays in the universe. Among them was a particularly strong source in the Cygnus constellation that was cataloged as Cygnus X-1. With time, astronomers found more and more of these X-ray sources. Since all sources emitted radiation in regular pulses, astronomers went so far as to believe they could be signals from alien civilizations. Very soon, however, they came to the conclusion that these objects had to be rapidly rotating neutron stars. Since then they are also referred to as pulsars. But if neutron stars actually existed, it was no longer totally unreasonable to believe in the existence of black holes.

In 1971 astronomers noticed a considerable change in the radiation intensity of Cygnus X-1. This seemed to rule out the possibility that it was a neutron star since their radiation pulse does not change that distinctly. Perhaps Cygnus X-1 was a black hole! Astronomers started to observe this particular source more thoroughly. It turned out that its position was almost identical with that of a "normal," very big star of about thirty times the mass of the Sun.

Path calculations showed that it had to be a double star system. A massive, bright star and an unseen companion emitting strong X-radiation orbit each other. The unseen object should have a mass of five to eight times that of the Sun. Since one cannot see it, it has to be very small in spite of its considerable mass. Since this mass is much too large for a white dwarf or a neutron star it is quite likely that Cygnus X-1 is a black hole.

However, this is not a safe bet yet. Astronomers argue that the strong radiation emitted by the black hole is produced by matter hurled off constantly from the surface of a massive, bright star—

perhaps one that is in the process of becoming a red giant—and sucked into the black hole. Nevertheless, this argumentation is indirect and therefore not definitive by far.

Maybe even the layman can now understand the excitement that currently prevails among astrophysicists and astronomers. In the 1990s new supertelescopes are expected not only to allow for even deeper penetration into the universe—18 billion light-years into the past—but also to deliver direct proof for the existence of black holes and perhaps even information about their structure. For the above assumption that black holes cannot emit radiation comes from the initial phases of the theoretical work on these mysterious objects.

In the 1970s Stephen Hawking proved on the basis of quantum mechanics that even black holes must emit radiation that is, however, too small to be detected by the available radio telescopes. Perhaps this will become possible with the new supertelescopes. The radiation emitted by black holes is called—after its theoretical discoverer—*Hawking radiation*. If these rays exist, they "do not come from within the black hole, but from the 'empty' space just outside the black hole's event horizon," Stephen Hawking writes. And he goes on:

> What we think of as "empty" space cannot be completely empty because that would mean that all the fields, such as the gravitational and electromagnetic fields, would have to be exactly zero. However, the value of a field and its rate of change with time are like the position and velocity of a particle: The uncertainty principle implies that the more accurately one knows one of these quantities, the less accurately one can know the other. So in empty space the field cannot be fixed at exactly zero, because then it would have a precise value (zero) and a precise rate of change (also zero). There must be a certain minimum amount of uncertainty, or quantum fluctuations, in the value of the field. One can think of these fluctuations as pairs of particles of light or gravity that appear together at some time, move apart, and then come together again and annihilate each other. These

particles are virtual particles like the particles that carry the gravitational force of the Sun: Unlike real particles, they cannot be observed directly with a particle detector.

Here our nonspecialist brains reach those familiar limits of which some of us may even have grown fond. For us, the black hole is located in our own heads. We have to accept the slightly mad idea that the cosmic vacuum contains more than just the interstellar matter particles flying around everywhere. Even though the electromagnetic and gravitational fields in the vacuum do not "do" anything specific, they nevertheless have to be there. They are energy at point zero which, according to the laws of quantum mechanics, cannot be exactly zero. This "zero-point energy" is the source of quantum fluctuations, that is, the spontaneous and unpredictable leaps of the field from zero to a state of excitation.

According to quantum mechanics, this state has to be interpreted as the formation of particle-antiparticle pairs. Usually, particles and antiparticles annihilate each other; the formation of such a pair therefore implies the destruction of both partners. In the area of an event horizon, however, this process is disturbed. It is possible that a particle falls into the black hole before it has annihilated itself and its partner. Its companion may suffer the same fate or it may escape the attraction of the black hole, thus making it seem as if the black hole itself had created and emitted this particle.

I have to admit that this simplified representation is itself very close to the "event horizon" of the permissible, for I was simply unable to comprehend the process of quantum fluctuation, that is, the causeless formation of particle-antiparticle pairs from zero-point energy. Even though quantum mechanics demands this process, since absolutely zero energy would be irreconcilable with the uncertainty principle, this does not make it any more understandable.

What is more, I do not know which particles and antiparticles are affected by it. Perhaps physicists do not know this for sure either. In any case, the absolute nothingness of the philosopher does not seem to exist in nature. Even in the most perfect vacuum there is still something, namely zero-point energy. Perhaps it should be associated with the philosphical term *idea,* that is, something spiritual. Quantum fluctuation in the vacuum takes place because zero-point energy must not be zero.

Nothingness does not exist. Nothingness is filled with options; it contains potential particles and antiparticles that only become real when they combine into pairs and annihilate each other. They only exist where they destroy each other. Otherwise they lie dormant in the potential and the probable. One could also call them "probability particles." Just as quantum mechanics cannot tell us why a radioactive material—uranium, for example—emits a particular particle at a particular instance and not another, it cannot explain why a specific particle-antiparticle pair is generated from zero-point energy at a specific moment.

Stephen Hawking's theory of black holes that radiate even though, according to general relativity, they should not do so was, as Hawking himself says, "the first example of a prediction that depended in an essential way on both the great theories of this century, general relativity and quantum mechanics." That black holes might result from the collapse of a star was a strictly logical consequence of the gravitational forces responsible for the collapse of great amounts of matter.

General relativity, which is a theory of gravitation, describes this process with mathematical exactitude, but cannot describe the final state of the black hole since gravity is infinite in a black hole. Einstein's formulas fail where singularities are concerned. What general relativity predicts—in this case, the black hole—is ultimately responsible for its failure. It does not incorporate the uncertainty principle that is necessary for describing the small-scale effects in nature. And the black hole is an example for these small-scale effects, the interactions of subatomic particles.

If a singularity like the black hole will be at all physically describable one day, it will probably be on the basis of quantum mechanics. Gravity, the only elementary force left in a black hole, has to be explained in terms of quantum mechanics just as the other three forces have been. So far gravity has resisted mathematical attribution to the effect of gravitational quanta (gravitons). Black holes could provide a means for theoretical physics to achieve this. In the case of the black hole singularity, particles sucked into the center move so fast that the gravity acting between them becomes as strong as the strong nuclear force, and therefore measurable.

Otherwise the effects of single gravitons in nature have not been experimentally detected; the available measuring devices are not accurate enough. Gravity is so weak that between the electron and the proton of a hydrogen atom, for example, it is 10^{39} times weaker than the electromagnetic force acting between the two particles. So far physicists hardly know anything about the quantum characteristics of gravity even though they are pretty sure that gravitational quanta (gravitons) exist. Black holes could become entrance gates to new theoretical territories. They may hide the answer to the question of what the big bang is and whether it really occurred.

THE UNIVERSE—A BLACK HOLE

Black holes do not only intrigue astrophysicists. Even the layman would like to know what might happen inside a black hole. General relativity and quantum mechanics, however, provide only rather discouraging predictions: Probably nothing happens at all, at least not for an observer inside the black hole. Consciousness cannot exist in a black hole. Everything that falls into a black hole loses its individuality and wholeness; it is torn up into its subatomic components and finally "boiled into quark soup."

To use a word like *finally*, however, is problematic. As we already know, general relativity predicts that time runs slower with increasing gravity. Time would therefore approach zero proportionally to the space-time curvature (and gravity), approaching infinity toward the center of a black hole, but only relative to an outside observer. An object nearing a black hole would become slower and seemingly come to a standstill when it reached the event horizon. For an outside observer, the journey to the black hole would take forever. The light emitted by the object would shift increasingly toward the red end; the object would become fainter and fainter until, passing the event horizon, it would become invisible. And that is, in fact, the end of all speculation; no object could be traced beyond the event horizon of a black hole.

Further speculation might be stimulated by imagining a spaceship that could resist being ripped apart inside the black hole, that is, by assuming the impossible. But even such a science fiction voyage into the interior of a black hole would probably be absolutely uneventful. The passengers on the spaceship would pass the event horizon without even noticing it. For them, time would go on as usual. They would continue falling toward the singularity at the center of the black hole, but the distance to the center would probably become greater and greater. They would never reach the singularity, the state beyond all known natural laws, because they are beings for which the natural laws are still valid.

As a part of nature I can only observe what obeys the laws of nature. But there would be no return from the black hole either. The spaceship would forever continue to fall toward the center and at the same time move away from it. Theoretically, there would be a single escape from this cosmic trap but only if the black hole is rotating. This solution is suggested by the equations of general relativity: The spaceship might fall through a "wormhole" and come out in another region of the universe. It would be hurled outside by the force of the angular momentum of the black hole.

"Outside," however, could be any place in the cosmic somewhere. Thus, the spaceship would travel millions or even billions of light-years in a single moment because the "wormhole" would have a different time structure than the universe. The equivalent of the black hole would be a white hole, the other end of the "wormhole." There the spaceship would reappear, simultaneously releasing great amounts of energy. This reminds me strongly of Edgar Allan Poe's famous maelstrom story where the escape from the whirlpool becomes possible by utilizing the centrifugal force inside the maelstrom. A reversed birth. Here astrophysics definitely stops being an exact science and enters the realm of superior science fiction. The boundaries are fluid, however, and that may be the reason why several great scientists have turned into great science fiction writers.

These speculations may be very stimulating, but they all proceed from the assumption that a body falling into a black hole maintains its material structure. But that would not be the case. These speculations only work if one ignores the only certain fact about black holes—that inside it nothing remains as it was. The most ingenious answer to the question of how the interior of a black hole might look comes from the physicist Kip Thorne: The entire universe represents the interior of a black hole, and there are lots of them. To know what the interior of a black hole looks like, we only have to look around us. The world is a hole, and man is right in the middle of it.

THE ANTHROPIC PRINCIPLE

The world is as we imagine it. The world is as we perceive it because we have been created by the world for the purpose of observing and understanding it. The universe had to create mankind, because without it, it would not be the universe. The tautology of such sentences circles around what modern astrophysics calls the anthropic principle. In a way, astrophysics uses it to escape the maelstrom of its own speculations by starting to argue in metaphysical terms. According to this principle, cosmic harmony only becomes understandable if one augments natural laws with the fact that man has appeared as an intelligent being in the universe and wants to understand it in order to understand himself.

It seems only fair to suspect that here man uses astrophysics to reestablish himself as the metaphysical pivot of the universe after the same science cruelly banned him from the cosmic center five hundred years ago. Even astrophysicists, however, do not agree on the range covered by the anthropic principle. Two anthropic principles exist: a weak one and a strong one. The weak principle essentially states that the universe is as old as it is because it took such a long time for an intelligent being like man to evolve. This process requires elements such as carbon and oxygen, which must initially be provided by a first generation of stars. Conditions necessary to support life are created only if a second generation of stars arises from the ruins of the first. This weak anthropic principle still lacks any metaphysical flavor.

Metaphysics are only incorporated in the strong anthropic principle that suggests the universe was specifically created for mankind. "It is almost irresistible for humans to believe that we have some special relation to the universe, that human life is not just a more-or-less farcical outcome of a chain of accidents reaching back to the first three minutes, but that we were somehow built in from the beginning," Steven Weinberg writes. Indeed, a complex interaction of natural laws was necessary to give rise to a being that is not simply there but becomes able, from a certain point of its development, to learn to understand these interactions.

The natural laws governing the universe are of such a kind that we can observe. Thus, we are entitled to speak of *our* universe. But that does not necessarily mean that there are no other universes with other natural laws. These universes would be beyond human observation. If they exist, they do not exist for us but only for themselves, because we can only observe phenomena that are governed by the same natural constants as we are. The scope of things we can expect to observe in our universe must therefore be limited by the physical conditions required for our existence. For example, man will never be able to discover beings in his universe with a fundamentally different biology since the biology that is possible in this universe is determined by a limited set of natural constants, or, more precisely, by the harmonious interaction between the micro-physical and macrophysical worlds.

The universe would look totally different—and the human species would never have evolved—if, for example, the electron charge or the mass ratio between proton and electron differed only slightly from the actual value. The elementary particles would have behaved differently in the hot early phase of the universe, and the proportion of helium and hydrogen during the first minutes of expansion would certainly have been different. If the forces of attraction between the elementary particles had been only minutely stronger, not hydrogen but helium would have predominated. In this case, stars would still have developed, but they would not have reached the stability necessary for producing the elementary building blocks of life.

Another crucial factor is the speed of expansion, which depends on the natural constant of the speed of light. If this constant was only slightly above or below the actual value, hydrogen would not have gathered into gas clouds and finally into stars and galaxies. This, too, is a prerequisite for life to evolve. We do not know why the natural constants have exactly those values and no others. They are only measurable, but cannot be traced back further theoretically. Why does the speed of light in the vacuum equal precisely 299.793 kilometers per second? We do not know, just as we do not know why the charge of an electron is exactly 1.602189×10^{-19} C (coulombs) or why the rest mass of the proton is 1.672614×10^{-31} kilograms as opposed to the electron's rest mass of 9.109534×10^{-31} kilograms.

The same is true for Planck's constant and all the other micro-physical and macrophysical constants. It looks as if these abstract numbers were carefully adjusted to make a universe possible that did not collapse immediately after its formation, and that even allowed for the development of life. But what if the whole universe, including mankind, was simply a product of chance, without a pur-

pose or goal! Well, it simply is. Only chance has led to a constellation favorable for the development of human life. The cosmos as a
whole is as much a result of chance as every single particle movement inside it. And the universal constants? Well, they could not
help but assume exactly the values they now have. A rather disen-
chanting thought, admittedly.

THE HIDDEN COSMOS

Here we have definitely crossed the border between physics and
metaphysics, even if we do not assume the presence of a God who
calculated the values of the natural constants before creating the
world. At least He must have done so if it was important to Him
that His world should be populated by living beings including Him
in their thoughts—and sometimes even in their prayers. God was
obviously not interested in a universe without life and without consciousness. If, however, this creative God was mainly concerned
with the intelligent being, man—as religion claims—one may ask
why it required such incredible expense, an incredible detour via a
universe that existed without mankind for 15 or 20 billion years.

It almost looks as if God had also created an impenetrable hiding-place for Himself, a shelter against the unquenchable thirst for
knowledge of a being which, by exactly this curiosity, gives the universe and ultimately also this God its meaning. Man can only be
imagined as an inquiring and developing being. If there was nothing
left to ask, he would stop being human. If there is a Creator, He has
taken this into account by fashioning such a complex universe that
there will never be an end to human questions. Such an end would
correspond to tracking God down in His cosmic hiding-place, to
finally understand His cosmic plan. If God exists, this will never
happen; it would be the proof that what mankind referred to as God
was just an enormous chimera of the human mind.

Whichever paths the human mind will follow in the future, all of
them will end before an ultimate abyss of unknowing. Man can
never escape his human nature and his mortality. As much as he

may expand his intellectual horizon, he will finally always realize that we are, as Niels Bohr said, "both spectators and actors in the great drama of existence." Man will always remain a mystery to himself. And if we are unable to understand the ultimate truths about ourselves, we cannot understand the cosmos of which we are a part.

Lincoln Barnett wrote in his book on Einstein:

> Man's inescapable impasse is that he himself is part of the world he seeks to explore; his body and proud brain are mosaics of the same elemental particles that compose the dark, drifting dust clouds of interstellar space; he is, in the final analysis, merely an ephemeral conformation of the primordial space-time field. Standing midway between macrocosm and microcosm he finds barriers on every side.

In this case, an infinitely wise Creator would have established the prerequisites for remaining a hidden God. Man will always be forced to either believe in Him or not believe in Him.

Once, when I looked up at the stars, the thought occurred to me that without this starry sky human existence would be unthinkable not only physically but also on a purely spiritual level. In a universe with only the Sun providing daylight, alternating with pitch-black darkness, man would probably never have learned to ask questions because there would have been nothing to ask about beyond his narrow earthly concerns. Put bluntly, without the night sky there would be no human culture because man would not be at the intersection of two infinities leading his mind toward the infinite on the one hand, and putting him in his place on the other. This position challenges man to probe both infinities intellectually.

"THE LIFE OF THE GODS IS MATHEMATICS"

Let us abandon the misty swamplands of metaphysics created by the concept of a personal God before we lose ourselves beyond redemption. The natural constants may be the proof of a divine origin of the universe but only for those whose "religiousness" requires such proofs. Physicists seek salvation in a different kind of metaphysics. One might call it a metaphysics of pure numbers, even a numerical magic, but this metaphysics is nevertheless based on strict physical facts. Physicists are quite uninhibited about referring to something as "magic" when they cannot trace it back further, that is, cannot explain why something is the way it is.

Nuclear physicists, for example, discovered very early that atomic nuclei are particularly stable if the number of protons or neutrons they contain is 2, 8, 20, 28, 50, 82, or 126. The helium nucleus, which is composed of 2 protons and 2 neutrons, is one of the most stable nuclei. Lead with its 82 protons is the stable end product from the disintegration of all radioactive elements occurring in nature. These seven numbers are called "magical numbers" in nuclear physics. But this is not the only example of "numerical magic."

Recurring magic numbers were also found when physicists looked for connections between the constant quantities on the atomic scale and those valid in large-scale physics. A pioneer in this search for recurring numbers that might express higher, harmonious relationships between the atomic and the cosmic structures was A. S. Eddington. He discovered that the numbers 136 and 137 are of special importance in Einstein's universe. These numbers, he pointed out, were closely related to a dimensionless number in nuclear physics encompassing the three natural constants: speed of light, electron charge, and Planck's quantum of action.

Eddington calculated, for example, that the number of particles in the universe should be 2.4×10^{79}. This number was the result of mathematically linking the radius of the universe with the number 136. Eddington found out that the basic natural constants can be impressively combined into a succession of pure numbers. An example would be the number 0.23×10^{40}. The square of this number, 5.29×10^{78}, approaches the total number of particles in the universe calculated by Eddington up to a factor of 4.

Two other pure numbers that he derived from the combination of atomic constants with Hubble's expansion constant are 4×10^{40} and 10^{80}. They, too, are closely related to the number of particles in the cosmos. The British astronomer Bernard Lovell commented on Eddington's scientific "number mysticism" as follows:

It is scarcely credible that the close relationships between these numbers derived from the constants of atomic structure and the scale of the entire universe can be accidental. Indeed the chance of coincidences between numbers of the order of 10^{40} derived in this manner can be disregarded. It is difficult to resist the conclusion that they represent some deep relation to the universe.

Chaos theory, which tries to detect a kind of hidden order in chaotic systems via endless computer calculations, has also managed to discover a magical number. It always turns up in the transition from an ordered to a chaotic state, regardless of the nature of the transition. It is—in abbreviated form—the number 4.669. It marks the borderline between order and chaos and is called, after its discoverer, the Feigenbaum constant. Nobody knows so far what 4.669 means or what deeper purpose it serves. But Eddington did not know what his numbers meant either.

One has a notion of its purpose, though. Even the most chaotic system may obey a mysterious higher reason that confronts us only in the form of a pure number: 4.669 is the result of random numerical experiments on the basis of an "abstract" mathematics, that is, a mathematics that does not only use real numbers but also complex numbers characterized by an imaginary portion i (the square root of -1).

The computer puts chaos through the mathematical wringer from two sides: a real one and an imaginary one. As much as the work of the chaos scientist and the astrophysicist differ, their aim is very similar: to incorporate the whole universe and all the systems contained in it from the smallest to the largest, the most simple to the most complex, the most ordered to the most chaotic, in a single abstract formula; to find something absolute and ultimate to which everything may be related with mathematical precision. In short, the whole world is to reside in a single number.

Natural constants as well as physics' magical numbers would then be the fingerprints the Creator has left upon his work. "The life of the Gods is mathematics," as Novalis said. In this case nature, in its essence, would have a purely spiritual purpose. "Subjectively, nature is not of the mind," Carl F. von Weizsäcker writes. "She does not think in mathematical terms. But objectively, nature is of the mind—she can be thought in mathematical terms. This is perhaps the deepest truth we know of nature." Mathematical symbols are the runes of the universal language in which the book of nature was written.

LIFE ELSEWHERE?

Even though, according to the anthropic principle, it looks as if the universe had been created for the purpose of producing intelligent beings, the term *anthropic* is misleading. Man does not necessarily have to be the only intelligent being in the universe. It seems, however, as if the astrophysicists who developed this more philosophical than scientific principle are not too interested in whether man is the only intelligent being in the cosmos or not. One probable reason for their lack of interest is that there is hardly any substantial basis for a theory of extraterrestrial life that would be more than pure fantasy.

Astrophysicists love to speculate, but only on the more or less safe ground of theoretical physics. Also, they will probably tell themselves that the question of extraterrestrial life is a matter for biology, not physics. Astrobiology, however, is a branch of science that develops extremely slowly; it is not even in its infancy yet. Even though the knowledge about biochemical requirements for the development of life has enormously increased, particularly in the last decade, information on the surface conditions of far-away celestial bodies is still very sparse.

Nevertheless, the question of whether extraterrestrial life exists is moving more and more into the center of astronomic research. So far, two basic assumptions about life in the cosmos are regarded as incontestable. First, organic life requires the existence of highly complex molecular combinations, mainly protein molecules and nucleic acids. Second, active and reproduceable life is bound to a rather narrow temperature range. At temperatures above 100 degrees Celsius, protein molecules and nucleic acids disintegrate into smaller molecules that decay into individual atoms at temperatures above several thousand degrees Celsius. At temperatures substantially below zero degrees Celsius, biochemical reactions become so slow that active life is no longer possible.

The ideal temperatures for organic life to evolve lie approximately between +25 and +45 degrees Celsius. All the higher-developed beings on Earth have body temperatures within this range, and every organism strives to maintain its characteristic temperature to fractions of one degree by means of highly complex temperature control systems. Apart from these two prerequisites for organic life there are others that are only of relative importance; they include, for example, the existence of a high-oxygen atmosphere or water.

There is no reason why the conditions that led to the development of life on Earth should not be present on planets in other star systems. After all, traces of formic acid, methanol, formaldehyde, cyanoacetylene, and other molecules have recently been detected in interstellar space. Formaldehyde, for example, is a genuine although very simple organic molecule; cyanoacetylene is already more complex. Theoretically, it is even possible that meteorites contain traces of formic acid.

As it now seems quite certain that there is no organic life on the other planets of our galaxy, considerations concentrate on areas outside our solar system. However, one is immediately confronted with the problem that nothing specific can be said about the number of planetary systems in the universe. The optimists among astronomers—actually only an optimist can become an astronomer—assume that probably all stars have planets that do not belong to double star systems, are not red giants or white dwarfs, and do not have too great a mass or luminosity.

Taking into account these limitations, only those stars with 2.5 to a hundredth of the mass of the Sun would be eligible. This is true for only a few percent of all stars, but considering the huge number of stars in the cosmos, it would still be a substantial number. In the "immediate" vicinity of our galaxy, however, only about twelve stars might have planets with organic life forms. These stars have long been monitored for artificially created radio signals but to no avail. This does not necessarily exclude the existence of lower life forms on these hypothetical planets, of course. After all, it seems pretty unlikely that intelligent beings exist on a faraway planet with a civilization that includes radio engineering.

It is questionable anyway whether civilizations necessarily have to invent radio engineering in the course of their development. Mankind only invented it a few decades ago. For millions of years, there has been intelligent life on Earth that was unable to make itself noticeable in outer space. For this reason alone, it is very unlikely that we will ever establish contact with an extraterrestrial intelligence. It becomes even less likely if we think about making contact with intelligent beings outside of our galaxy. The galaxy closest to ours, the Andromeda nebula, is 2.5 million light-years away from us. Signals would take 2.5 million years to cover that distance. It is highly unlikely that technical civilizations can be maintained at all over such time spans.

The statistical average for the duration of highly developed technical civilizations is about one hundred thousand years, which seems already pretty optimistic considering that our technical civilization is only a hundred years old, and there are more and more voices claiming that it is not going to last another hundred years. If an extraterrestrial intelligence should really capture our radio signals, it would probably do so at a time when the only remaining traces of our civilization would be, at best, decaying cola cans, plastic bags, and tires.

The possibility of making contact with another intelligence is therefore primarily dependent on how long our civilization will last. Certainly there would be no adventure more fascinating for humanity than to communicate with or even meet intelligent extraterrestrial beings. The spiritual shocks caused by such an encounter are inconceivable. Above all, those religions that obsessively insist on regarding man as the crown of God's creation would probably collapse. It would be the end of all anthropocentric theologies. But it would not necessarily be the end of religion.

Cosmic religiousness, as defined by Einstein, would have found its extraterrestrial vindication, so to speak. To know that we share the cosmos with other thinking beings would perhaps provide the consolation that human beings so far have tried to find in the different religious systems. Perhaps man created religion only because he could not bear the thought of being all alone in the infinite depths of the universe.

As little as this may interest astronomers, during the heroic times of manned space travel one did not fail to attach small golden plaques bearing messages to extraterrestrial beings to the machinery left in space. An almost childish naivete considering that these devices did not even pass the threshold of our earthly home, or flew around in our front yard at best. A pair of rather comic-looking cosmic messengers adorns also the plaques aboard the American space probes "Pioneer 10" and "Pioneer 11"; in 1973 and 1974 they circled Jupiter, and were sent on an infinite journey into interstellar space afterward.

The probes "Voyager 1" and "Voyager 2" followed later. The latter left our planetary system in August 1989, after it had circled Neptune, in the direction of a star with the catalog number "Ross 248." It will arrive at this star in the year 42155. The messengers on the plaques are naked—like Adam and Eve before the Fall—not underneath a fig tree but before the contours of the probe, which is meant to say: This thing has been built by us. Adam lifts his right hand in greeting; Eve does not. Thus, the extraterrestrials also get to know something about the gender-specific roles on Earth. One can only hope that they do not interpret the greeting as a threatening gesture.

At the lower edge of the plaque is a drawing of our planetary system, showing from which planet the probe was dispatched. In the upper left corner, the symbol for neutral hydrogen atoms indicates how incredibly intelligent we are. A truly interstellar message in a bottle! But what would happen if alien guests from outer space really followed up this invitation? If we assume that these extraterrestrial guests possess the same underdeveloped ethics but more sophisticated weaponry, there would be cause for panic! Perhaps before inviting unknown guests one should make sure that they are "better people" than we are.

It is also typical that we automatically take it for granted that another high—or even higher—intelligence is at all interested in us. Who knows, we may have been discovered a long time ago but dismissed as unimportant by our discoverers for existing on too low a level of galactic and intergalactic intellectual development. Perhaps there is a big party going on in our Milky Way to which we simply have not been invited. It might be that we make as poor an impression on extraterrestrials who happen to drop by once in a while as on the supernatural narrator in Douglas Adams' novel *The Hitchhiker's Guide to the Galaxy:*

> Far out in the uncharted backwaters of the unfashionable end of the Western Spiral arm of the Galaxy lies a small unregarded yellow sun. Orbiting this at a distance of roughly ninety-two million miles is an utterly insignificant little blue green planet whose ape-descended life forms are so amazingly primitive that they still think digital watches are a pretty neat idea. The planet has—or rather had—a problem, which was this: Most of the people living on it were unhappy for pretty much of the time. Many solutions were suggested for this problem, but most of these were largely connected with the movements of small green pieces of paper,

which is odd because on the whole it wasn't the small green pieces of paper that were unhappy. And so the problem remained; lots of the people were mean, and most of them were miserable, even the ones with digital watches. Many were increasingly of the opinion that they'd all made a big mistake coming down from the trees in the first place. And some said that even the trees had been a bad move, and that no one should ever have left the oceans.

Man As the
Intersection of the Four Elements
One gets the impression
that modern physics is based on assumptions
which somehow resemble the smile
of a cat that is not there.
[ALBERT EINSTEIN]

CONCLUSION

Theories and speculations on black holes in particular create the impression that astrophysicists endeavor to become modern mythologists, mythographs in the literal sense of the word, storytellers. Along with science fiction writers, they fill the vacuum created by the renunciation of the old myths. Nobody seems able to manage without myths. Human beings want to listen to stories, preferably those that lead them far from the misery and limitations of earthly existence. The science fiction sky is basically just a high-tech heaven.

It would be wrong to assume that myths cease to exist where science commences. Even the scientist cannot help but risk hypotheses, telling tales when certain knowledge is not yet available. But by so doing he enters the dangerous no-man's-land between knowledge and faith.

Physics and astrophysics inevitably acquire a metaphysical character when they promise answers to supposedly final questions, questions about the origin and purpose of the universe, about the smallest and the largest things, about a primary force acting in everything. The question about the origin has always been at the center of metaphysics. Origin is the great fixation of Western thought. "Elementary" terminology is central to modern physics: elementary forces, elementary particles.... Not since Greek antiquity have science and philosophy been as close as in our century of quantum physics and relativity. But whether an ailing philosophy can be revived by science's artificial respiration remains to be seen. At times it seems that modern physics is the last serious advocate of the mythical and metaphysical. Like religion, it is governed by dreams of the absolute.

In the metaphorical terms of modern astrophysics—black hole, red giant, white dwarf—its mythologizing tendencies become apparent, reminding us strongly of archaic realms of legend. Objects from the dark depths of the universe are given names drawn from the dark depths of an ancient world. Black holes might just as well be called "collapsars" or "poststellar singularities" or "antistars"; but "black hole" sounds much more exciting and mysterious.

Black hole is a rather primitive term, arousing a sense of foreboding in all of us. The humorous astrophysical proposition, for example, that black holes have no hairs (it means that the size and shape of a black hole are solely dependent on its mass and speed of rotation, not on the characteristics of the star that gave rise to it by way of its collapse) introduces the primal womb of old myths as metaphor of origin, longing, and fear. The black hole appears as the "hairless" entrance into a primary cosmic uterus in which everything valid outside is negated: a mythical site of dissolution and, perhaps, redemption, a symbol for the abyss but also a place of hope for cosmic rebirth.

Of course, such metaphorical terms are not crucial to the scientist; scientists are not dependent on a symbolic language for they have the language of mathematics. These colorful terms have been created for us laymen, to keep us interested. Because we feel lost in the tangle of scientific terminology, we cling to these hauntingly vivid terms. Formulas do not sink in, but metaphors do. Often we link those metaphors to incorrect ideas, or invest them with a meaning they do not have for the scientist. Science uses metaphors mainly where findings are still vague. Metaphors are landmarks for scientific insecurity or perplexity, the gray area where myths flourish.

But what is the meaning of this longing for myths, be they old or new? I believe it is something very simple. Man longs for certainty, for solid proof that there is a higher, spiritual world that will outlast this finite, earthly one. Myths are stories enveloping the uncertain with a pretense of certainty. For at heart, man does not want to believe. He wants to *know* that God exists. Faith is a demanding affair, a never-ending, lifelong effort, at least if the intellect does not want to submit to rigid dogma or be content with a child's faith. It should be a faith not opposed to reason and the knowledge of our time. The longing for myths and mysticism expresses the desire to abandon this painful effort of believing and the hope to be redeemed from the heavy burden of keeping the faith. For this purpose, some dig up the old myths, and others create new ones. Their motivation is always the same: a need for clarity of thought, control, predictability, and security.

For many people today, the fascination of old myths and mysteries, ancient mystic rituals, cults, and rites lies probably in their promise of direct access to the supernatural. One only has to attend specific magical ceremonies, endure certain initiation rites to sharpen one's senses for the supernatural. If only one follows this path passionately—one could also say fanatically—enough, then a "different reality" will finally reveal itself. This is called revelation or enlightenment. It renders faith invalid for now the incomprehensible has been comprehended and the inconceivable grasped. The mysteries of the universe have been revealed, its secret basis drained. For the mystic, there are no mysteries; he has seen God and therefore deified himself to a certain extent. Now he feels comfortable; now nothing in this earthly world can affect him for he has been moved by the absolute.

Very often the obsession for knowledge is even more pronounced in the followers of so-called esoteric sciences than in natural scientists. Even God is subjected to human knowledge—an incredible arrogance, if one thinks about it. True, science also strives for an ultimate and absolute knowledge of all natural phenomena, but it does so with the awareness that the natural laws as we defined them do not have to be valid under all circumstances, that there is no such thing as nature per se.

On its long and rocky path, science has learned that every scientific theory is temporally limited and must never claim to be final. After all, nature itself is not final. Just as all things in nature perish—or rather change—so every scientific theory has to "perish with necessity." *Panta rhei*—everything flows. Absolute knowledge of nature may be the ultimate goal of science, but inwardly it knows that the desire to construct a complete scientific picture of the entire universe will not be fulfilled. It would be a spiritual catastrophe for the human species. There would be nothing left to ask, to search for, to believe in. The completely explained world would be a completely meaningless world. To live in a world without mysteries would be the epitome of a meaningless life.

The so-called esoteric sciences, on the other hand, promise knowledge of the ultimate things. They offer formulae for obtaining this knowledge through pseudoscientific methods. The "heavenly powers," or rather, their earthly manifestations, are "scientifically" detected. Methods applied are necessarily rigid and dogmatic. The factor that frequently forces science to redesign or even rebuild its edifice is omitted in the occult sciences: experiment.

The experiment keeps science moving; its theories are not rigid and dogmatic but subject to constant change. The dogmatism of esoteric sciences or rigid theological systems prevents such creative change. They are fundamentally scholastic and always reveal the narrow-mindedness and hair-splitting attitude characteristic of a book learning which functions only as long as the dogmas on which it is based remain untouched. If one submits to such a closed system one must also perceive the world as a closed system. Nothing falls outside it because nothing is allowed to fall out. There are no universal mysteries left. And that is precisely what makes these systems so irksome, bloodless, and dull.

Of course, it is true that scientific knowledge cannot really satisfy man's metaphysical longing. But does this longing have to be satisfied at all? Is it not possible that its significance lies in its remaining unfulfilled? And if science fails to explain the ultimate mystery of the beginning of the universe, it should not be blamed for it; on the contrary, this is a proof of its honesty and the incredible demand for truth it imposes upon itself. Science leaves it to the faith of every individual to implant his personal linchpin in the mosaic of the world.

Esoterics like to refer to Goethe when trying to justify their hunger for absolute knowledge. For Goethe, too, employed scientific methods to penetrate areas not immediately accessible to our senses, trying to find a comprehensive principle with which to explain the world. But as passionately as he conducted his work in various scientific disciplines, he always suggested the existence of so-called primary phenomena that man may discover but never explain.

According to Goethe, man should not step outside the realm of sensual facts; he should enjoy the world order he has found but not become obsessed with a final analytical explanation. He said: "The scientist should leave the primary phenomena in their eternal serenity and glory untouched." And, in a different context: "Joyful admiration is not incited by the obsession to explain." But how does the scientist know that he deals with a "primary phenomenon"? Is there an objective standard for determining the universal validity of such a phenomenon? Goethe himself did not provide answers to this question. Perhaps it is not so vital.

What is important is that Goethe, as well, proclaimed something of an anthropic principle, stating that the world exists only to the extent that it is accessible to the human senses. "Primary phenomena" mark the limits of sensory perception. Questions reaching beyond them are pointless. In Goethe's own words:

> The highest goal that man can achieve is amazement, and when he is amazed by the primary phenomenon, he should be content. A higher reward cannot be granted, and further he should not inquire. This is the limit. But men are seldom satisfied by the sight of the primary phenomenon. They believe there

should be more, and they resemble children who, having looked into a mirror, immediately turn it around to see what is on the other side.

One could compare the "occult scientists" with researchers trying to find out how the mirror image of the world is created by looking behind the mirror.

But there are also those equally harassed by an insatiable longing for ultimate metaphysical knowledge who hold their reason too dear to trade it for a dubious "secret knowledge." And they may wish that the findings of modern science unveil the ultimate secrets. "Religious" revelation by strict reason appears to be a contradiction in terms. But who can say—perhaps it is not a contradiction at all. For modern physics has already disclosed parts of a "different reality," to speak in the fashionable parlance of the occult sciences. In so doing, however, it necessarily had to shift its field of research into realms traditionally reserved for philosophy and theology.

In fact, there have been few distinguished scientists in this century who did not occasionally comment on philosophical and religious questions. Essentially, all the leading physicists of our century have been physicist-philosophers. In the fringe areas of modern science, philosophical and religious questions arise automatically. For many people, this seems to promote an attitude of religious expectation, mainly toward nuclear physics and astrophysics. Perhaps, some may think, physics can tell me once and for all whether God exists or not.

As with relapses into mythical and mystical thinking in past epochs, here, too, a deep religious exhaustion leads people to expect solid proof for the unprovable. In a way, modern science adds fuel to this hope. In particular, where the beginning of the universe is concerned, physicists tend to introduce the concept of God into scientific discussion—above all in discussions with the layman.

The British astrophysicist Stephen Hawking, for example, seems to be convinced that physics will succeed in the foreseeable future to find a complete theory of the universe that also includes its beginnings. After a certain amount of time, he believes, this theory "should ... be understandable in broad principle by everyone, not just a few scientists. Then we shall all, philosophers, scientists, and just ordinary people, be able to take part in the discussion of the question of why it is that we and the universe exist. If we find the answer to that, it would be the ultimate triumph of human reason—for then we should know the mind of God."

Unfortunately, Hawking does not realize that this would also be man's triumph over God. For if God's plan was comprehensible, it would no longer be divine, just as a comprehensible God would no longer be God. The possibility that nature itself may reveal structures so far unimaginable for us does not seem to occur to Hawking. Max Planck, for example, was much more careful in this respect, and much more modest about the potentialities of human reason. In a lecture held in 1926 he said:

First of all, we should not take it for granted that a system of physical laws exists at all, or, if it has existed so far, that it will exist in the same manner in the future. It is quite possible, and we could not do anything against it, that nature will one day outwit us with a totally unprecedented event, and that, despite all efforts, we shall never be able to impose any kind of systematic order upon the resulting confusion. In this case, science would be forced to declare bankruptcy.

In an interview, Carl F. von Weizsäcker even envisaged the possibility that, in a distant future, people might regard current science as a primitive myth. In the end, all theory up to and including the quarks can be seen as a specific form of mythology.

Hawking's case is a striking example for the vast myth-hunger of the nonspecialist audience. The stunning success of his book *A Brief History of Time* probably does not indicate a sudden awakening of public interest in astrophysics. Rather, it expresses a diffuse religious need, a longing for new myths in those who are no longer satisfied with the old ones. Of course, that this longing concentrated particularly on the physicist Hawking has something to do with his personal background. Hawking has all the right credentials as a scientific mythopoet. And he is perfectly suited for being mythified himself. "A 'genius of the century like Albert Einstein'... a scientist on the trail of the 'world formula,' a man who, against all medical prognoses, has been living with an incurable, lethal nerve disease for the past twenty years, in short, a myth—Stephen Hawking." So reads the jacket blurb for the German translation of his book.

From a man who is still alive though the doctors gave up on him long ago, one does not only expect information on the latest scientific findings—one knows one is not going to understand them anyway. That is not the point. What matters is that Hawking is surrounded by an aura of miracle. Such a wondrous scientist must have a hotline to the miraculous. The admirable energy with which this man searches for the "world formula" must surely draw on superhuman sources, bound as he is to a wheelchair, able to communicate only via a voice synthesizer. And what such a man says about the beginning of the universe and about God can only be true. In this respect, Hawking's book must have been a disappointment for many. For Hawking cannot offer an answer to the question of whether God exists, either. The answer to the ultimate questions, awaited by so many, has been postponed again. Science has quite a precise idea of what the universe *is,* but it still has difficulties answering *why* it is so. Even Hawking cannot provide anything new here.

Scientists can rarely be accused of trying to advocate a new mysticism. But some of the basic findings of modern physics actually possess a mystical touch that is the stronger the more our definitions of "reality" are overthrown. Just take the electron, an almost sturdy particle compared with the neutrino or photon—not to mention the quarks! But even in the case of the electron, the concept of a tiny matter-corpuscle becomes nonsensical. The main characteristic of elementary particles is precisely their intangibility. They are not only the elementary substance of matter but they are something entirely insubstantial.

The "inconceivable concept" of the electron as a "wave of matter" alone touches upon a metaphysical dimension in which shape, in the familiar sense, no longer exists. These "waves of matter" are more than shape; they are metashape, shapes to which we can no longer attribute a substantial content—only a spiritual one. That is because they lack the substance that might move in waves, such as is the case with a wave of water. At the most, one could regard them as waves of probability, but this does not make them any more "real."

Thus in quantum mechanics we now witness a kind of recovery of the spiritual in physical phenomena after materialists had long hoped that everything, even the spiritual, could be explained by purely mechanical actions between matter. In modern physics, however, mechanistic images are no longer applicable. In the microrange, matter can no longer be explained materialistically. Even matter receives its order by something spiritual that can only be described mathematically. Elementary particles have an ideal nature rather than a substantial one.

In an interview, Herwig Schopper, former head of the European Center for Nuclear Research (CERN), had the following to say on the matter:

> The exciting thing about elementary particle physics is that we advance into unknown areas, that we explore new territories about which nothing can be predicted with certainty. We do not know yet how to explain the extremly differing masses of elementary particles. There are highly interesting theories, claiming that matter and force-carrying particles should not be regarded as two separate worlds but as variations of one and the same primary particle. However, this "super-symmetry" would require an as yet unknown partner for every particle we already know. Perhaps we are now at the threshold of yet another world pic-

ture. Basically, we still think of particles as small lumps of matter, just as Democritus did. In the new theories, symmetry plays a much more important role. Actually, it is no longer appropriate to think of quarks as particles as defined by Democritus because they can no longer be viewed separately. Their binding energy is stronger than their mass energy. This means that if you try to separate two quarks, the energy released will constantly generate new pairs of quarks and antiquarks, and you will never really succeed in separating the original quarks. The dominance of symmetry leads us back to Platonic thinking which is centered around ideas.

In any case, the religious concept of an all-encompassing spirit or logos does not contradict modern physics; on the contrary, it represents a quite convincing conclusion from the current state of elementary particle physics. This does not mean, of course, that theological doctrines could be derived from physical knowledge or even by means of modern physical experiments.

Once we have familiarized ourselves with the idea that in the microworld, matter evaporates into the spiritual and ideal, it takes only a small step toward a "spiritual physics" that is no longer concerned with physical strictness. Indeed, there have always been attempts to elaborate the metaphysical contents of modern physics into a kind of "scientific religion" or "scientific mysticism." The most famous example is the "neognostic physics" developed by the French nuclear physicist Jean E. Charon. His basic thesis says that in order to explain elementary particles entirely and satisfactorily, one cannot avoid "introducing, in addition to the space-time of matter, a special kind of space-time structure" that possesses "all the characteristic features of the spiritual."

In other words, electrons are matter particles endowed with a kind of elementary consciousness. The elementary particle as elementary "spiriticle." Like black holes, Charon says, electrons are closed microcosms with a space-time structure that no longer obeys the known natural laws. They can store information on their own "history," the sum total of all interactions with other particles since the beginning of their existence. Naturally, this gives rise to the question of why only electrons possess this magical characteristic, and not the other particles such as photons or neutrinos.

Be that as it may, the intention is immediately obvious—a "scientific" provision for the human longing after immortality. "My thoughts *are* the thoughts of my electrons," Charon, the physicist-prophet, proclaims. And this means simply: My mind is as immortal as the electrons I am composed of. It remains unclear, though, what benefits this knowledge is supposed to provide. What is the use of a mind that is split up into innumerable electronic mind-particles? Electronic immortality has little consolation to offer. And consolation is, ultimately, the goal of all transcendental theories and spiritual hypotheses.

It is always the same with scientific superstition: It tries to transform the uncertain and mysterious into knowledge by means of pseudoscientific methods. Mysteries or secrets are taboo. Knowledge is what matters, albeit only a secret knowledge. This attitude speculates with a general longing for transcendental certainty, particularly in a time where the traditional religious belief in a hereafter has become weak and fragile. The likes of Charon offer a kind of space-time or quantum theology as compensation for a disintegrating religious faith.

Scientific superstition is not a new phenomenon. In fact, it is very old; astrology is one of its best-known and most enduring varieties. The source of scientific superstition can always be found in science itself, mainly where it fails to present unassailable knowledge and has to rely on hypotheses. Modern occultism has only become so popular because it is modeled on science. Modern mystics use a pseudoscientific methodology and terminology for their nonscientific purposes, busily observing, measuring, and calculating with the help of complex tables. And they do it with such an obsession that finally they believe in this hocus-pocus themselves.

Astrology, for example, utilizes exactly that chunk of astronomical knowledge that is mysterious enough by itself: the knowledge about the gravitational fields between celestial bodies. Philosophers like Leibniz or Huygens rejected gravity, as described by Newton, because they believed that, as a long-range force, it belonged to the realm of the occult. It contradicted, like all things occult, the causal order in nature. Until today, gravity could only be explained in terms of relativity, via the unimaginable concept of four-dimensional space-time and its curvature. Such concepts provide an ideal hotbed for scientific superstition. A perfect breeding ground for spirits and the levitating mind, the "fourth dimension" became a catchall catchphrase for the modern occultist.

Of course, it is not superstitious to speak of a spiritual fourth dimension. There is no reason why human consciousness should not reach a supramental level, or consider a spiritual fourth dimension after proof for a physical fourth dimension has long been provided. Superstition flourishes only when a physical dimension is used to prove the existence of a purely spiritual dimension. Superstition is muddled thinking that tries to pay homage to the transcendental by forcing it down to the physical level.

Of course, everybody is free to believe what he wants to believe. In a certain sense, "scientific" mysticism is also an expression of creative imagination. It becomes dubious, however, when a scientist betrays the basic mandate of science: to establish hypotheses from a flawless mathematical basis. Every science, Kant said, "contains as much truth as it contains mathematics." Pseudosciences are characterized by a lack of this mathematical basis. In Charon's hypotheses it is missing altogether. Of course, science has never exclusively moved along mathematical lines. Intuition, too, is a practicable path. All great scientific deeds were probably linked to intuitive knowledge in one way or the other but invariably supported by a mathematical intelligence.

"The measurable and the unmeasurable are ... in harmony, and one notices, indeed, that they are different methods of viewing the one and unseparated whole. If such a harmony exists, man cannot only gain insights into the meaning of universality but he can also—

and this is much more important—discover and realize the truth contained in these insights in every phase and every manifestation of his life." This was written by the American physicist David Bohm.

Einstein's cosmic religiousness might be compared to gaining an idea of the unfathomable, conveyed by an understanding of the measurable. This does not leave room for an omnipotent personal God or other supernatural beings. Why should it? A personal God is only necessary on a lower spiritual level. The world is "godly" enough without a personal God. The British biologist and philosopher Julian Huxley writes:

> Many people assert that this abandonment of the god hypothesis means the abandonment of all religion and all moral sanctions. This is simply not true. But it does mean, once our relief at jettisoning an outdated piece of ideological furniture is over, that we must construct something to take its place. Though gods and God in any meaningful sense seem destined to disappear, the stuff of divinity out of which they have grown and developed remains.

This "divinity" in the universe, however, would no longer be a supernatural principle, which religions have always systematized, interpreted, and employed for earthly purposes at will, but an ultimate and unimaginable principle beyond nature. And Julian Huxley continues:

> A humanist evolution-centred religion too needs divinity, but divinity without God. It must strip the divine of the theistic qualities which man has anthropomorphically projected into it, search for its habitations in every aspect of existence, elicit it, and establish fruitful contact with its manifestations. Divinity is the chief raw material out of which gods have been fashioned. Today we must melt down the gods and refashion the material into new and effective organs of religion, enabling man to exist freely and fully on the spiritual level as well as on the material.

Could a faith be possible that is not centered around the belief in something specific? Such a faith would perhaps simply represent the capacity to be constantly in awe before nature. A capacity that we increasingly lose because nature gets lost, not least our own. Religiousness would be to admire the sublime, the "genius" of nature, the order of the whole. Religiousness would simply be a true worldview, observing and admiring the world, including its terrible aspects that we must always resist anew. Faith as "intuition" in the original sense, as a spontaneous appreciation, a thorough observation of objects, conditions, and relationships. It would be a faith that atheists too could adopt and that might enable us to sense forces behind the objects observed that are more powerful than "divine" personification could ever be. There would never be a name for them, however.

Science could indeed become midwife to a new religiousness in a new epoch. It would be a religiousness without catechism, a spirituality without spiritism. It would be a religiousness without ideology, teachers, or priests, without parishes, associations, or memberships, without cultic rites and ritual cults. In short, it would be a rather modest and quiet religiousness, extremely ascetic in form and content. "The most powerful in the world is what can neither be seen nor heard or touched," Lao-tzu says. Our knowledge of the physical world demands this metaphysical asceticism ever more emphatically.

Man can do well without the theistic God since He is only a human construction anyway—in fact, a rather frightening one. For this God, as a supernatural subject, turns us into mere objects. The Protestant theologian Paul Tillich says:

> He deprives me of my subjectivity because he is all-powerful and all-knowing.... This is the God Nietzsche said had to be killed because nobody can tolerate being made into a mere object of absolute knowledge and absolute control. This is the deepest root of atheism. It is an atheism which is justified as the reaction against ideological theism and its disturbing implications. It is also the deepest root of the Existentialist despair and the widespread anxiety of meaninglessness in our period.

This God, Tillich claims, must Himself be transcended: "The God above God is the object of all mystical longing, but mysticism also must be transcended in order to reach him."

As a Protestant theologian, however, Paul Tillich cannot avoid offering a Christian-theological solution. Even Tillich's "absolute faith" in a God above the God of theism can only be a Christian faith. But is it not necessary, on the way to an absolute faith, to not only transcend the theistic God as well as any kind of mysticism and theological system but also Christianity itself to approach what might be called cosmic religiousness? In this respect, Tillich, too, holds an exclusively Christian monologue.

Even though the God of Christian theism has to be transcended, He nevertheless remains undoubtedly a Christian "God-above-God." This is paradoxical and naive to boot. An absolute faith cannot be a faith bound to a specific confession. After all, Christianity does not have an absolute metaphysical constitution elevating it beyond all other religions. The dismal state of Christianity would alone deny this. Theologian Otto Wolff says:

> Modern Western man, secularized and de-individualized, standardized and technicalized, without a metaphysical centre and without an eros-relation, depersonalized and deprived of individuality, shares the general state of consciousness, which is encrusted in rationality, even where he is still a part of the centrally Christian or inner-ecclesiastical realm. And what makes him irrefutably conscious of his direct participation in this unspirituality is his disability to establish a truly reviving and creatively meaningful relationship between the world of his faith and his everyday existence.

The Christian proof of truth is only an internal one. All religions are equally true or equally false. Cosmic religiousness, as defined by Einstein, would be a religious universalism, free of dogma and prejudices, beyond religious pathos and fanaticism. It would harbor, so to speak, the essence of all religious truths that manage to pass the filter of modern science undamaged. At its core, it would perhaps be no more than an honest solidarity in the search for the truth of real humanity; and this truth would certainly begin at a point where all human beings are given the chance of a decent life.

Mankind is still far from this point, though. All our questions about true meaning and the true God and true religiousness will remain a discussion typical of an affluent and well-fed society as long as the majority of human beings do not know where the next meal is coming from. But how often has this been said and written down!

In the introduction to this book, it was mentioned that man finds himself at the junction of two infinities, and that he has to determine his spiritual home relative to these infinities. Now, at the end, it should be noted that there is yet another and no less important point of reference: the world in which we live. However, everyone lives not in the world as a whole but in the more or less limited space of his everyday world. There our small, often miserable activities are played out. We do this and that, go about our work, struggle with major and minor crises, amuse ourselves, fulfill desires and create new ones, make decisions and are affected by decisions, meet people and lose track of others.

We are more or less touched by the conditions of the world, cheered by events here, frightened by events there. We get excited over this and that, but rarely for very long. We forget; we become insensitive. In general, we forget a great deal and very quickly. Nevertheless, we have small and bigger hopes—the big ones for ourselves, the small ones for others. We would like to maintain hopes for the world as well, but in this case we somehow hope as if we are not part of it. We prefer to look for private escape routes, as if they might lead us out of the world.

And so the days pass, one after the other. The state of our planet requires universal solutions, but they are not in sight. Somehow it is going to work, we think. Unfortunately, this "somehow" is no indication of a growing knowledge. And what is knowledge, anyway! Where does it enter daily life? Science and religion—that sounds universal, but also slightly pompous. My insignificant days are not part of science—and neither of religion, if one thinks about it. Cosmology makes everyday life appear small and unimportant. And religions have always endeavored to declare everyday life trivial.

But for every one of us, everyday life represents the real world. For me, the universe is the life that I lead. What have I to do with the big bang? Why should I grapple with space-time and quanta? If something throws me off balance, it is everyday life, and that is a process that is hard to describe in quantum-mechanical terms. Astronomers may gain as much knowledge about the universe as they like; for me the universe resides in my head. Unfathomable as the cosmos is, for me it never extends beyond my brainpan. It is merely one of the innumerable images in my mind. The everyday world, that is the real world.

"Everyday world," that is easily written down. As if we know what everyday reality really is. *Reality* is an incredibly effective term, but also a dangerously convenient one. It leads us to believe in universality and certainty, but if we take a closer look, we begin to suspect that even everyday events fade into indeterminacy, that even the most concrete things have a transcendental content. We sense a purpose in the most banal things, and are conscious of a vague responsibility in our most trivial actions.

And just like that, our small, ever-so-concrete days acquire a cosmic-religious dimension. And thus we are again at the center of a whirlpool of thoughts that do not lead us anywhere. For if this anywhere would have a name, it would be the meaning valid for every single one of us. And such a meaning cannot, indeed must not, exist. The existence of an unambiguous meaning would turn us into its slaves. Man would lose his mind over this meaning. The unrealizable quest for meaning represents an insoluble basic paradox of human existence. It is a paradox because there actually is a meaning of life that is valid for all of us: death. But man cannot accept death as a meaning; on the contrary, man asks for a meaning because he knows he is mortal.

And yet, mortality is self-evidently the absolute meaning of life. If we were not mortal, our life would be totally meaningless. Any single activity would be meaningless for we could just as well do it later. Being mortal, however, we are forced to give shape to our lives and to make use of our short life span. Death is the terrible meaning of life. This entails, though, that life itself, every single, unique, and individual life, represents the embodiment of this paradoxical meaning. Life itself is the meaning of life. The inability to understand and accept this forces man to look for a meaning in another world.

The hereafter is a human construction, born of man's existential despair. But even this is just words, empty phrases, meaningless incantations. The point is: Where do they affect our lives? Do we not constantly violate our own convictions? So we have read a stack of books on physics and astronomy and philosophy and religion— but where are the threads leading back into our lives, strengthening the fabric of our existence? We arrive back at the same old, worn-out, and empty words: faith, love, humor. They, too, are more easily written down than lived, and they are accompanied by large question marks.

Is it true that nothing can stand in the way of love, not even the cosmos in its powerful magnitude, that even the fixed stars will evaporate in its fire? And faith is supposed to move mountains? What are mountains, anyway! And humor? Does it really enable us to bear the weight of the world? No, by itself, each of these spiritual giants is powerless and in need of support.

Martin Buber said that faith alone leads to bigotry and humor alone to cynicism. But faith *and* humor, that would be a mixture with which life could be mastered. Love he did not mention, perhaps because, in his opinion, it is automatically created by the combination of faith and humor. That is at least possible. In any case, love alone leads to obsession.

The deep crisis of Christianity may be connected to the fact that it does not admit humor and has never accepted the erotic aspect of love. The crisis of modern science may be connected to its failure to introduce humor as a universal constant of nature. Research is done too obsessively and with too little humor, governed as it is by the false belief that human existence per se can be reduced to a formula. I have a dark feeling, though, that a humorous quantum of action is hidden in nature that refuses to be mathematically defined. It guarantees that behind every secret that man regards as the ultimate one, another "ultimate" secret will appear, each time accompanied by an engaging, not at all scornful, laughter. But it will only be audible for those who are endowed with truly "spiritual" ears.

A Jewish proverb says: "Man thinks, and God laughs."

INDEX

KODANSHA GLOBE

International in scope, this series offers distinguished books that explore the lives, customs, and mindsets of peoples and cultures around the world.

MAN MEETS DOG
Konrad Lorenz
Illustrated by Konrad Lorenz
and Annie Eisenmenger
New introduction by
Donald McCaig
Translated by
Marjorie Kerr Wilson
1-56836-051-7
$12.00

SARAJEVO, EXODUS OF A CITY
Dzevad Karahasan
Afterword by
Slavenka Drakulić
Translated by
Slobodan Drakulić
1-56836-057-6
$10.00

MERCHANT PRINCES
An Intimate History of Jewish Families Who Built Great Department Stores
Leon Harris
New introduction by
Kenneth Libo
New foreword by
Oscar Handlin
1-56836-044-4
$14.00

THE FORBIDDEN EXPERIMENT
The Story of the Wild Boy of Aveyron
Roger Shattuck
New introduction by
Douglas Keith Candland
1-56836-048-7
$13.00

TURKESTAN REUNION
Eleanor Holgate Lattimore
Illustrations by Eleanor Frances Lattimore
1-56836-053-3
$13.00

HIGH TARTARY
Owen Lattimore
Original photographs by
Owen Lattimore
New introduction by
Orville Schell
1-56836-054-1
$15.00

GOD'S LAUGHTER
Physics, Religion, and the Cosmos
Gerhard Staguhn
1-56836-045-2
$13.00

THE FOUR-CORNERED FALCON
Essays on the Interior West and the Natural Scene
Reg Saner
1-56836-049-5
$13.00

THE CROSSING PLACE
A Journey Among the Armenians
Philip Marsden
New introduction by
Peter Sourian
1-56836-052-5
$13.00

TRACING IT HOME
A Chinese Journey
Lynn Pan
1-56836-043-6
$12.00

TRESPASSERS ON THE ROOF OF THE WORLD
The Secret Exploration of Tibet
Peter Hopkirk
1-56836-050-9
$13.00

To order, contact your local bookseller or call 1-800-788-6262 (mention code G1). For a complete listing of titles, please contact the Kodansha Editorial Department at Kodansha America, Inc., 114 Fifth Avenue, New York, NY 10011.